Handbook *for* Butterfly Watchers

D1413085

Books by Robert Michael Pyle

Watching Washington Butterflies

*The Audubon Society Field Guide
to North American Butterflies*

*IUCN Invertebrate Red Data Book
(with S. M. Wells and N. M. Collins)*

Handbook for Butterfly Watchers

*Field Guide to the Butterflies Coloring Book
(with S. A. Hughes and Roger Tory Peterson)*

Wintergreen: Listening to the Land's Heart

Sponsored by the
Roger Tory Peterson Institute

HANDBOOK

for

BUTTERFLY WATCHERS

Robert Michael Pyle

Illustrations by
Sarah Anne Hughes

HOUGHTON MIFFLIN COMPANY
Boston / New York

For information about permission to reproduce selections
from this book, write to Permissions, Houghton Mifflin
Company, 215 Park Avenue South, New York, New York 10003.

Library of Congress Cataloging-in-Publication Data
Pyle, Robert Michael.
Handbook for butterfly watchers / Robert Michael Pyle ;
illustrations by Sarah Anne Hughes ; sponsored by the
Roger Tory Peterson Institute.
p.   cm.
Includes index.
ISBN 0-395-61629-8 (pbk.)
1. Butterfly watching — Handbooks, manuals, etc.
2. Butterflies — Popular works.   I. Roger Tory Peterson
Institute.   II. Title.
QL544.P95   1992   92-4919
595.78'9 — dc20   CIP

Printed in the United States of America

AGM 10 9 8 7 6

For Marvyne,
a true friend of butterflies
and all nature,
and to the memory of
John Heath,
butterfly watcher, mapper,
and conservationist
nonpareil

Contents

The Roger Tory Peterson Institute

is a nonprofit organization

dedicated to informing society

about the natural world

through the

study and teaching

of natural history.

Acknowledgments

I wish to thank Charles Remington for having shown me what there is to see in butterflies for more than thirty years; Harry Foster for his real interest in the book and for shepherding this new, paperback edition through to publication; Roger Tory Peterson, a great butterfly watcher, for his kind words of encouragement to us all; Sally Hughes for her elegant drawings; the family Chu of Boulder—Steve, Jan, Ray, and Amy—for their valuable comments on the text and constant support; and lots of friends, such as Karölis Bagdonas, Boyce Drummond, Linc Brower, John Hay, Mary Jane Foley, Ron Wahl, Ray Stanford, Paul Opler, Joan and Bill DeWind, Angus Hutton, and Audrey and Jim Benedict, for fun in the field while learning from them.

I further thank Larry Orsak, Larry Gall, Paul Ehrlich, and Dennis Murphy for their helpful criticism of the first edition; John Lane for assisting in its repair; and the Evergreen Aurelians and David Myers for helping me to understand the butterflies of home.

Special thanks to Bilak Bokis for paperweighting, lap warming, and keyboard support; to Fayette Krause for his constant encouragement; and to Thea Pyle for her loving care and assistance with the revision and with the author.

Finally, I wish to thank and to honor all those who have gone afield with me to find these dazzling fliers, helping to keep my passion ever fresh and allowing themselves to be, like me, beguiled.

Foreword

Butterflies have much in common with birds; both are vivid expressions of life. And like birds, butterflies are sensitive indicators of the environment, sending out signals when things are out of kilter. Butterfly watching can be as addictive as bird watching except during the colder months when butterflies are conspicuously absent. These flamboyant insects crave warmth; most of them are sun worshipers, and when bird activity slacks down during the heat of the day butterflies are at their best.

Prior to the turn of the century, those few individuals who professed an interest in birds relied mainly on the shotgun. Audubon, who with Alexander Wilson started it all in America, once implied that it was not a really good day if he shot fewer than 100 birds. And yet it was the national society which bears Audubon's name that was most responsible for the shift from the shotgun to the binocular. "A bird in the bush is worth two in the hand" became its motto.

It has taken another generation or two—about 50 years—for butterfly collecting to evolve into butterfly watching. When I was a teenager, sixty years ago, butterflies were to be pursued, popped into a cyanide jar, and pinned in a tray. They were possessed, but seldom watched, unless they were out of reach of my net. As a result I knew little about their way of life. However, collecting was important in those days, and still is, for the purpose of establishing a critical taxonomy and also to gain a fairly precise knowledge of butterfly distribution; but I am sure that my own compulsion to catch butterflies was more akin to stamp collecting or egg collecting. Or could it have been something more subtle? In my youth, netting butterflies was usually a schoolboys' hobby that seldom survived the early teens. I have wondered—could it be that these psychedelic nymphs symbolize an adolescent boy's dreams of the fair sex, gossamer and floss creatures to be pursued and—just possibly—possessed? Certainly, however, in these more liberated times butterflies are no longer primarily a boy's hobby. Many birders of both sexes are now applying their field skills to the Lepidoptera, and those who have not done so are missing a lot.

Observing butterflies can take as many directions as bird watching. It can be a science, an esthetic experience, a recreation, a game, or much more. If you bring scientific expertise to bear on your activity you might presume to call yourself a lepidopterist or an entomologist, whereas if you simply watch the butterflies in your garden and plant some buddleias or zinnias to attract them, you are more akin to the person who feeds birds. Or, if you are really serious about it, you can design and plant a garden solely for butterflies, as my wife Ginny did. She seduced those butterflies that followed the little woodland road that winds past my studio. After her experiments with various nectar producing flowers and larval food plants, 20 to 25 species of butterflies became regular visitors. Her success was excellent for our part of Connecticut where there are relatively few butterflies to delight the eye and lift the spirit.

I blame the paucity of butterflies in our area on the lack of open spaces except along the highways where unfortunately the verges are periodically mowed and sometimes sprayed to keep down the vegetation. Where a number of states—Texas and Massachusetts, for example—encourage wildflowers along the roads and highways, Connecticut takes a dim view of "noxious weeds." Perhaps if the garden clubs would take a hand as they did in some of the other states we could turn things around. If we had more roadside flowers we would undoubtedly have more butterflies. In these days of spraying and "pest control" the Lepidoptera need our help.

Photography is one of the most satisfying spin-offs of the butterfly game. It is more tangible than the list and a good substitute for the specimen tray. Building up a file of transparencies satisfies the collecting instinct, but it can do more than that if you have a good eye and an esthetic sense. There is an immediacy about taking wildlife pictures; there is action. And unlike birds, butterflies are easy to capture on film without using a long telephoto lens. However, my own favorite lenses for this work are the Micro-Nikkor 105mm and the Micro-Nikkor 200mm, which allow frame-filling shots without crowding the butterfly into flight.

Perhaps no one has done more to popularize butterfly watching than Robert Pyle, author of this handbook. He had already aired many of his ideas ten years ago in *Watching Washington Butterflies*, but as that modest little book applied only to the butterflies of the Northwest it was inevitable that he should expand things for a larger audience; hence this new book. During the intervening years he has authored *The Audubon Society Field Guide to North American Butterflies* and *A Field Guide to Butterflies Coloring Book*, illustrated by Sarah Anne Hughes. Incidentally, the coloring book is not just for kids. It will sharpen your observations and condition your memory for the days you spend outdoors. By filling in the colors during evenings at home, or on winter days before the first Mourning Cloaks of early spring make their appearance, you will be better informed about the various butterflies that will emerge as the season advances.

Dr. Pyle was the founding president of the Xerces Society, a national organization for the promotion of butterfly watching and conservation. One of its special projects has been a yearly butterfly census or butterfly count conducted in various places across the land, usually in early July. These counts will eventually tell us much about the population dynamics of butterflies, their ups and downs, their cycles. It is a pity that counts of this sort were not taken prior to the 1950s so that we might have had a more accurate assessment of the impact of DDT and other biocides as well as any subsequent recovery that has taken place. We lack the baselines we might have had.

Whereas there are nearly 9,000 species of birds in the world, there are perhaps twice as many butterflies, somewhere between 15,000 and 20,000 species. No continent save Antarctica is devoid of butterflies; they are widespread from desert oases to alpine meadows. Strangely enough, however, some of the more remote islands, such as the Pribilofs and the outer Aleutians, lack these insects even though they are carpeted with wildflowers.

The greatest number of butterflies is in the tropics, and no observant person can ignore them as he or she walks the jungle trails. Nowhere have I seen more butterflies than around Explorer's Inn on one of the tributaries of the Amazon in Peru. I found myself giving more time to photographing them with my Nikon than I did to ogling through my binocular the tanagers, toucans, parrots, and other avian goodies that disported in the treetops above. One morning when I wished to wash the stickiness from my perspiring hands with beer, the only liquid available, a huge blue morpho attempted to alight on my fingertips.

There is no doubt that butterfly watching is fun, but we must thank Robert Pyle for pointing the way and giving us tips so that our butterfly observations might be more meaningful.

—*Roger Tory Peterson*

Handbook *for* Butterfly Watchers

1

Why Watch Butterflies?

A butterfly passes by, and only a few heads turn—what a great pity. Most people are simply not aware of anything smaller than a robin; their senses are not adjusted to take in small wonders. Even naturalists tend to be attuned to the greater spectacles, to the exclusion of the lesser. As Vladimir Nabokov observed in his memoirs, "It is astonishing how few people notice butterflies." Yet those who miss butterflies miss one of the greatest spectacles of all, in sheer wonder and beauty if not in size.

Few other subjects in the realms of nature or craft offer the degree of aesthetic pleasure to be gained from observing butterflies. In a jaded world, butterfly watching furnishes a simple and refreshing pathway to fascination. Not an escape, but a fresh kind of connection with reality, butterfly watching provides a new nature alternative.

Seeking out and observing butterflies gives one a unique window on the world. One cannot become a butterfly lover without at the same time growing sensitive to the animals, plants, soils, landforms, weather, and climate—and the habitats they all make up together. So the watcher of butterflies soon becomes a botanist, a geologist, a reader of clouds—in effect, a general naturalist. I know of few pursuits out-of-doors that lead one quite as a matter of course down so many avenues. And this means that the lepidopterist gains as well an appreciation for the landscape as a whole

A mating pair of Painted Crescents takes flight. The larger, stronger female carries. Such observations make butterfly watching endlessly fascinating.

and an understanding of the imperative for thoughtful and caring stewardship.

Perhaps I have made it sound as if you cannot participate in this activity without energetically pursuing a dozen others as well, when all you want to do is watch a butterfly. Actually, butterflying can be as rigorous or as relaxed as you wish to make it. An example from the birthplace of butterfly studies, Great Britain, will illustrate this point. For the past decade or so I have been fortunate to live in England much of the time and therefore have done a lot of my butterfly watching there. One would think that all challenges entomological would long since have been met in this small, well-inspected land and that butterfly researchers would have run out of field problems to solve. Such is not at all the case. Much remains to be learned, particularly of species that are rare and becoming rarer; and despite the excellent British butterfly mapping system (see Chapter 9), Britain's wilder landscapes still hold some secrets and physical challenges for the field lepidopterist.

One day in July 1972 I found myself in pursuit of the Heath Fritillary in northwest Devon. My survey of this threatened species presaged an intensive program for its study and recovery that is still going on. I was exploring locales known to have been frequented by the small orange-and-black brocade butterfly to see whether it still occupied any of its domains. On a hot, crystalline morning I started up a steep slope, bound for a moor purple with heather and overlooking the Irish Sea, buoyant with hope and exhilaration. An hour later I was deeply enmeshed in the worst brier patch I evér hope to see from the inside. Sixteen species of thorns, brambles, and stickers turned my gentle Devon ramble into the worst outdoor ordeal I have ever experienced—New Guinea swamps and North Sea storms included. I emerged scratched and bloody, none the wiser about the Heath Fritillary and seriously doubting the sensibleness of my profession. It was an adventure one could appreciate only in retrospect.

Yet just last spring, I experienced another English butterfly experience of the most serene kind. Seated on a white lawn chair in the garden of a Cambridgeshire pub on a golden May day, a pint of fine East Anglian ale in hand and in a state of utter repose, I watched a Brimstone flutter onto the scene. The lemon-yellow butterfly dallied among the nectarless blossoms of like-colored daffodils and mauve crocuses. A fruitless foray for the butterfly perhaps, but a rich and memorable experience for me.

Likewise, butterflying can be as intellectually demanding as you wish, or you can approach it on a strictly appreciative basis. The study of butterflies has led to enlightenment on matters medical, genetic, behavioral, and ecological, and has prompted major strides in evolutionary understanding. For scientists such as Professors Sir Cyril Clarke and Paul Ehrlich the contemplation and observation of butterflies was no less stimulating or rewarding than the study of the most arcane atomic particles or stellar phenomena. On the other hand, poets have always approached butterflies on an emotional, appreciative level, where feelings are as significant as facts. This gestalt or zen level of butterfly appreciation is accessible to anyone willing to contradict that scientist-poet Nabokov and notice butterflies. For most of us, butterfly watching is something between pure science and pure feeling: a chance to sharpen our powers of observation, to learn something new and intriguing, while experiencing aesthetic pleasure and feeling good about what we are doing.

A birder with whom I once discussed butterfly watching scoffed at my ideas. "Butterflies are there only in summer," he claimed, "whereas birds are always around." How wrong he was. The active adult flight of butterflies extends in the north from early spring to late autumn, while in the south they fly year-round. Even in cold northern winters, Mourning Cloaks and their hibernating relatives may come out on sunny days. And of course, paying attention to butterflies means, in the broader sense, being aware of their eggs, caterpillars, and chrysalids—the whole life cycle of the most remarkable changelings on earth. Seeking out the early stages in winter makes butterfly watching an activity for all seasons.

"Well, then," countered the skeptical birder, "what about geography? I can find birds in any habitat. Surely butterflies hang out in few places other than flowery meadows." Wrong again. The only bird habitat devoid of butterflies is the Antarctic. Butterflies can even be spotted over open water; Christopher Columbus, Charles Darwin, and many others have reported great clouds of sulphurs far out at sea. Butterflies have come to dwell in virtually every terrestrial habitat except icefields. Indeed, they are at least as abundant and diverse as birds in rigorous habitats such as the High Arctic, the Arctic-Alpine, and the desert.

"And weather?" The birder's attack was flagging. It is true enough that butterflies strongly prefer sunny weather and that clouds discourage many species even on warm days. Butterfly watching in the rain tends to be a fairly futile activity. But even then, as in winter, caterpillars are abroad on the land. And locating the resting place of a sheltered butterfly in a thundershower, beneath a leaf or high in mountain turf, is an experience that—although infrequent—is magical.

"Surely," the birder finally challenged, "you can't find butterflies at night? At least we can prowl for owls and nightjars in the wee hours." I told him about zebra butterflies, which roost communally in Florida and may be found in their striking, striped nocturnal assemblages with the aid of a flashlight, or by watching them bed down at dusk. I mentioned crepuscular nymphs in New Guinea that I watched well into the tropical twilight and the night-feeding fritillary larvae that come out to browse on violets only after the sun goes down. If that's not enough for the night-person, consider moths, butterflies' counterparts of the shadow-world. Moths number among them many beauties; they are mostly nocturnal, and at least ten times more numerous and diverse than diurnal butterflies. And one more thing. With butterflies, you needn't make excuses for missing that 5 A.M. field trip: unlike birds, they begin their day's activity at the very civilized hour of eight or nine o'clock.

The birder was beaten. He has since become an avid butterfly watcher, and finds that butterflies and birds complement each other nicely as field pursuits. In fact, a number of Audubon Society chapters now stage annual or even more frequent butterfly field trips. I led Seattle Audubon's first such walk on May Day, 1970, and it has proved popular ever since. Although butterflies are not likely to edge out birds as the most watched creatures, they have begun to be discovered, and not found wanting.

Butterflies may be the least appreciated of the three great, colorful outdoor pleasures: birds, butterflies, and wildflowers. Yet in many ways they may be thought of whimsically as a mixture of the other two groups. Not so bewilderingly various as wildflowers, yet just as diverse as birds in North America and more so worldwide; as colorful and many-patterned as flowers, yet rather more active; as fascinating as birds in their behavior, but much easier to approach and watch close-up. Hazel Wolf, doyenne of the Seattle Audubon Society, has called butterflies, "wildflowers with wings." They might just as easily be thought of as the birds of the invertebrate world; in fact, butterflies and birds even share the trait of having the female carry the sex-determining chromosome—unlike virtually any other animal.

So while birdwatching and wildflower appreciation far outnumber butterflying in number of devotees, they offer no greater fascination, color, or intrigue. Perhaps their greater popularity was due in part to the availability of many more field guides on birds and flowers, but that is less true today. Too, these other organisms are often simply more conspicuous; often it takes a teacher or interpreter to point out butterflies to the inexperienced.

I teach with butterflies—about the land, about biology, about the creatures themselves and how they react to human uses of the world. One of my great pleasures is being able to extend even a handicapped person's observations of butterflies, for these are not joys for the able-bodied alone. In a later chapter I will discuss butterfly experiences for the blind and disabled. The mere fact that I can do so signals that virtually everyone, some with a bit of help, can enjoy butterflies.

Even though butterfly "watching" can be done with fingers or smell, most of us are fortunate to do so with sight. Yet observation in the strict sense only begins to suggest the pleasures and peace that attention to butterflies can bring. Seldom photographed until recently, butterflies offer photographers an incomparable array of color and form for image-making. Butterfly photography is challenging, to say the least, but its satisfactions far outstrip its difficulties. Then there is the rearing of butterflies from eggs, larvae, or pupae. No other miracle in nature begins to approach, in my view, the sheer wonder of Lepidoptera metamorphosis. To see it happen before your eyes can be a transcendental experience.

Both gardeners and entomologists in England have long engaged in butterfly gardening, whereby the resources in the garden are carefully managed to lure and keep more butterflies than might otherwise come. New World gardeners are beginning to discover the delights of this practice.

Beyond watching, depicting, gardening, and rearing, some proportion of butterfly lovers will go on to sample and study their subjects in a scientific manner. This is not necessary in order to enjoy butterflies fully, but it is true that from an early sense of wonder followed by open-eyed watching many a biologist is born.

My own conversion to a lifelong butterfly-person and biologist came early, but not before I'd sortied elsewhere with less than satisfying results. As a very young boy my strongest passions were reserved for two categories of things: seashells and suits of armor. Both commodities were singularly uncommon in my native Colorado. I kept my habits alive with acquisitions from shell shops, museums, and the printed page. Then one day while wandering in a new park near my suburban home, I spotted and wondered at little whirring, bluish objects among the weeds. Later I found a brilliant butterfly, dead and dried with wings spread open, on a pitcher's mound in the same park. These harbingers turned out to be Checkered Skippers and a Viceroy respectively. Soon I began to see great chocolate and vanilla Mourning Cloaks, salmon-spotted Painted Ladies, astonishing Black Swallowtails, and little blue butterflies ("Blue!" I marveled) along the fencerows. It began to dawn on me that butterflies might provide a more fruitful field for a Denver lad than medieval armor or conchology. One day my stepbrother announced that he was going to begin an insect collection. I offered to "do" the butterflies. So at age eleven I went

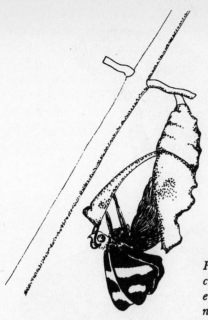

Red Admiral eclosing from its chrysalis. Few sights are as engrossing or enlightening as a new butterfly emerging.

afield along a local ditch with net in hand, and I've never regretted it.

In the years that followed, my grandfather used to ask in jest whether there was any money in butterflies. I doubted it, and I was mostly right. But butterflies have brought me a different kind of reward that I value much more. It is serenity, and it provides perhaps the best advertisement of all for becoming involved with butterflies. Personal peace is hard to find in the frenetic world we have made. Yet for me, no moments are more peaceful than those I spend among the butterflies, whether in Edenic landscapes or vacant lots. From my own experience, I commend spending time with the gentle, beguiling butterflies to anyone with tension to dissipate or stress to dispel. In our stress-ridden society, there are numerous prescriptions for peace of mind. I have found nature study, and in particular the contemplation of butterflies, to be the best tonic in my own search for serenity. It is just as effective, incidentally, in banishing boredom. Butterflies are simply never boring.

Mimicry is one of the most fascinating tales in butterfly evolution. In this set, the model is the distasteful, metallic blue Pipevine Swallowtail (center). The Red-spotted Purple (above) and female Diana Fritillary (below) have diverged from their close relatives by becoming blue mimics of the Pipevine Swallowtail in order to gain protection from birds.

I recall one particularly grueling international conservation meeting when I felt quite worn down by the concerns and conflicts involved. I fled for an afternoon's walk up a narrow valley above Lake Geneva. In a tiny Swiss meadow, an early April Orange-tip wafted over pink cardamine, its host plant. I was able to coax the splendid fresh insect onto my finger; not a scale was missing from its bright orange-and-linen wings. All my cares dissolved, and I returned from the meadow fully refreshed and reminded of the reasons for working to conserve such places for butterflies and people.

So you are convinced, I hope. You are going to go forth to watch butterflies. Why do you need a book to tell you how? You can watch butterflies with no help whatever. But in the quarter-century I've carried on a serious affair with butterflies, I have picked up a few things I believe I can share—things that may help to make your watching easier, richer, more revealing, and ultimately more satisfying. In short, this book is offered as a tool for the greater enjoyment of a new activity in your outdoor repertory. Or if you already pay attention to butterflies—maybe you have for twice as long as I—consider this my half of a conversation in which we tell each other what we have learned.

My hopes for this book were elegantly summed up by Samuel Hubbard Scudder in the introduction to his charming book *Frail Children of the Air*, published in 1897: "To gain for our butterflies a deeper interest and closer attention on the part of the observing public is the simple object of the present volume."

2

About Butterflies

I thought I knew something of what butterflies were about until I went to Papua New Guinea. Butterflies, I quickly found, can be practically like birds, in their biology as well as their size. The giant birdwings of New Guinea made me completely rethink my concept of butterflies. This happened again when I first went to Mexico to see the winter clusters of migratory Monarchs. No longer were butterflies individual, silent things: They were trees, boulders, whole walls; they were the forest floor and the sky itself. And they made such a collective fluttering that one could hear them all day as a soft whir, like stirring leaves.

Butterflies turn their watchers into iconoclasts. One has to be constantly prepared to alter one's view and give up cherished beliefs about these animals. Nor does this happen only with wondrous butterflies in exotic locales. Lately my opinion of butterflies has expanded once again—in my own garden, by the generally despised European Cabbage Butterfly. I grow enough crucifers for both of us and welcome *Pieris rapae* as part of my garden fauna. One day in late October, while observing Small Whites (as the English call them) still on the wing and laying eggs on weedy crucifers in a disturbed spot, it occurred to me that this adaptable animal just might develop a winter generation. In the mild Maritime Northwest, I could imagine it evolving the capability of exploiting winter without hibernating. The host plants are there all year, and in a year of above average sunshine and little frost, such a development could indeed come to pass. In fact, at least one Cabbage White has been spotted in January. But a non-hibernating winter butterfly in northern climes? There we go, changing our butterfly mind-set once again.

The simple fact is that butterflies are different from anything else, even moths, and exhibit characteristics unique in nature. They display protective adaptations almost beyond imagining, and they comprise a visual array that quite overwhelms our capacities for assimilation and appreciation. Early in the voyage of the *Beagle,* after a few weeks ashore in Brazil, Charles Darwin was forced to admit that "it is wearisome to be in a fresh rapture at every turn of the road; but you must be that or nothing." It can be that way with butterflies.

There are some 15,000 to 20,000 species of butterflies. The catalog of models runs far beyond that number, as males and females differ, as do populations from place to place and season to season. And of course every species has four manifestations (egg, larva, pupa, adult) due to its metamorphosis. One often hears the senseless phrase "the butterfly," referring to "butterflies." There simply is no such thing—no standard model, no average type, and certainly no *typical* butterfly. To stereotype these animals as "the butterfly" makes them all seem like different flavors of fritillaries, separate shades of swallowtails. That they are nothing of the kind should be obvious by now, but don't take my word: Your own time spent among the butterflies will convince you far better.

Their individual qualities aside, butterflies are all derived from common ancestors. Therefore they do share certain characteristics. I may not be able to produce for you a "typical" butterfly, but I hope in this chapter to introduce you to some of the traits that distinguish butterflies from other animals. By learning these you can build a mental framework on which to hang all those amazing variations you will observe for yourself.

This discourse on butterfly biology will be brief and simple. Related subjects such as ecology and ethology (behavior) will be amplified elsewhere in this book. Other books are available to anyone wishing greater detail on butterfly structure and life-style, and a number of these are listed in the section on further reading. To dwell too much on these details here would detract from the space available for discussing what is, after all, the subject: watching and enjoying butterflies. Yet a modest acquaintance with the butterflies as living organisms will help to explain what you see in them.

In the first place, butterflies are animals. Thus they share common descent with everything from protozoans to whales and humans. In looking for closer relationships, it is important to distinguish between analogy and homology. Analogies are structures with similar function that have arisen independently; homologies are structures derived from the same ancestral structures. So while butterflies are winged, brightly "feathered" with scales, and share with birds the unusual trait of having the sex-determining chromosome carried by the female, they of course bear no close relationship to birds. Their wings are merely analogous, as are feathers and scales in a remoter way, and their genetic situation is coincidental. On the other hand, the wings and many other structures of butterflies are indeed homologous with those of other higher insects, although modified differently. Butterflies, like dragonflies and grasshoppers, are insects. But dragonflies and grasshoppers are more primitive, while butterflies and moths are considered among the more sophisticated, highly evolved groups, more closely related to bees, beetles, and flies, and particularly to caddisflies, from which they may well be derived.

Fossil butterflies similar to modern species are known from the Miocene age, and butterflies as a group are thought to have originated between 50 and 100 million years ago. They relate not only to insects but also to the larger, encompassing group of animals known as arthropods, all of which share traits including the lack of an internal skeleton and jointed legs, usually with a hard outer chitinous shell. Arthropods include crabs and spiders as well as insects and other groups. Within the Phylum Arthropoda and the Class Insecta, butterflies belong to the Order Lepidoptera (Greek *lepis*=scale, *ptera*=wing). This order also includes moths, whose traits will be discussed in Chapter 17. It has been suggested that butterflies are just one of several subgroups of moths that have evolved to fly by day and to do certain things differently from most of the others. Their clubbed antennae and lack of a linking structure (frenulum) between the fore- and hindwings distinguish butterflies from moths. Together they make up the second or third largest order of insects, after beetles and perhaps bees, ants, and wasps. Insects as a whole outnumber all other living things by at least a factor of ten. Lepidoptera, as you can see, are a very important group of insects and they are often considered by biologists to be the most evolutionarily advanced of the lot.

To sum up, butterflies belong to the Kingdom Animalia, the Phylum Arthropoda, the Class Insecta, the Order Lepidoptera. Their suborder is called Rhopalocera, and within it there are two superfamilies, the Papilionoidea ("true" butterflies) and the Hesperioidea (skippers). True butterflies comprise from four to about a dozen families, depending upon the authority consulted; skippers, two families (skippers are small, fleet, thick-bodied and short-winged butterflies once erroneously thought to be links between butterflies and moths). Families are the major groupings of butterflies. In the broad sense these are as follows: Papilionidae (swallowtails and parnassians; Pieridae (whites and sulphurs); Lycaenidae (gossamer-wings and metalmarks); Nymphalidae (brush-footed butterflies); Hesperiidae (skippers); and Megathymidae (giant skippers). So while the species diversity of butterflies is quite high, the number of general groupings to learn is modest —a boon to the watcher.

Nearly all animals change markedly from juvenile to adult, but nowhere is this more pronounced than among butterflies. Many insects (for example, bugs and grasshoppers) go through a relatively gradual change, the growing nymphs progressively coming to resemble the adults. In this they are like higher animals and might therefore be thought to be advanced. In fact, insects with incomplete (hemimetabolous) metamorphosis are the primitive ones. More advanced, or more highly evolved, groups possess complete (holometabolous) metamorphosis. This might better be called profound metamorphosis, which it surely is. Such insects change radically between the earliest stage and the adult. The basic advance this brought insects was the ability to exploit two virtually separate ecological niches during their lives—in effect, to perform as two separate sorts of animals. This increased their adaptability, versatility, and ability to cope with environmental change.

No insects display profound metamorphosis more impressively than the Lepidoptera. More will be said about this and about the individual life history stages in Chapter 13, on rearing. Essentially it works like this: Having been laid on or near the host plant by the female, the egg (ovum; plural, ova) consists of a minute sphere, turban, spindle, or obloid. It may be plain or highly ornamented. When it hatches, the tiny caterpillar (larva; plural, larvae) emerges. In many instances it makes its first meal of the eggshell and then goes to work feeding on the host plant. The larva is a wormlike animal, naked, hairy, or spiny, with six short true legs in front and eight prolegs farther back, plus a pair of grasping false legs on the last of thirteen segments. The head of the caterpillar carries minute, simple eyes and antennae and a silk spinneret, besides the powerful cutting-and-chewing mandibles. These are important since the primary function of the larva is conversion of plant material into animal tissue; it eats prodigiously.

The skin of insects is composed of chitin, a material limited in its elasticity. So when a certain size is reached, the caterpillar's skin splits and sheds, and out comes a bigger caterpillar. The new skin is temporarily soft to accommodate a spurt of growth, while the old one looks like a rumpled, discarded suit with helmet and goggles; the hard head capsule comes off intact. Each growth stage of a caterpillar, between molts, is known as an instar, and there are generally four to six instars.

The final instar larva ceases eating, wanders about, and spins a silk pad from which it will hang either upside down or diagonally, head up. In the latter case a silken girdle like a lineman's belt encircles its trunk; the posterior attachment, consisting of little hooks enmeshed in a button of silk, is known as the cremaster. When the skin is molted this time, the next stage, the chrysalis, is revealed and is left hanging immobile. The chrysalis (plural, chrysalids) is also known as the pupa (plural, pupae). In many moths and a very few butterflies, the pupa will be enclosed within in a silken bag (known as a cocoon) rather than suspended naked.

The most dramatic part of the profound metamorphosis takes place within the pupa. Not long after its formation, one can look closely at a chrysalis and detect the outlines of several adult fea-

An array of typical butterfly eggs. Clockwise from top: tortoiseshell, blue, swallowtail, two skippers, white.

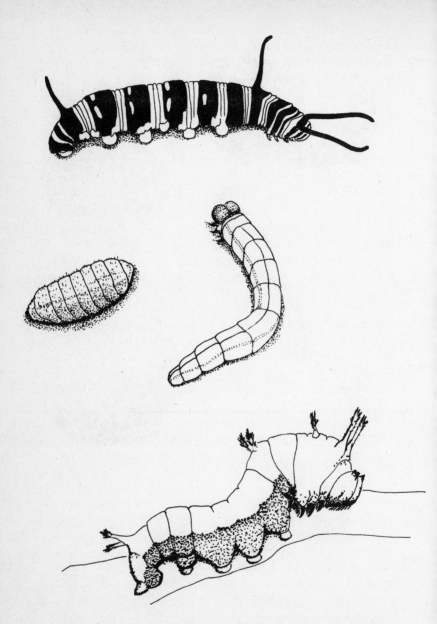

An array of butterfly caterpillars. Clockwise from top: Queen, Long-tailed Skipper, California Sister, Common Blue.

tures: the wings (in miniature), the eyes, the tongue, the antennae, and the body segments. Reasonable people long thought that the material within was molded into shape by these externally etched casts. Nothing of the sort actually happens. The outer "cast" actually comes before the fact of full development of the structures themselves, as they are beginning to form within. But the structures grow into the pupal shell, rather than being molded by it.

Some small parts of the larva correspond to those in the adult. For example, tiny groups of cells known as imaginal buds or pads (the adult is also known as the imago) are present in the larva and will develop into the legs and wings of the adult. The growth of the pads is stimulated by a change in the hormonal climate within the creature, which is now a closed, almost air-and-water-tight package. The same chemical changes that signal the development of adult tissues and organs also call for the breakdown of most larval tissues. So if you were to see inside an early pupa, you would not see an insect in transition from caterpillar to butterfly—a sort of butterfly-worm cross, as many people imagine. Rather, you would see a homogeneous-looking stew with a few formative structures at the edge, firmly attached to the pupal case. In other words, the transition from larva to imago involves a basic dissolution of one animal and reconstitution of another. It is this feature that imbues the process with much of its miracle-like quality.

The appearance of the pupa and the length of time it persists both vary greatly. A Mourning Cloak's thorny sepulcher is a short-term mummification, giving rise to the butterfly about two or three weeks after pupation. The nude little pellet of a hair-streak's pupa may last six months or more before cracking, while some swallowtail chrysalids, resembling slivers of wood, are capable of enduring a second winter in unfavorable years. Whenever it occurs (unless it has dessicated, rotted, been parasitized, eaten, or otherwise frustrated), the outcome of a chrysalis is a butterfly. I will postpone the exciting story of the perilous emergence of the adult, along with a discussion of the number of generations in a year, until Chapter 13. By now you can see that there is much more to a butterfly than its adult incarnation, although that is the only part most people consider. A butterfly's body retains some resemblance to that of a larva, in that it is still tubelike, with a simple digestive tract and direct air supply to every cell via tracheoles leading from the outside air pores, known as spiracles. The adult body, however—like that of all insects—is clearly organized into three parts: the head, thorax, and abdomen.

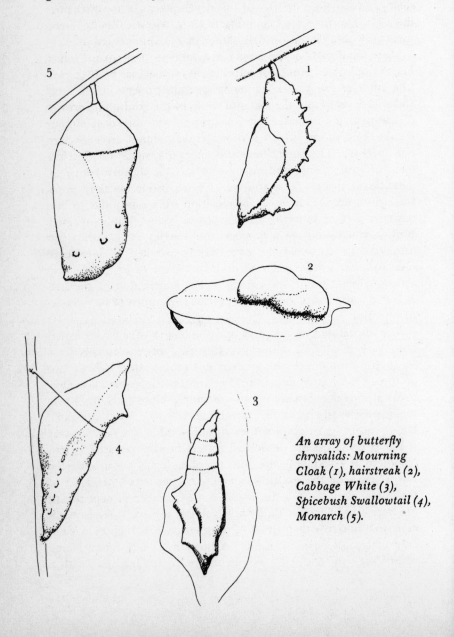

An array of butterfly chrysalids: Mourning Cloak (1), hairstreak (2), Cabbage White (3), Spicebush Swallowtail (4), Monarch (5).

The butterfly head is conspicuous for four sets of structures: the eyes, antennae, palpi, and proboscis. The large, globular eyes are called compound because they consist of some thousands of optical receivers known as ommatidia, each ending in a hexagonal lens or facet on the surface of the eye. An optic nerve carries the visual message from the ommatidia to the brain, where it is received as an integrated, erect image. A butterfly's vision is quite sharp at close quarters, but because acuity depends on the number of facets aimed at the object, butterflies are very near-sighted. Their color vision has been experimentally proven, and in addition to all the wavelengths we can see, butterflies can see far into the ultraviolet as well as infrared.

Tiny, simple eyes called ocelli occur on the head of both larva and adult, but these can do little more than perceive light and dark. Vision plays an extremely important role in the lives of butterflies, notably in the location of mates and food sources. Anyone who swings a net at butterflies soon comes to appreciate their sharp eyes and quick reflexes. But other senses are important to butterflies as well.

In this close-up of a brush-footed butterfly's head, the following structures are easily visible: striped, compound eyes; proboscis coiled between the furry palpi; and base of the antennal shaft.

Between the eyes and above and behind them originate the antennae. The so-called "feelers" are actually smellers for the most part, feeling being the function of small hairs called sensing setae that occur all over the insect. The antennae may have a balance and orientation purpose as well as an olfactory one. Butterfly antennae are segmented and end in thickened knobs. Whether slender and gently tapered or thick and abrupt, the knobs distinguish butterflies at once from nearly all moths.

Also situated between the eyes, but below them, is the proboscis. This is also a paired structure, since two halves of its long sucking tube become hooked together to form a central canal upon emergence of the adult. The proboscis may be coiled like a watchspring, tight against the face, to protect it. When in use it is extended with muscles to probe the nectaries of flowers or other substances. When outstretched in this manner the proboscis behaves like a drinking straw in drawing fluids up and into the throat. Commonly 1 or 2 centimeters long in butterflies, the proboscis may extend to 30 centimeters in certain hawkmoths.

On either side of the proboscis you will see a furry member called a labial palp. The two palpi line up along the butterfly's face and seem to have little mobility. No single purpose has been agreed upon for the mustachelike palpi, but I have often wondered whether their role is not simply to protect that vital structure, the tongue.

Within the head lies a brain of two parts. Ancestral, primitive insects had a ganglion of nerves gathered in each segment, and in butterflies three of these have fused to form quite a respectable and modern brain—a brain that is analogous, however, not homologous to our own. From the brain a pair of nerve cords runs backward and meets in more or less fused ganglia along the thorax and abdomen; thence nerves radiate out into the rest of the animal, including the wings. Also running back down the body of the insect, from the proboscis, is the esophagus leading to the gut.

The thorax, behind the head, is body part number two and is the anchor point for both wings and legs. The wings attach to the sides of the thorax. Four in number, they are what we notice most about a butterfly and what enable it to live as it does. The forewings are generally larger and more elongated than the rounded hindwings, and attach above the latter. The hindwings

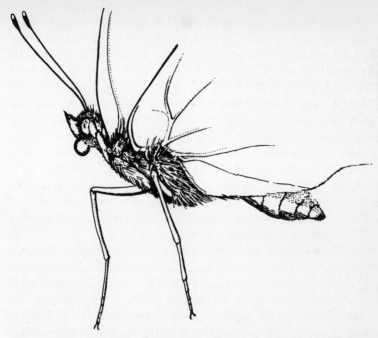

Try to pick out these features of basic butterfly anatomy: Head, antennae, palpi, eyes, proboscis, dwarfed forelegs (it is a brush-footed butterfly), legs, tarsi, thorax, abdomen, forewing, hindwing, wing veins.

fit in below so that when you see a butterfly with wings folded above its back—the most frequent posture—you are observing the underside (ventral) of the hindwings (secondaries) (see figure above). The upper side (dorsal) of the forewings (primaries) is presented when the butterfly opens its wing (see page 31). It is important to get this geography right in order to situate field marks correctly. The wings consist of parallel membranes most of which merged upon drying, except along the veins, or nervules. These prominent canals through the wings originally pumped or carried fluid into them to expand them upon emergence. They continue to carry some haemolymph, perhaps as a means of passive solar heat conduction. But they also carry some nerves. The configuration of the veins remains rather constant within closely related groups of butterflies, so they comprise a useful tool for the taxonomist seeking to delineate such relationships.

The wing membranes are covered by millions of close-ranked, simply socketed scales. These minute shingles give Lepidoptera their chief distinguishing characteristic. While they do not assist greatly in flight, and exist chiefly to imbue butterflies with their coloration, a theory has been advanced recently suggesting their utility in helping a butterfly escape from spider webs. Indeed, the scales do come away freely, giving rise to the uniform childhood experience of the "powder" on a butterfly's wings; and spiders are major predators of butterflies. A special class of scales, known as sex scales, scent scales, or androconia, convey pheromones (hormonal perfumes) from tiny glands in the wings. These play a part in courting and mating readiness. Androconia may be scattered through the other scales, or gathered into velvety scent patches sometimes called stigmata.

Scales, as we have discovered, give a butterfly its color. Browns, oranges, yellows, blacks, whites, and other earthy tones come from pigments carried in the scales. These absorb certain wavelengths of light and reflect others, making the colors we see. Metallic and iridescent colors such as bright blues, greens, purples, and silvers are created differently by ridged, three-dimensional structural scales. These refract the light like prisms, yielding rainbow colors with no basis in pigment. A structurally colored butterfly may seem brilliant viewed from one angle, but when the sun strikes it a little differently it goes drab.

I will never forget the first blue *Morpho* butterfly I ever saw. It was in Costa Rica along a forest pathway. The famous flash of flying sapphire was instantly recognizable. But as the *Morpho* flapped down the dappled path, passing in and out of sunbeams, it looked alternately like incandescent blue foil and a big brown moth. At last it left the jungle and sailed out over the Caribbean, where the blue remained steady, intensified by the indigo-water backdrop. Our common little blues at home are colored the same way.

Carpeting the wings with vast numbers of intricate scales may seem an expensive way for nature to endow these insects with color. But the many adaptive purposes to which butterflies put color surely justifies the physiological cost. And while pure aesthetics played no role in evolution, the scales and their hues and patterns surely afford us one of the most compelling reasons for watching butterflies—though by no means the only ones, as I will show later when discussing butterfly watching for the color-blind.

Beneath the wings, three legs are attached to each side of the lower thorax. Each leg consists of a coxa, trochanter, femur, tibia, and tarsus. The tarsus bears tiny claws for clinging. In the family Nymphalidae, the first pair of legs is reduced to useless, brush-like paws. Male blues and some other butterflies share this trait with the brush-footed butterflies. The legs are primarily used for walking and climbing while the butterfly is feeding, and for clinging while drying its wings, mating, or roosting. In addition, the fact that the rear pair of legs can taste substances with which they come in contact is well established. This ability is used in food and host plant recognition.

Within the thorax pumps a heart—a simple organ for circulating haemolymph through the body cavity—and the strong, well-developed flight muscles. Somewhat more complex is the abdomen. It contains, in addition to nerve ganglia, the digestive tract, an air sac, and the internal reproductive organs. There are ten abdominal segments, the last two of which are modified into the external genitalia. In the male, these consist of a pair of claspers for gripping the female, between which the penis emerges, connecting with the fused testes inside. The ovaries of the females connect to the outside via the vagina on the eighth segment and the ovipositor on the ninth. The tenth segment has a third opening, the anus. In copulation, the male transfers a packet of sperm called a spermatophore into the female's genitalia. This packet is capable of fertilizing eggs long after the actual coupling. Both male and female genitalia are useful to the taxonomist. They vary less than wing patterns within species, and as conservative structures, they change slowly with evolution and thus show relationships over time. Courtship and mating, one of the most beautiful aspects of butterfly behavior, will be described in Chapter 11.

One additional quality of the adult butterfly that should be mentioned here is its longevity. I am frequently asked, "How long does a butterfly live?" The question is a relative one, since any butterfly clearly could be destroyed by a storm on the morning of its emergence or have fair skies and a long life. But what is long for a butterfly? One tabulation for British butterflies suggested an average lifespan of two weeks in the adult phase, and that may be as good a figure as any. Particularly dainty species might manage a few days only, while robust swallowtails could be vital for a month or two. I suspect most butterflies fly for something under a month. However, there are dramatic exceptions. Nymphalids that overwinter as adults necessarily live in that stage at least from October until March, and more likely two or three months more. These include Mourning Cloaks, anglewings, and their relatives. I saw a particularly tattered Milbert's Tortoiseshell in late August last summer; it may have been a candidate for spanning a calendar year as an adult, since it had likely overwintered. Tropical longwing butterflies that ingest pollen (see Chapter 11) and the giant birdwings of New Guinea commonly live on the wing in excess of six months. Certainly the migratory generation of the Monarch must be among our longest-lived butterflies. Flying south in August or September, northward again in April and May, winter Monarchs may see ten months between the chrysalis and the day they die. The butterfly as a fragile, ephemeral creature remains a good image, but clearly there is enormous variation around a norm of perhaps a fortnight's flight.

We have followed the life history of butterflies from egg to egg production in the adult, and learned a little of each stage. By now you know something of the nature of butterflies. To learn more, the best way is to go out and watch. And when you think you know butterflies, keep watching. From time to time, you'll see something to change your mind.

3

Watching vs. Catching

One day some summers ago I was sampling butterflies for a research project in a national recreation area in Washington State. A young park ranger, spotting my net, braked and got out to cite me for breaking regulations. I informed him that, whereas the adjoining national park was indeed off limits to collecting, a NRA was not. He radioed headquarters, checked his rulebook, and finally conceded that I was correct. "Even so," said the ranger, "we've got a new book in the office that says you should *watch* butterflies instead of collecting them." I replied that I'd written the book in question (*Watching Washington Butterflies*) and that if he read it clearly, he would see that both watching and catching butterflies have their place. We parted amicably, but not before he confided that a woman camper down the road had complained that "some hippie's up there catching all the butterflies."

People knowing of my fondness for butterflies and my commitment to their conservation often are taken aback to see me with a net. It seems to them that collecting and conservation must be inimical. Decades of public education and activist attention to vertebrate conservation have led to the commonplace conclusion that natural history collectors are evil wastrels or, at the least, antediluvian churls. Of course, ethics and needs have changed since Darwin and John James Audubon collected large numbers of creatures to document their science and art. If all the birders in the country were still collectors, many of our less common birds might be in greater peril than they are. But all this has to do with vertebrates. Those who castigate butterfly netters seldom have any idea of invertebrate population biology. The difference is immense, and makes an entirely fresh consideration of the problem necessary.

First, let's consider the virtues of butterfly collecting; then we can ask what harm collecting actually does. The tradition of amassing butterfly specimens goes back at least to the seventeenth century, and in our own lifetimes, to most of our childhoods. Therein lie two of the major values of collecting. Scientifically speaking, there is an unbroken line of nearly three hundred years of lepidopterology, which means butterflies and moths are among the great storehouses of insights into the natural world. One might think that, in all that time and with all those boxes of dead, dried butterflies, we would have learned all there is to learn from specimens. While it may be true that much more remains to be learned from living butterflies than pinned ones, it is far from the case that the latter have nothing left to contribute. Entomology is, in some ways, still in the Dark Ages compared to vertebrate science. To stop collecting now would be to keep it there, since many aspects of the study—including taxonomy, morphology, physiology, and genetics—can be elucidated only through the examination of specimens. And since insects are our greatest competitors for food and fiber, as well as some of our most powerful natural allies, it would indeed be foolhardy to stem the advances of entomology. As I will show later, basic biological research with butterflies has contributed significantly to several branches of science and medicine.

Second, it is certain that more young people get their starts on the road toward a career or lifelong involvement with biology through insect collecting than by any other stimulus. Insects offer the last great accessible, free, unlicensed, and basically unrestricted resource for youthful investigators. Kids normally begin gathering "trophies" in their early field-play. Later this usually gives way to a state where looking is enough, and then all too often to blinkered adulthood. But for a few, collecting gives the gratification necessary for lifelong studies. To ban it would prove disas-

This Zebra Swallowtail has lost one tail to a bird's misguided attack. Such a flaw would disqualify the specimen for many collectors, enhance its value to others. The watcher can enjoy and learn from a butterfly in any condition.

trous at a time when we need a public more—not less—acquainted with the living world and its parts.

Ironically, butterfly collecting (when properly carried out and applied) can even serve conservation. Many young collectors go on to become dedicated professional or citizen conservationists, because they come to understand the specialness and fragility of habitats. It is equally true that you cannot conserve something without knowing what it is, where it is, and where it isn't. A dune katydid in California became extinct before it had even been scientifically described. Fortunately, specimens in museums were able to provide information about the lost creature, adding motivation to save the remaining fragment of habitat and the endangered butterfly that lives in it. Annually, dozens or scores or hundreds of insect species probably disappear in the tropics, unbeknown to scientists. In order to conserve natural diversity, this diversity must first be recognized—and since three-quarters or more of the creatures on earth are insects, collecting must continue in order that we may characterize the special landscapes we are so rapidly losing, especially tropical rainforests. This way, efforts to set aside and manage reserves will be more informed.

My own doctoral dissertation aimed to correlate butterfly distribution with that of nature reserves in Washington (this led to my encounter with the ranger). By plotting 10,000 records of butterfly occurrences in the state, I was able to demonstrate that there were natural butterfly provinces whose reserve coverage differed drastically. One section of the northern mountains has 17 percent of its area committed to parks and reserves, for example, while another, just as distinctive, has less than 0.1 percent. Yet managers regarded them as equal. Drawing attention to the neglected regions has helped to bring about new reserves. Thus the thousands of collectors' data I employed became direct tools of land conservation. And there are lepidopterists all over North America who are working with their local chapters of The Nature Conservancy to provide similar clues.

Given that it has such redeeming qualities, what is the actual impact of collecting upon butterfly populations? Many invertebrate biologists, concerned about the future of their resource as well as possible regulations, have raised this question recently. The fundamental fact is that most butterflies and other insects reproduce their numbers so rapidly and efficiently that direct taking of individuals can have little impact on a healthy population. Predators—from spiders to dragonflies to birds—have infinitely greater speed, appetite, and success than all the collectors put together. And automobiles, lawnmowers, and garden sprays kill more than collectors do. Only one federally endangered butterfly, Mitchell's Marsh Satyr, has been listed because of the impact of collectors. It was much reduced already from wetland drainage. Conservationists who have studied the question have concluded that collectors simply could not deplete a population badly unless it were already very small and insular, ecologically stressed, or otherwise independently at risk. Habitat alteration, on the other hand, has placed many colonies in just that position, so care and restraint must be exercised with rare varieties. But assuming that they possess a measure of common sense and responsibility, collectors are normally the least of a butterfly species' worries. (Chapter

15 discusses butterfly and moth conservation and what you can do to help.)

Although I am mostly a watcher and photographer of butterflies these days, it is important to clarify these points about collecting so as not to perpetuate mistaken assumptions. Ill-informed collecting bans divert attention from genuine conservation problems while lessening the benefits to be gained from careful collecting.

Many butterfly enthusiasts, however, simply do not wish to collect. For one thing, it takes time. Properly curated, a collection requires spreading, labeling, and periodic fumigating. While lifelong lepidopterists derive considerable satisfaction from these tasks, they become tedious to others. Once the youthful hunt loses its bloom, most beginners leave their collections to the attentions of the carpet beetles that will soon devour them without curating. Then too, going about with a butterfly net arouses attention, sometimes derogatory or derisive in nature. I have grown tough-hided in this respect. Sometimes the attention can be welcome, bringing lodging, rides, and interesting encounters. But as Edwin Way Teale, Pulitzer Prize-winning nature writer, pointed out in his book *Springtime in Britain*, inconspicuousness is the best policy for a naturalist who wishes to observe unimpeded. Carrying an insect net is no way to remain inconspicuous. For youngsters, the attention of their friends often assumes the form of peer pressure, leading to the premature loss of many a young naturalist from the ranks of entomology.

Perhaps the greatest deterrent to collecting among people I know is simply displeasure over killing butterflies. This is something I have struggled with for years. No one, I am convinced, *likes* to kill a butterfly, but collectors become more or less inured to the act of dispatch as a necessity of their hobby or profession. Most do so with some degree of compunction. (It is interesting that many people who condemn butterfly killing think nothing of killing a salmon, an earthworm, or a moth.) I have found that if I think about or watch a given butterfly for very long, I become incapable of making it a specimen. True enough, most butterflies you catch will have fulfilled their reproductive function and be near their natural demise in any case. But the fact remains that it's no fun, any way you look at it, to hasten it. One alternative is to collect road-kills only. Often these remain in near-perfect condition. A friend in New Jersey loves to collect but cannot abide killing butterflies, so he bicycles along the shoulders of roads, gathering the road-killed butterflies he spies. In this way he has collected most of the species of butterflies ever found in New Jersey.

This book provides another alternative to butterfly collecting. Through observation, you can achieve many of the joys previously considered the sole province of the insect collector. In fact, I hope to show that certain things can be learned through careful watching that no quantity of preserved specimens will reveal. Even on a taxonomic level, the actual differences between closely allied species may be less open to illumination by dissection than by painstaking comparison of behavior. In such instances cooperation between watchers and catchers is called for. After all, it needn't be an either/or thing: One can do both, as inclination and necessity indicate.

I collect selectively in certain parts of Colorado, in Washington, and in New Guinea, where I have long-term interests in faunistic research (what lives where and why). And I catch representatives of satyr butterflies and hook-tip moths, groups in which I have particular evolutionary interest. In other places and with other faunas, I chiefly watch, because I prefer it. Sometimes it is difficult for conscientious lepidopterists to get over feeling that they ought to be sampling when they would really rather just watch. In fact, one of the greatest liabilities of collecting is that it teaches one to nab now and ask questions later. There is scarcely a lepidopterist in my acquaintance whose work would not benefit from more observation prior to the act of capture. I am sometimes surprised by how little some of my colleagues, so elegantly versed in spots and genitalic processes, know about their subjects' behavior in the field. And so I recommend the practice of careful observation to those who would catch as well as merely watch.

The important thing is for each person to decide how to relate to butterflies to attain the greatest satisfaction, and to allow others to do the same. Motivations differ. There are those who think scientific sampling is okay but that "postage stamp" collecting of butterflies is indefensible; others abide the hobbyist but ostracize the commercial collector. Our taste may be offended by bric-

Our largest western butterfly, the Two-tailed Tiger Swallowtail—what is its greatest value to you? As a spectacular specimen, a photograph, or the image of a free-flying butterfly?

a-brac and kitsch artifacts that seem to violate butterflies' free spirits by associating them with commercial vulgarity. Yet in Papua New Guinea, careful cultivation of butterflies as a renewable resource makes a genuine contribution to village economics while conserving habitat and wild stocks of butterflies as well. The aim of this project, on which I have worked, is to ensure that more butterflies from the "farms" are released in the wild than killed to sell. Marketing is done by a government agency that oversees prices as well as conservation. So there are two sides to butterfly commercialism.

It strikes me as curiously self-righteous to favor one motive above another so long as the effect on the resource is the same. The Xerces Society, an international insect conservation group, opposes "only that collecting which can be shown or reasonably expected to damage populations," and I think this is a reasonable criterion. Conservation should be the touchstone, and the population is the unit of conservation. Any action that jeopardizes a whole group of animals or plants is clearly against the public interest, and should therefore be discouraged or regulated.

If you do choose to collect, you should observe certain conventions and courtesies to protect the resource as well as the rights of others. Suggested behavior is summarized in the following guidelines for collectors, adopted in 1982 by the Executive Board of the Lepidopterists' Society. By observing the guidelines, collectors can minimize their impact on populations of butterflies and on the environment that supports them.

The Lepidopterists' Society

STATEMENT
of the
COMMITTEE ON COLLECTING POLICY

PREAMBLE

Our ethical responsibility to assess and preserve natural resources, for the maintenance of biological diversity in perpetuity, and for the increase of knowledge, requires that lepidopterists examine the rationale and practices of collecting Lepidoptera, for the purpose of governing their own activities.

To this end, the following guidelines are outlined, based on these premises:

0.1 *Lepidoptera are a renewable natural resource.*

0.2 *Any interaction with a natural resource should be in a manner not harmful to the perpetuation of that resource.*

0.3 *The collection of Lepidoptera*

    0.31 *is a means of introducing children and adults to awareness and study of their natural environment;*

    0.32 *has an essential role in the elucidation of scientific information, both for its own sake and as a basis from which to develop rational means for protectng the environment, its resources, human health and the world food supply;*

Published in the *News* of the Lepidopterists' Society, No. 5, Sept./Oct. 1982. Reproduced courtesy of the Lepidopterists' Society.

0.33 *is a recreational activity which can generally be pursued in a manner not detrimental to the resource involved.*

GUIDELINES

PURPOSES OF COLLECTING (consistent with the above):

1.1 *To create a reference collection for study and appreciation.*

1.2 *To document regional diversity, frequency, and variability of species, and as voucher material for published records.*

1.3 *To document faunal representation in environments undergoing or threatened with alteration by man or natural forces.*

1.4 *To participate in development of regional checklists and institutional reference collections.*

1.5 *To complement a planned research endeavor.*

1.6 *To aid in dissemination of educational information.*

1.7 *To augment understanding of taxonomic and ecologic relationships for medical and economic purposes.*

RESTRAINTS AS TO NUMBERS:

2.1 *Collection (of adults or of immature stages) should be limited to sampling, not depleting, the population concerned, numbers collected should be consistent with, and not excessive for, the purpose of the collecting.*

2.2 *When collecting where the extent and/or the fragility of the population is unknown, caution and restraint should be exercised.*

COLLECTING METHODS:

3.1 *Field collecting should be selective. When consistent with the reasons for the particular collecting, males should be taken in preference to females.*

3.2 *Bait or light traps should be live-traps and should be visited regularly; released material should be dispersed to reduce predation by birds.*

3.3 *The use of Malaise or other killing traps should be limited to planned studies.*

LIVE MATERIAL:

4.1 *Rearing to elucidate life histories and to obtain series of immature stages and adults is to be encouraged, provided that collection of the rearing stock is in keeping with these guidelines.*

4.2 *Reared material in excess of need should be released, but only in the region where it originated, and in suitable habitat.*

ENVIRONMENTAL AND LEGAL CONSIDERATIONS:

5.1 *Protection of the supporting habitat must be recognized as the* sine qua non *of protection of a species.*

5.2 *Collecting should be performed in a manner such as to minimize trampling or other damage to the habitat or to specific foodplants.*

5.3 *Property rights and sensibilities of others must be respected (including those of photographers and butterfly-watchers).*

5.4 *Regulations relating to publicly controlled areas and to individual species and habitats must be complied with.*

5.5 *Compliance with agricultural, customs, medical and other regulations should be attained prior to importing live material.*

RESPONSIBILITY FOR COLLECTED MATERIAL:

6.1 *All material should be preserved with full data attached, including parentage of immatures when known.*

6.2 *All material should be protected from physical damage and deterioration, as by light, molds, and museum pests.*

6.3 *Collections should be made available for examination by qualified researchers.*

6.4 *Collections or specimens, and their associated written and photographic records, should be willed or offered to the care of an appropriate scientific institution, if the collector lacks space or loses interest, or in anticipation of death.*

6.5 *Type specimens, especially holotype or allotype, should be deposited in appropriate scientific institutions.*

RELATED ACTIVITIES OF COLLECTORS:

7.1 *Collecting should include permanently recorded field notes regarding habitat, conditions, and other pertinent information.*

7.2 *Recording of observations of behavior and of biological interactions should receive as high priority as collecting.*

7.3 *Photographic records, with full data, are to be encouraged.*

7.4 *Education of the public regarding collecting and conservation, as reciprocally beneficial activities, should be undertaken whenever possible.*

TRAFFIC IN LEPIDOPTERAN SPECIMENS:

8.1 *Collection of specimens for exchange or sale should be performed in accordance with these guidelines.*

8.2 *Rearing of specimens for exchange or sale should be from stock obtained in a manner consistent with these guidelines, and so documented.*

8.3 *Mass collecting of Lepidoptera for commercial purposes, and collection or use of specimens for creation of saleable artifacts, are not included among the purposes of the Society.*

The guidelines are meant not to regulate lepidopterists but to remove the need for regulation by asking them to consider their actions carefully. They are worth reading even if you think you know what you are doing. While teaching an early spring insect course at Lake Louise, Alberta, recently, I was rather desperate because of the lack of insects so soon after snowmelt. Unaware of a gentleman on the opposite side of the bush, I swept a pussy willow for the flies on its yellow catkins. To my horror, I realized that this man was trying to photograph the same pussy willow and the insects coming for its pollen. He was irate, I was mortified, and only my students enjoyed the spectacle.

In sum, the title of this book does not suggest that I am adamantly opposed to collecting. I believe that collecting has its place for children, hobbyists, and scientists. But for butterfly lovers who fall somewhere between the kids and the professors, who have no desire to enmesh butterflies in nets or impale them on pins, watching may furnish the best way to enjoy these fascinating animals.

4

How to Find Butterflies

The cool, foggy maritime regions of Maine and Washington, where I now live, are often considered America's poorest places for watching butterflies. One can go out and find places with all the attributes I am about to describe, where butterflies really should be teeming—and see next to none. Indeed, they may be absent altogether in a sunny, flowery meadow seemingly designed for butterflies. Yet one keeps hoping, and sallies forth each time with renewed expectations. Just often enough to reinforce such behavior, such places yield enough interesting butterflies to maintain interest and enthusiasm. Yet the low rate of gratification is trying for a butterfly watcher who has had the pleasure of tropical forays. I have made it a long-term goal to understand the reasons for the relative butterfly poverty of the Maritime Northwest, and this quest in itself helps add interest.

Having been raised in the prolific butterfly country of Colorado, it took me a long time to get used to the subtlety of the western Washington fauna. Yet the fact is, you can get skunked anywhere. I remember a brilliant morning in a Colorado canyon, where thistles abounded in purple masses in the sunshine. I fully expected to see scores of fritillaries, swallowtails, and other beauties tippling on the fulsome flowers. But all I saw was a single wood nymph. One goes where butterflies by all rights should be, and when they don't show, it can be very vexing.

By its very vexation, however, such an experience implies that as a rule, butterflies usually *are* where they ought to be. In fact, except for those off-days and off-places, finding butterflies is mostly a matter of knowing where they should be. That, in turn, means learning what they need and what they like. For wherever such resources occur, in the right range and season, you will be most likely to find the butterflies you seek.

What does a butterfly need? Each stage in its life history—egg, larva, pupa, and adult—has its own ecological requirements. For the egg and the chrysalis (pupa), this consists essentially of the right kind of substrate for attachment, safe from the weather and predators and reasonably near the host plant. The host plant is the chief requirement of the caterpillar (larva). Most species are very selective in this regard, but given the right plant at the right stage of growth, and cover for resting beneath when inactive, the caterpillar is happy.

The needs of adult butterflies are somewhat more general but also more complex. One is obviously nectar, so flowers are the most conspicuous draw. But adults are nearly as likely to drink of other substances, among them scat, carrion, sap, rotting fruit, aphid honeydew, as well as the moisture around mud puddles, seeps, or shorelines. From nectar and sap they gain starches, and a few tropical longwings are known to be able to consume pollen as a direct protein source. Scat and carrion may contribute amino acids. It appears that the common practice of mud-puddling furnishes salts necessary to the diets of male butterflies in particular. Satyrs nectar less than others; blues and swallowtails are great puddlers; nymphs love fruit and sap.

Mud puddles, seeps, and damp sand patches often prove to be productive butterfly grounds. These puddlers are three species of blues, but swallowtails, skippers, and sulphurs join "mud-puddle clubs" just as avidly, sometimes in large numbers.

Physical traits of the landscape are important to some butterflies. Since storms account for a high proportion of butterfly mortality, shelter figures in their needs. When the sun shines, butterflies bask, favoring spots that have proper exposure and high reflectivity. Hibernating species such as Mourning Cloaks need suitable wintering crannies where they will be snug from storm and ice. When they emerge in spring they will seek mates. Careful observation has confirmed that many courting butterflies utilize specific features of their landscape for orientation and to locate one another. For example, Anise Swallowtails and many other species engage in hilltopping; that is, the males seek prominences in the countryside and fly up to and around the summits of hills. Females are thought to enter the arena briefly to be mated. Males of other species select special perches from which they either dart out at passing potential mates or patrol a set course back and forth. Rockslide and canyon butterflies commonly zigzag up and soar down the same paths time and again, all in the pursuit of females.

Where half a dozen species of white butterflies dwell on the same desert tract, they tend to situate by species around subtle features such as rises and arroyos, so as to sort out with their own kind. In Great Britain, the regal Purple Emperor butterfly has been found to utilize a "Master Oak" in its courtship, though the larvae feed on sallows (a kind of willow); cut the oaks and the Emperors abdicate. Similarly, the Threatened Oregon Silverspot employs violets in scarce salt-spray coastal meadows for its host plant; but adult interactions take place largely within sheltered, nectar-bearing clearings in the nearby forest. This double ecological requirement is not an uncommon state of affairs.

You can see by now that the needs of butterflies are not as simple as just a patch of posies in the sunshine. But, speaking of the sun, I should say that bright sunlight may be counted the least variable preference of butterflies in general. Whether it is simply to raise their night-chilled blood temperatures and warm their flight muscles, to give maximum photo-orientation and vision, or to provide some evidence that lethal thunderstorms are not at hand, sunshine seems to be a profound prerequisite for flight on the part of many species. True, a few will fly in overcast; others will flout clouds, rain, and even snow; still others thrive in deep, dark rain forest. But even on hot days with a covering of clouds, most butterflies refuse to come out of hiding, and the coming of clouds over the sun heralds a vanishing act for butterflies abroad moments before. In the case of some arctic-alpine species, it is truly astonishing how quickly they disappear and how deeply into the sedges they burrow as soon as vagrant clouds obscure the sun.

Taken together, these factors, along with water and oxygen, make up the needs of butterflies and constitute the components of their environment. Find them, and you are likely to find the animals themselves. To sum up: A good butterfly spot is a sunny, warm place where abundant flowers bloom, where moisture is present and a wide array of herbaceous and woody plants grows. The presence of stumps and hollows, sun-struck banks or walls, and perhaps some mammals make it even better. The larger the habitat the better, since localities tend to lose species as they become fragmented and hemmed in by urban influences. A spot with these qualities (unless, perhaps, it lies in western Washington) is unlikely to disappoint you in your search for butterflies. And let us add one note: Herbicides and/or insecticides can ruin the picture. If a site has been recently or regularly sprayed, its capacity for holding butterflies will have been greatly diminished. A powerline right-of-way can be a butterfly paradise if managed by mowing, barren if by spraying. The same goes for roadsides.

From the features mentioned above, we compile a list of potentially good kinds of butterfly watching spots:

Arboretums	Gardens	Rights-of-way
Bogs	Glades	(powerline, pipe-
Burns	Gravel pits	line, railway)
Campuses	Hilltops	Riverbars
Canals	Marshes	Roadsides
Canyons	Meadows	Seeps
Cemeteries	Mud puddles	Shorelines
Clearings (small)	Open woods	Swamps
Creeks	Orchards	Talus
Deltas	Parks	Thicket edges
Deserts	Pastures	Trails
Ditches	Plains	Tundra
Farmyards	Prairies	Vacant lots
Fields	Quarries	Waterfalls
		Wineries

Why wineries and farmyards? Because butterflies go for sweet spills as much as for manure. This list is accompanied in my mind by images of successful butterfly spotting in each of the kinds of places mentioned. You will notice that it includes both natural and anthropogenic (human-influenced) kinds of features. Other things being equal, nature reserves, wilderness areas, and national parks offer better prospects than the developed landscape. Parts of the latter, however, can be rewarding. This is particularly true where man-made features have grown gradually among the natural elements of the countryside, as in much of the British Isles. Butterflies do adapt, some more than others, given half a chance. As Chapter 15 on conservation points out, specialist species can drop out when disturbed. But artificial conditions may actually enhance habitat for others, especially those generalist and weedy species capable of rapidly colonizing suitable host plants when the opportunity presents itself.

For example, it has been found that one of the few plants able to revegetate the wasted mine spoils in the collieries of South Wales is *Buddleia davidii,* the butterfly bush. Few other plants are esteemed so highly as nectar sources by butterfly gardeners. Peacock butterflies, Red Admirals, and Small Tortoiseshells all flock to its pungent purple spikes of flowers. Happily, all three of these British butterflies feed on stinging nettles in the larval stage, and this plant also thrives in the industrial landscape. So among the relatively few organisms able to adapt and prosper in this hostile anthropogenic environment is a trio of brightly colored nymphs.

Likewise, common leguminous crops such as red clover and alfalfa have proven to be fine larval hosts for several of our native sulphur butterflies and blues, and other butterflies treat their nectar as ambrosia. Unnatural influences can also open the forest canopy and admit more sunshine, thus favoring butterflies. A small forest clearing may be a boon, but the vast clearcuts of the Pacific Northwest overdo it and tend to be devoid of butterflies. Rights-of-way and roadsides are very good for butterflies (as all lepidopterists know) because they emulate and extend the "edge effect" in ecology: Edges, or ecotones between habitat types, provide the greatest variety of vegetation in both species and structure, and therefore a greater number of niches than may be found in more homogenous habitats on either side. This effect may be nulli-fied by a lack of natural habitats in propinquity, as sources of species. That is, if the whole landscape becomes one great "edge" of secondary scrub, as is happening in much of the tropics, then a uniform, poor, and monotonous fauna results.

The foregoing gives you an idea of the range of places where you can expect to find butterflies in season. You can do even better with a little knowledge about the specific preferences of individual kinds of butterflies. Just how specific are they?

If you think of a Painted Lady, the answer is "not very." Its alternate common name, in fact, is the Cosmopolitan Butterfly. Butterfly collectors learn not to be surprised to find Painted Ladies anywhere. A highly emigratory animal whose larvae consume weedy thistles and whose adults reproduce rapidly and fly with swiftness and power, the Painted Lady can be found almost any-where except in the deep tropics and on the arctic icecaps. Even open water fails to deter its movements. Similarly, I am incapable of being surprised by Milbert's Tortoiseshell and where it occurs in the United States. A hardy, cold-tolerant nettle-feeder, this flame-rimmed brown butterfly is just as content in the high arctic-alpine as down on the arid plains or deep in the northwoods.

Most butterflies are not so adaptable. The majority choose a single species or genus of plant as larval host, while few will accept or survive on plants outside a given family. Obviously, learning these plants (named in butterfly field guides insofar as they are known) is the seminal step in finding the butterflies they support. The application of such knowledge can be very pleasur-able. I recall the first time I sought the little Hoary Elfin in western Washington, when I was new to the region. I knew the host plant was kinnikinnick, an evergreen heath. No sooner had I stepped out of my car beside a roadside patch of the shiny stuff than a pair of the frosted brown hairstreaks rose and circled over the shrub. I got a photograph and a deep sense of satisfaction. Finding butter-flies is a constant treasure hunt, and foodplants provide the pri-mary clues.

There are others. How choosy are butterflies about their nectar? "One person's poison . . ." applies somewhat to flower-sugars, al-though butterflies are less choosy in this way than toward larval hosts. Still, my observations tell me that they exercise more choice

*The Painted Lady, also
known as the Cosmopolitan
Butterfly, may turn up in
almost any habitat or locality
in prolific years. Thistles
serve both as nectar sources
for adults and as larval hosts.*

about nectar than a lot of lepidopterists have commonly believed. Certainly not every butterfly is a sucker for any drink going. So I seek swallowtails at thistles and wild cherries and phlox, silverspots at horse mint and asters, blues at composites and clovers, and hairstreaks at bee-balm and clematis. Generally the wild or naturalized relatives of good garden sources are attractive. You will quickly learn which flowers work well in your area, both as general attractants and as draws for particular kinds. A visit to a botanic garden or floral park can be helpful in this respect; you can read the label on the plant while you watch the butterfly drink from it. You will also learn which flowers to ignore, since butterflies ignore them: roses and hydrangeas, dahlias and peonies, and most double ornamental hybrids. But do not write off anything altogether, for surprises occur: In the past year I have witnessed butterflies visiting a wild rose, a daffodil, and ox-eye daisies—all flowers I love but had considered worthless for butterfly watching. There comes a point when you will be as inexorably drawn by certain flowers as the butterflies themselves. A patch of dogbane in a mountain canyon, a bed of marigolds in a city park—these will become irresistible, and you will simply have to have a look.

Few situations offer better butterfly finding than sunny, flowery spots with lots of readily accessible nectar. Here a pair of Red-banded Hair-streaks, normally very flighty, nectar peacefully on a composite.

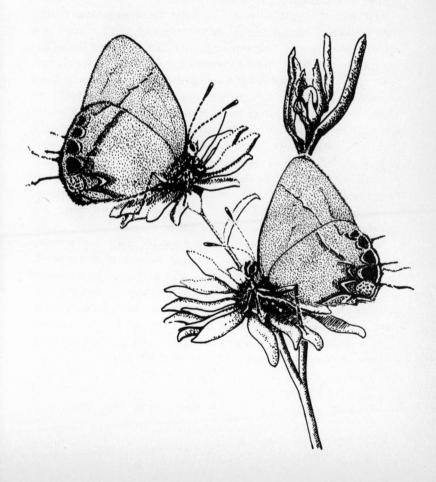

Suppose you have figured out the physical and biological requirements of a species of butterfly and visited a promising locale on a sunny day, checked out the right plants and features, and still fail to find it. Does that mean it doesn't occur there? No; negative evidence never establishes anything. There could be several possible explanations. Annual variation in weather can severely diminish populations in bad years. A late, dry winter followed by a cold, wet, prolonged spring makes for a summer low in butterflies; and they may not recover their average numbers for a year or two. Parasite cycles also cause great fluctuations in population. The glorious purple Colorado Hairstreak was absent from its traditional metropolis in Deer Creek Canyon west of Denver for years—and parasite cycles are as likely an explanation as any. Now it has repopulated the area.

Remember too that butterflies have specific flight periods lasting days or weeks, though actual dates vary with temperature and rainfall. Most species have one or more generations per year. Certain northern and mountain varieties are biennial, requiring two years to metamorphose fully. When all the individuals of a biennial species are in phase, they appear only every other year. Phase varies from place to place, so there are ranges in Canada where Chryxus Arctics fly only in odd years, others with even-numbered flight years, still others where they fly every year. Both single- and multi-brooded species emerge earlier or later depending on local conditions, and might or might not overlap. Also, flight periods tend to recede with both latitude and elevation—the later the date, the higher you hunt. So don't write off a spot without giving it a fair chance and thinking about seasonality.

Now consider a situation in which a species really does seem to be missing from an apparently suitable habitat, after repeated, careful searches in different seasons and years. If the reason is anthropogenic, it should be obvious: bulldozing, paving, logging, or some other gross change may have taken place. Spraying may leave fewer obvious signs, unless it was a herbicide that turns the green vegetation to an ugly, twisted yellow. But if nothing of the sort has interposed, the cause must be sought elsewhere. It is crucial to realize that animals are distributed not only in time but also in space according to very specific criteria. Each species has its proper range as well as habitat and time of flight. Again, the

Painted Lady tries to break this rule, but most butterflies lack such ubiquity. While some are distributed around the Northern Hemisphere, such as the Red Admiral, and others all up and down the New World, like the Common Checkered Skipper, the greater share occupy more restricted ranges. Endemics are those whose range consists solely of some very narrowly defined area—an island, say, or part of a state. The Avalon Hairstreak, confined to Santa Catalina Island and the Uncompaghre Fritillary of Colorado's San Juan Mountains vie as our narrowest endemics. Most species fall somewhere in the middle and are neither endemic nor cosmopolitan.

So geographic considerations may foil your search. You may be within the general range of a species as indicated in the field guides, but it might never have reached a suitable locality where you think it should be. Invisible barriers of moisture, temperature regime, or some combination of climatic factors—or physical barriers such as major rivers or ranges—can keep butterflies out. I suspect this is the case with many of the butterflies absent from western Washington: Too densely forested, cool, and cloudy for many species' liking, it also lies in a biogeographical backwater, tucked away in the corner of the country. Yet I wonder, why does the Ochre Ringlet, present in all the surrounding counties of Washington and Oregon, eschew the county in which I live, when habitats seem to abound? Why does Mitchell's Marsh Satyr survive in the few remaining marshes of suitable quality in Michigan and Ohio, and perhaps New Jersey, while never having been seen in intervening Pennsylvania? These are the kinds of questions that astute observers can help to solve.

You will save time and frustration, not to mention precious days of sunshine and leisure, if you consult lepidopterists in your region as well as the lists, records, and maps compiled by local and state butterfly clubs. Sources and contacts appear in the Appendix. But don't rely exclusively on second-hand hints. Collectors tend to be rather unadventurous, visiting year after year tried and trusted localities where they know they can find their quarry. The names of such spots are passed on like precious embers until they become general knowledge, embedded in the local lepidopterological folklore. I find that much of the pleasure is in the searching and that a day out-of-doors is never misspent. So unless your heart

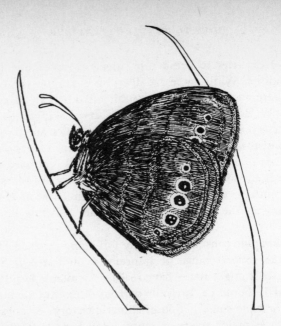

Mitchell's Marsh Satyr is an example of a butterfly that must be sought in a few, specialized settings. Severely restricted by drainage of wetlands, it has retreated to a few tamarack bogs in the upper Midwest and New Jersey.

is set on finding only a specific butterfly in your limited time off, I recommend a bit of casting about on your own as well as visiting the great old spots the "pros" will recommend. In this way your own field savvy will grow faster and you may very well contribute something new.

There are tools you can use to enhance the success and enjoyment of your search. Learn to read and use U.S. Geologic Survey topographic maps (topo sheets). This is vital for accurate record-keeping, and it also helps in finding exciting places. If you know that a particular sort of butterfly is a denizen of territory above a given elevation, you follow the contours on the map to find potentially accessible alpine localities, such as glacial basins or long ridges with plenty of room for rambling. Roads and trails are shown on the topo sheets as well as land-use designations to tell whether permits are required or mining might be in progress. A wealth of information either appears on or may be inferred from these maps. County or public agency maps may also help to distin-

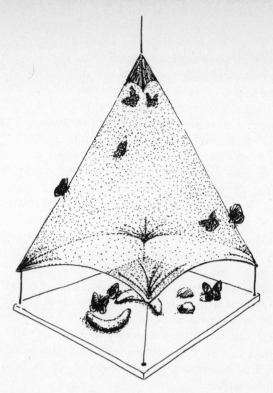

A simple design for a butterfly trap, to be suspended from a branch.
Overripe fruit attracts Red Admirals and others, which then become
entrapped in the netting. Good for close observation.

guish private lands from public. Some naturalists are using
LANDSAT infrared photographs along with maps to locate promising patches of certain vegetation types. Needless to say, but necessary to emphasize, you should always carry a compass and know how
to use it both to make the best use of maps and to avoid getting lost.

Another set of tools can help you to attract butterflies once you
arrive in a good place. Rotted fruits or a mixture similar to mothing sugar (see chapters 11 and 17) may be placed out to attract
more individuals than you might otherwise see. Such baits set on
a stump in a dappled glade may well attract wood nymphs and
brush-footed butterflies. You can bait a platform suspended beneath an inverted butterfly net hung from a branch, and find Red
Admirals, Commas, and other tipplers waiting for you in the net

when you return (see page 47). A Malaise trap is an elaborate gauze tent erected in such a way that insects fly up and in, not out. As with the bait trap, such a device enables you to find out what lives in a locality and to see butterflies thus caught up close. The animals are not hurt and they may then be released. Taiwanese professional collectors urinate on mountain paths and display brightly colored bits of cloth to lure male swallowtails and others. These techniques can work just as well elsewhere, assuming the social setting allows for such behavior.

None of the baits, traps, or tricks, however, furnish the same degree of pleasure and wonderment as a natural, unpremeditated encounter. You must determine your own favorite ways of locating butterflies. The important thing to remember is that most places contain unique butterfly charms that you can discover if you are open to them. It may be as easy as opening your eyes in a summer meadow redolent with clover and aflutter with bright wings or as challenging as ferreting out a single bush and its butterfly in a backcountry canyon. Success is certain with practice and some decent habitats to visit. You cannot help but gain a sense of the landscape, and in so doing, you will come to see the land through the eyes of butterflies.

This means that eventually you will even be able to find butterflies during inclement weather. Think of where you would take shelter from pelting rain or hail if you were a delicate, dextrous creature. As a small boy, I once took shelter from a devastating hailstorm with my brother in a great hollow cottonwood tree. It saved our lives. Butterflies do the same. And I recall another stormy afternoon in the same vicinity when my young butterfly partner found a Black Swallowtail in the downpour: it had taken shelter from the thunderstorm beneath a broad elm leaf. Our electricity went out during the storm, but that rainy-day butterfly lit up our afternoon. Sally Hughes is especially good at finding butterflies during bad weather. One sodden afternoon on the tundra of the Olympic Mountains, after days of rain, we decided to look for butterflies anyway. She managed to find a High Mountain Blue that had burrowed down into the mosses and grasses of the alpine turf. She tucked it back; the butterfly was too cold to move, and no doubt it remained there until the sun finally shone. Sometime later I watched a West Coast Lady fly into a cherry tree

Inclement weather provides a challenge in butterfly finding. Here a Regal Fritillary takes shelter beneath the umbrella of a dried umbel.

as the clouds gathered. Sure enough, the rain came, but the Lady was snug with her wings folded tight beneath the green umbrella of a leaf.

Even winter isn't a good enough excuse for giving up on butterfly watching until spring. A number of butterflies—certain nymphalids (brush-foots) in North America and also the yellow

Brimstone (a pierid) in Europe—overwinter as adults. Some of these will fly about on a sunny day in midwinter. Records are few, since even lepidopterists tend to put on butterfly-blinders north of the frost-free latitudes between November and April. Not so Professor A. B. Klots, however. The author of the Peterson field guide to eastern butterflies reports in that small classic an occasion when he found six species of butterflies in a New England dump— during February! I encourage people to watch for butterflies in winter as well as summer. A midwinter butterfly walk holds out no guarantee of success; but it offers at least the possibility, in a season when the sight of one live butterfly can do as much for the spirit as a whole meadowful in June.

And what of those chronically unrewarding places, like western Washington and Maine? In truth, even they are not so bad if one persists. A venerable lepidopterist in Maine knows just where to find special Down East butterflies such as the little metallic mauve Bog Copper and the fabled Katahdin Arctic. I can take you to see swallowtails breeding on Seaside Angelica around Willapa Bay, and show you milky, ruby-spotted Clodius Parnassians in my front yard. Often, the pleasure in butterfly watching is a matter of adjusting expectations to local realities. If I could do it between Colorado and the Maritime Northwest—not to mention New Guinea—you can surely do it anywhere.

5

Watching Butterflies

In the previous chapter I urged you to try to see the landscape as a butterfly might, to spot the resources it would seek for itself. Now I would like you to "think like a butterfly"—that is, put yourself in a butterfly's place, as it adapts to the array of perils and opportunities that present themselves. If you can do so, you will soon come to understand the ways to behave so as to cause the least disturbance to the butterflies you wish to see up close.

Clothing makes a difference, to start with. We know that butterflies see in color and are sensitive to the ultraviolet range of light. This means that the old maxim that one should dress drably while pursuing wildlife (unless hunting!) applies here. I have found that bright clothing is more likely to put butterflies to flight than earth-toned fabrics. This can, however, be turned to your advantage, since males, especially, may be attracted to bright swatches of cloth. I won't soon forget the brilliant blue Ulysses Swallowtails that darted at my blue denim cap again and again in New Guinea. Red hats and shirts attract many a nymph in search of flowers. A bright bandanna may serve as an effective lure to bring butterflies closer. But such behavior may not be particularly conducive to close observation, since the inspecting butterflies more often dart and flit away again than settle. It may not be simply tradition that dictates the khaki color field clothing worn by many field entomologists.

A Ulysses Swallowtail, or Mountain Emperor, darts at the blue hat of a New Guinea visitor. Garments may serve to attract inquisitive butterflies.

Even a very colorful outfit need not spoil your efforts if you truly take care in other respects. Clothing is less important than comportment. And the cardinal rule is to move with stealth, deliberation, and fluidity. Whether watching, netting, or photographing butterflies, the principle is the same: Rapid movements startle butterflies. Even if you merely brush away a fly, or jerk your head, quick movements are likely to spook your quarry and put it to flight in the opposite direction. Bright clothing intensifies the startle effect of movement. So in order to maximize proximity and period of contact, you must learn to approach butterflies slyly and slowly, making every shift of limb as natural and slow-motion as you can. Never let your shadow fall across a perched butterfly if you can help it, as this is almost guaranteed to disturb it.

Indeed the whole point is to approach butterflies when they are alighted on some surface. Once in flight, they become obviously much more difficult to observe (except that you will no doubt want to follow flight patterns as well, to learn their methods and varieties). When you come across a flitting or soaring butterfly, the first step is to await its landing. You will soon learn that angle-wings, skippers, and hairstreaks tend to return to their perches, while sulphurs and swallowtails, once gone, are likely lost from sight. So station yourself near likely spots for nectaring, basking, or perching, and await the arrival of butterflies; or, intercepting them in flight, follow ever so slowly and unthreateningly and hope they will soon alight. Then make the calculated, slothlike approach I described above. If the insect takes wing, wait for a few moments to see whether it will reappear. If not, start over. Eventually you should manage to get a good look at even the wildest species. But if you barge ahead, brash and nervous in your actions, or over-confident, you may never succeed.

During the writing of this book a warm day came when I felt the need to get out. Since it was late fall, few butterflies were about. Across the river, I spied a cinnamon flash that could only be an anglewing getting ready to bed down for the winter. I saw it settle on a dried weed, but in crossing a stream and climbing the slippery bank I frightened it and it flew off. Yet the habit of anglewings is to hang about. So I searched and searched, and at last I spotted the reddish-golden, raggedy-edged Satyr Anglewing basking on the bank and sipping from the mud where cattle had passed. It had no intention of leaving soon. I weaseled my way very close and in the end spent an enchanted half hour at a range of inches, watching its russet wings with their inky spots and lilac tips, and its pulsing body covered with shiny green-bronze fur. The filament of a tongue probed the damp earth as the spot-tipped antennae tapped the air and the ground before the bright nymph. I left with the anglewing still in place. It was difficult to leave, but I find a special satisfaction in leaving a butterfly undisturbed after watching it well.

People tend to be astonished when I show them just how close they can get to a living butterfly. With care, there is no reason why you should not be able to watch most species from a meter or two, while to come within inches is not at all rare. The ultimate is to be able to touch a butterfly gently, to feel the soft downiness of its fringes, the delicate touch of its tarsi. Wipe a little sweat

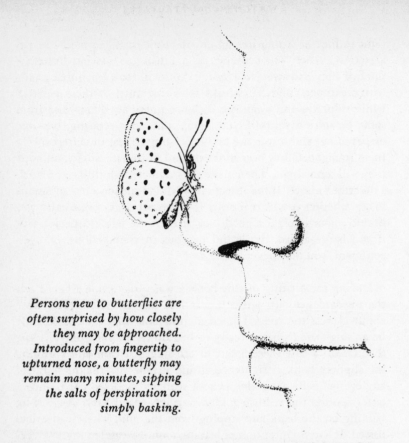

Persons new to butterflies are often surprised by how closely they may be approached. Introduced from fingertip to upturned nose, a butterfly may remain many minutes, sipping the salts of perspiration or simply basking.

onto your forefinger and place it before a perched butterfly so that it is encouraged to climb aboard. When the hind feet touch the saltiness of the perspiration, chances are its proboscis will uncoil and begin to drink. Blues behave in an especially gratifying way when thus treated, particularly if they are already mudding. From there it is an easy matter to transfer the sipper to nose, forehead, or flower. I have unashamedly used this trick many times to introduce skeptical children to the joys of butterflies. Once they see it happen, parents want to try as well.

Such encounters are satisfying and fun, but the main thing is to gain proximity—a foot is as good as a nose—so that you can clearly see the characteristics of the living butterfly. To see the loose scatter of sapphire scales in the ebony setting of a swallowtail's hindwing, like stars in a distant, dispersed galaxy—such a sight cannot be duplicated in a collector's cabinet with the same aesthetic impact. The probing of mud or blossom with the living, pumping proboscis conveys the vital moment-to-moment existence of butterflies as organisms of nature. Or the unexpected may occur. While watching an amethyst Colorado Hairstreak basking on a shiny green scrub oak leaf, a field class of mine witnessed a rarely observed event. A large robber fly appeared from nowhere, seized the strong and wary hairstreak before our eyes, and absconded with it.

Certain conditions help to guarantee success. Foremost is not being hurried, so you can exercise patience. All this does not happen at once; you have to give it time and undistracted attention. Another is solitude. Much can be seen by pairs or coteries of watchers, as I know from my annual butterfly classes. Yet the loner is likely to see more or see it longer, undistracted and unhindered by the rash motions of others. This must be balanced against the joy of sharing the experience. I love to be afield with children, but their sheer unbridled enthusiasm does little to foster butterflies' equanimity. Nothing pleases me more than seeing someone's eyes light up, who was blind to butterflies before; yet also I need to observe butterflies alone. I advise taking time for both the shared and solo moments.

Dogs may be delightful field companions, undemanding of conversation, but they tend to spot your quarry for you and put it to flight. The only two pooches with whom I have spent much time out-of-doors, a border collie and a dalmatian, were much better at shying butterflies than at pointing quietly while I watched. My cat, on the other hand, has more than once actually captured a butterfly I was engaged in observing. Uninvited spoilers show up as well. The passage of a bird or a grasshopper will likely startle a butterfly. Many times I have been focusing on a flower feeder, only to have it shoved off by a bumblebee or irritated by a fly intent upon it as a perch.

Different species vary in their tolerance of intruders; some will shoulder their way to the nectar past bees and wasps, while others clear out at the least competition. Perhaps the most common form of disturbance consists of other butterflies, especially those of the same species. Unable to resist a quick look at a potential mate, males especially spring up to encircle newcomers. The challenged and challenger often disappear together. Should you happen to have a territorial post under surveillance rather than a mere nectar stop, one or the other will normally reappear—usually the butterfly who held the patch in the first place.

When you go afield in search of butterflies, two basic approaches help in spotting them. Both are wholly applicable to nature perception in general, so butterfly watching provides good discipline for becoming a broader, more observant field naturalist. First, it helps to adjust your scale of attention downward. Most people, even those who look beyond the man-made, focus on big, spectacular things that catch their attention. They fail to see the fairy world of minute mushrooms and micromoths. Small wonder! Our sensations are bombarded constantly with superlatives. The scale of our urban habitat is such that only the stupendous and garish can vie for attention with the megalithic and brash. So when we go to the parks, we see giant sequoias and Half Dome but we often miss the seedlings and the pebbles. In order to rejoice in the sublimity of butterflies, you need to look down and think small. Then in a sense you *become* small, able to step among anemones without bruising them, able to touch a butterfly without harming it. Warning: Once you have found this scale of operation, the world will never look quite the same to you. You may become a slower hiker and an impossibly distracted gardener. I personally think it's worth it.

The second, more demanding task is to pick your way visually among the artifacts of the landscape so as to spot your targets. This means seeking disconformities among all the ordinary objects that might be butterflies. You have to acquire a search image. Let's say you arrive in a meadow on a bright, warm morning. The scene is a complicated tapestry of parti-colored flowers, dozens of shades of green, breeze-tossed vegetation, and buzzing, flapping, moving images of insects. How do you pick out a butterfly from all this? An insect's image in a field guide may not have a lot to do with how it looks in the field, wings folded or flapping, definitely not holding still. But I cannot really tell you how to acquire a butterfly search image. It comes only through watching. To start with, pick an object you think is a butterfly, tune out everything else, then simply stick with it through all its gyrations. It will not be long until butterflies fairly leap out at you from the living mosaic, and not much longer until you have a pretty good idea of approximately what they are at first glimpse. This is where the butterfly gestalt enters in; I will continue the discussion of the subject in Chapter 7 on identification.

Before moving on from recognition, a word to the wise about imposters. A number of other insects rather resemble butterflies while in flight, and some discrimination is called for in sorting them out from the real thing. Of day-flying and bright moths, you will learn more later. One group deserving mention here is that of the vapourers or tussock moths. So butterflylike are these bright chestnut diurnals that many a lepidopterist has been titillated by the promise of some unexpected hairstreak or copper. Alas, they are always just furry old tussocks; but they have their own beauty, with great plumelike antennae on the males and bright white spots on their russet forewings. (The females are flightless.) They also have their own manner of flight, rather frenetic and unbalanced, that eventually gives you their measure.

Any number of clear-winged insects, flashing in the sun, can give you pause for an instant—especially dragon- and damselflies. Caddisflies, hoverflies, and wasps can also be deceiving for an instant or at a distance. Perhaps the most perennial spoofs are the black-and-yellow-winged Carolina Grasshopper (*Dissosteira carolina*) and its banded relatives. Exhibiting the same general pattern as the Mourning Cloak butterfly, these hoppers distract the eye a thousand times a season. Again, they are worth watching in their own right—try to spot them among the gravel when they alight!— and easy to tell apart in time.

When any of these deceptive insects are numerous they can try your visual dexterity. Even certain butterflies, when extraordinarily abundant, vex the watcher on the lookout for something new. Painted Ladies can be that way in an eruptive year. Collectors tend to term such commonplace species "junkbugs" or "trash"— derogations of which I wholeheartedly disapprove. This year's junkbug may be next year's rarity, due to the fluctuating nature of many species' numbers. We should take advantage of the bumper years with frequent, intensive observation.

The opposite situation occurs when there are no butterflies apparent. Then the search image is confronted with a different chal-

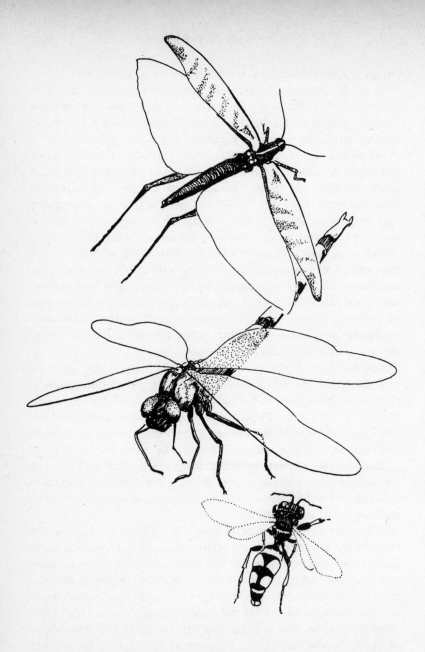

Acquiring a search image for butterflies means learning to distinguish them quickly from other flying objects. Common distractions include grasshoppers, dragonflies, and wasps.

lenge. I am reminded of a day one recent spring when I came upon a little glade among the alders, a suntrap that looked so suited to butterflies I could scarcely believe there would be none. At first glance, not an insect stirred. Looking closer, from ten meters away, sure enough I spied the golden wedge of a Dun Skipper basking on a low alder leaf. It turned out to be a new record of occurrence for southwest Washington, yet at first it was all but invisible. It pays to look carefully before entering such a likely-looking spot, for if you charge ahead you may chase away any butterflies that might have been there.

My advice in this chapter has dwelt upon patience and taking time. I do not want to create the impression that short walks and odd moments are worthless for this pursuit. The fact is that none of us has more hours in the day then twenty-four, and there are bound to be many occasions when you can spare only minutes instead of one or more of those hours. Take heart: A lot of rewarding, if tantalizing, butterfly watching can be done in stolen moments.

Whenever you find yourself at loose ends for a spell, consider the butterflying prospects nearby. Taking a bus, train, or plane trip? I always investigate the precincts of the depot even on short layovers, and usually find something worth watching. Outside a Florida airport, Long-tailed Skippers were the reward; in New Orleans, Phaon Crescentspots beside the Mississippi levee a short walk from the concourse. Waiting for a car repair? Nothing more boring, but in a vacant lot beside a Connecticut garage I found my first European Small Skippers; and in Portland, a brief walk under the same circumstances let me see Woodland Skippers on a dozen different backgrounds from sword ferns to lavender. When the car is back on the road, remember that highway rest areas are well worth exploring while stretching your legs on a long trip.

A recent pause at a roadside picnic area near Washington's Stevens Pass treated me to close-up comparative views of three species of anglewings. Side by side, they were stocking their energy supplies for hibernation by visiting something a picnicker's dog had left behind.

Some of my most memorable spare-time butterfly watching took place a couple of summers ago in Hayes, Kansas. I had just an hour at my motel between engagements, shortly before sunset on a cool summer day. It had been a rainy week and the prairie was resplendent with native wildflowers. A patch of that near-original prairie nestled along a watercourse between the commercial strip and a subdivision. I had a go. Immigrant Dwarf Yellows flew all about. A big, fresh Variegated Fritillary showed its white-netted side as it sought warmth by basking in the last of the day's rays. Gray Hairstreaks, Tailed Blues, and crescentspots chased one another and visited the profusion of grassland blossoms. A swallowtail, a lady, and several sulphurs sailed by. I counted three or four skippers among the score of species I'd tallied before it was time to go. My trip was much richer for that hour.

More recently, I found myself stranded in a shopping mall in Vancouver, Washington. My wife, Thea, had business in an office block across from the sprawling mercantile palace. I only hoped it would be quick. Then I noticed a formal garden of petunias and ageratum in a lawn before the offices. I got out of the car, knelt to sniff the sweet pink and purple trumpets of the petunias, and spotted skippers on the ageratum. They were of a type abundant throughout the Northwest in late summer, numerous in my own garden; but I never tire of watching their precise and edgy behavior. Then I saw something different—a little longer-winged, bigger overall, patterned more sharply. Thea emerged and the two of us amused the office captives as we crawled about on our knees, observing closely, finally seeing three of the oddities well. As I suspected, these interlopers turned out to be Sachems—a species of tawny skipper never before recorded in Washington State. "A state record," I kept saying on the way home, "and in a mall!"

By all means take the time, if you have it, to watch deliberately. If not, see how butterflies close to home or highway can help you salvage odd moments. A pop phrase I dislike but that is useful here is "quality time"—referring, I presume, to high-quality, as opposed to lower-quality, experience. Whether a week in the wilds or an hour in a vacant lot, all time spent with butterflies is "quality time." This is a highly sensual business you are setting about. So think small, move slowly, look sharply, be patient—and prepare for extraordinary pleasures.

6

Butterfly Watching Equipment

One day during my studies of insect conservation and butterfly farming in Papua New Guinea, Sally Hughes and I set out to see the world's largest butterfly, Queen Alexandra's Birdwing. *Ornithoptera alexandrae* flies only on the Papuan coastal plain, where its rain forest habitat has diminished sharply due to oil palm planting and logging. We were hoping to discover a means for its long-term survival, but first we hoped to glimpse the huge insect in the field. The brilliant aquamarine and black males span eight or nine inches, while the salt-and-pepper females may exceed a foot in wingspread.

A village butterfly farmer named Jeremiah, well aware that this biggest of birdwings is fully protected by the government, assured himself of our credentials, then guided us into the bush. An hour passed. We saw the host plant, *Aristolochia schlechteri*, a vine with long, narrow leaves and seed pods. He showed us a chrysalis the size of my thumb. But there was no sign of the great butterfly itself. Then, when we were nearly back to the village, disappointed yet hopeful, Jeremiah gestured excitedly toward the forest canopy. Way above, perhaps a hundred feet over our heads, a mammoth dark shadow of a butterfly was soaring. "It's *alexandrae*," someone cheered, and so it was. In and out of tropical sunbeams, for a few minutes, twirled the largest butterfly in the world. Then it vanished into the bush, and we never saw another.

I have never been so glad for a pair of binoculars in the field as I was then. Without them, I could have gotten a sense of the size of the birdwing and watched its flight pattern, but that's about all. With binoculars I was able to make out pattern and shape as well as size—I even fancied I saw the scarlet patch of fur on the female Alexandra's thorax—and to feel as if I were flying with her as she surveyed her shrinking jungle world.

All you really need for butterfly watching are your eyes—and even the unsighted can enjoy butterflies, as I will show later. However, your experience may very well be enhanced by carefully chosen accouterments. As I discussed in the previous chapter, the first consideration is clothing. Comfort, visibility, safety from exposure, and ease of movement are all important factors. Bright colors exacerbate the disturbing effects of rapid movements, but may also serve to attract inquisitive butterflies. Two additional thoughts on color relate to safety. A bright shirt or jacket would be more easily seen were one to become lost; and in the autumn, any outdoors person is well advised to wear colors difficult to confuse with deerhide for even the most trigger-happy or drunken hunter. For this purpose, I own a bright scarlet poplin vest; its many pockets are handy for notebooks and pencils and forceps.

Always take warm clothing if your itinerary offers the slightest chance of a night under the stars or a rising storm. I learned this lesson on an extended butterfly walk last summer. I'd hiked from 8,500′ to 13,000′ in the Front Range of the Colorado Rockies, in order to study the all-black Magdalena Alpine butterfly. I am especially drawn to *Erebia magdalena* and its alpine heights. My siren called me higher and higher, and no thunderstorms threatened in the western sky. The day's walk was a great success; I'd seen the ebony Magdalena on a vast mountainface rockslide where it was much at home; watched Milbert's Tortoiseshells dogging the alpines in vain courtships, not giving them a moment's rest; and studied the big spiders that sling their orbs between the granite boulders, occasionally snagging a Magdalena. But now the sun was dropping behind Long's Peak, and it became clear that I would not be able to trace my steps back down a vertical mile of talus and stony bristlecone pine forest before nightfall. I chose instead a descent over the backside of Mount Meeker into well-named Wild Basin, whence a broad pack trail led down to the

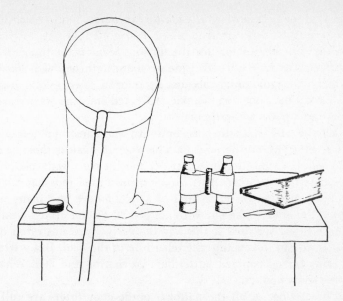

Essential items of equipment for the butterfly enthusiast: hand lens, net, binoculars, forceps, notebook.

lodge. I reached the valley as dusk faded into darkness, but a foaming cascade separated me from the trail. I could only bivouac. I did so, and made a long but simple exit at dawn. There was no real problem, but there might have been had I not carried my goose-down parka in my day-pack, for the temperature of the high country air dropped to the thirties. Hypothermia is the commonest cause of accidental death among outdoor recreationists. A bright, warm, sunny morning and a gentle butterfly walk seem to give little cause for such precautions. But temperatures fall fast as the sun sinks, and fine-weather frolics often take us farther than we intended. It is always best to be adequately prepared for cool or wet weather.

In general, pick field clothing that will repel thorns, shed stickers, prevent sunburn, dry fast, and allow you to move as fluidly as I urged you to do earlier. Cotton is good; wool is better if the temperature permits. I prefer to wear shorts from about April to October, but biting insects, briers, and other assaults on the skin often dictate otherwise. You will work out your own best field outfit as you experiment. Comfort is paramount—remember, you're in this for enjoyment.

Shoe yourself suitably for the terrain. Many is the time I have worn sandals for a little roadside stroll and returned with soaked, scratched feet and ankles because I was lured down a slope or into a wet meadow. Speaking of ankles, a twisted one can spoil a season, so consider boots with support.

A word or two about hats: Sunburn and sunstroke defeat the purpose of any outing, and hats help guard against them. They also help to keep biting insects at bay and cut glare from spectacles, binoculars, and camera lens. In a pinch, a capacious hat can be clamped over an insect in lieu of a net. I have had many, lost many, but always take one with me even if I don't always wear it. I have never yet used it the way the early Aurelians often did; that is, to pin insects into the felt while in the field. But a friend of mine carries papered butterflies, for sharing and later release, in her straw bonnet.

The catalogs of all the national outdoor outfitters are full of indomitably attractive, irrepressively healthy people looking good in their duds. Good looks are fine, but more important are comfort, protection, and practicality.

Next to consider are optics. Complementing the wondrous human eye is certainly gilding the lily in some respects, but it is true that things can be seen with extra lenses that our single lens cannot resolve. I do consider sunglasses a hindrance to nature observation because they tend to alter natural colors. For the same reason I deplore tinted windows in cars, buses, and trains. Photosensitive glasses that darken without changing hue can be a genuine aid, however; they lessen eye fatigue and actually intensify real colors until near dusk. Bi- and tri-focalists complain of the difficulty of close detail observation, but I have known numbers of each who have overcome their polyvisioned status; it takes practice, concentration, and determination. I am often surprised by naturalists who fail to clean their eyeglasses, then complain they cannot see well. A stream and a dry cotton bandanna can make everything brighter. Contact lenses may be the answer for those who find that glasses come between them and butterflies in more ways than one.

It often happens in nature that we cannot get as close to objects or creatures as we would like, due to wariness, difficulty of access, or scale. This is when binoculars, telescopes, microscopes, and hand lenses come into their own. Telescopes have relatively little to offer the butterfly watcher, except that a spotting scope may be trained upon a stationary nectaring or basking butterfly too far away to examine otherwise and difficult to approach. Binoculars, however, have a great deal to recommend them, and I am constantly amazed by how little they are employed by lepidopterists. Indeed I am the only lepidopterist I know who routinely carries them. Most collectors, as I have said before, are too busy catching to bother much with watching. Even so, binoculars would save them many a chase after misidentified or tatty specimens. For the watcher—as for the birder—they are all but essential. Henry David Thoreau observed nature without field glasses, so obviously there is much to be seen with the trained naked eye. But even more may be discerned with the judicious use of binoculars.

The best binoculars for butterfly watching are those that focus closely. This usually means lower magnification, in itself not a problem if you can get physically near the subject. The pair I have used for a decade (and hope to use for the rest of my life) focus to within about two meters, and magnify by six times. Because they have overhead or roof prisms, they gather more light than like-sized conventional types. This means they are better at dawn and dusk (important for moth watchers) and in heavy cloud. The right-hand ocular normally focuses closer than the two together—in this case down to my outstretched boot. In the independent focusing of the oculars lies much of the success in using binoculars. Many beginning birders and others never come to terms with this procedure and therefore give up the use of the instrument or resign themselves to a blurry image. This is a pity because it is not hard to do once you get the hang of it. Here's how:

First, close your right eye (or hold a card over it) while you focus the left-hand ocular using the central adjustment screw. Then close your left eye while you focus the right-hand ocular with its own screw adjustment, being sure to focus on the same subject. Thereafter, both oculars will be focused in concert by the central screw. Anytime the right ocular is changed, as when you use it to focus as closely as possible or when someone else uses the binoculars, the dual adjustment must be repeated. It only takes a few seconds and makes everything sharper thereafter. If you simply cannot arrive at a clear, coordinated image, it may mean your binoculars are out of alignment and need servicing.

Another common problem occurs when people use binoculars with glasses. Try first to focus with your glasses removed, since for many people binoculars will correct vision as well as telescope the scene. (Astigmatism may prevent this.) Special eyepiece fittings are available for adapting binoculars to glasses without narrowing the field of vision.

A third difficulty that causes neophytes to abandon binoculars is that of locating the subject to be scrutinized. I try to spot a larger, recognizable feature near the butterfly, such as a flower clump or a leafy twig or a distinctive stone, with which to orient myself in the picture. Scanning the field back and forth and up and down is another method.

The most common mistake is shifting around by far too much— several degrees at a time—instead of gradually. Again: Be a sloth, a patient one. Soon you will find yourself using field glasses as naturally as your own two eyes. And you will find that they enable you to see things you never thought you could. They will save you pushing through a painful thistle patch to watch Painted Ladies or fritillaries at drink, and allow you to follow the flight of a vagrant without sprinting and scaring it off for good. For the flightiest species, your glass may provide the only chance you will get for a good look.

Conversely, what happens when you can get right on top of a butterfly, closer than your eyes will focus? In the lab, the answer is a microscope. Binocular or dissecting scopes are of the greatest value to naturalists, but since for the most part they are made for use indoors, they are beyond the range of this book. The field counterpart is much simpler and cheaper.

No naturalist should be without a handlens. Available at low cost from two- to ten-power magnification, these implements take a little practice for proper use. The trick is to hold the lens very close to your eye, then move your subject or yourself until the image comes into sharp focus. A handlens brings whole worlds to your notice, small wonders otherwise passed over. But butterflies?

Surely these symbols of fickle flight and flickering speed cannot be stayed for scrutiny beneath the lens? Not all butterflies always, but some, sometimes. Especially those individuals engrossed at nectar or mud may be so closely encountered.

Suppose you come upon a galaxy of blues papering a puddle. You stealthily kneel beside them, disturbing a few on the edge, but they soon resettle. You offer a sweaty finger, and a sapphire crawls on and begins sucking your sweat for salt. That's when you whip out your handlens and see things most people only behold in books. Turquoise spots resolve into fields of individual iridescent scales; a fuzzy margin becomes a fringe of soft, ermine hairs. The butterfly's face, with large, spotted eyes and delicate, furred palpi, comes clear. A swallowtail on a thistle may present a similar opportunity. Then if you are clever you may be able to watch the proboscis probe each floret in turn, see how the tarsi cling, and make out the segments of the gracefully curved antennae. Looking through binoculars backwards produces the same effect. Some naturalists prefer to use magnifying glasses, but most such glasses are too weak. Opti-visors, worn like goggles, free the hands while conferring full-time magnification. Whichever tool is used, the ability to see things really closely is a precious one.

In the eyes of many naturalists, a butterfly net is a symbol of murderous intent and wasteful taking. We have already considered the virtues and vices of collecting, so you have seen that a net can be a positive tool, even a complement to conservation. But you may not realize a net's utility to the noncollector. Even if you have no intention of collecting insects, a net can be an invaluable tool for butterfly appreciation. Very simply, a butterfly in the hand is considerably simpler to examine than one in the bush. This can be accomplished with no harm done to the temporary captive, if care is taken in handling.

The proper technique involves holding the butterfly gently between thumb and forefinger, gripping the thorax with wings above the back, being careful not to squeeze. The touch is a learned one that quickly becomes instinctive. The same is true of using the net in the first place to ensnare the insect you wish to examine.

Approach a butterfly to be netted in the same deliberate manner you use for watching. Chasing seldom works; butterflies are much more fleet and graceful than we. Instead, wait for it to perch on a flower or the ground. If the latter, clamp the net quickly over the insect, then lift the bag into which it should fly. Or if a butterfly has alighted above the ground, sweep the net at and past the target so that the follow-through carries it deep into the net bag. If you must make an aerial shot, it is better to swing from behind the flier than head-on, because butterflies are expert at avoiding oncoming objects. Mourning Cloaks especially will consistently evade the most deftly handled head-on shots. Whatever stroke you choose, the secret is to move slowly until the instant of the swing, then strike with great speed and resolution. The "victim" should come to no harm from this exercise.

I will not discuss net design in detail here. Commercial varieties are available, or you can make your own from any sort of pole, spring steel, and netting. The best type is tough but allows air to pass through freely so you can swing it fast without creating a parachute effect. Once you own a net and gain a little facility with it, you will be surprised at the versatility it affords your insect activities.

One more tool essential both for observing the butterfly closely and for protecting it is the forceps, or tweezers. Many kinds and styles are available, from eyebrow pluckers to a jeweler's fine-pointed forceps. I favor broad, spatulate stamp tongs over most kinds of biological forceps, which tend to be too sharp or serrated —features that can damage delicate wings. The stamp tongs hold tightly and safely. To remove a butterfly from a flower, a puddle-margin, or a fold of the net with tweezers, clamp all four wings together where they join the body, with the legs showing. If you can see the legs, the wings are properly placed over the back. Be sure to grip all four wings, or the free ones will flap, likely causing injury. Also be careful not to get any of the netting in the forceps with the wings or you will surely tear them. Most people are afraid to hold the forceps tightly enough at first, inadvertently allowing the butterfly to pull free. You cannot hurt a butterfly by holding it tightly, if you are holding it properly, so clamp it solidly. Then when you wish you may simply place it back on a leaf or a blossom, or launch it on the breeze.

Since it is easy to lose forceps, I suggest that you wrap a string

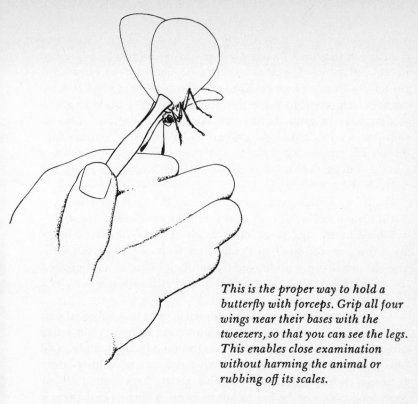

This is the proper way to hold a butterfly with forceps. Grip all four wings near their bases with the tweezers, so that you can see the legs. This enables close examination without harming the animal or rubbing off its scales.

around the base and through the arms, or pass it through a hole drilled through the base; then wear them around your neck or tied to a belt loop. Be careful not to use a fiber that will cut if it gets caught on a branch or otherwise pulls against your skin. It is a good idea always to have a spare pair along in your field bag. Field bags are handy for carrying everything else as well. Among my acquaintances they vary from great heavy surplus canvas bags to bellybags to elegant leather pouches.

Suppose you have caught a butterfly and would like to take it home to keep alive for a while, or to coax a female to lay eggs. You would be ill-advised to place it in the traditional jam jar, with or without holes punched in the lid, as it leaves too much room for the butterfly to struggle, flap, and get hurt. Instead, use paper envelopes such as collectors employ. You have a choice of either glassine envelopes or paper triangles. The former have the advantage of being see-through; the latter may be hand-made in a hurry. Butterflies will stay alive in "papers" for a day or more if kept fairly cool. I used to send live consignments of Hackberry Butterflies from Denver to Knoxville, with high survival success. Light refrigeration (not freezing!) will enhance longevity, and a feeding may be given before you release your captives. Instructions appear in Chapter 13 on rearing. *Note:* Never release butterflies far from where you found them. They probably won't survive, but if they do they may influence local gene pools and upset distributional studies.

For carrying papered live butterflies in the field, you will want a stiff container that offers protection from crushing. Film, Band-aid, hard candy, and many other kinds of metal or plastic boxes serve this purpose well. In Papua New Guinea I was given a triangular metal box with hinged lid and belt loops. It was designed for carrying birdwings, so I can fit a sandwich into it as well as a supply of papers.

The butterfly watcher's kit is completed, or at least rounded out, by plant containers or other containers for bringing home live caterpillars, eggs, or pupae, as well as fresh food plant samples. Old film tins work well for eggs or small larva, but something larger is necessary for bigger game. Zip-loc plastic bags work well for fresh food plants to be fed to larvae later. A small plant press is useful for taking back specimens of host plants and nectar sources for identification.

Maps for the region to be visited, a compass, field guides, and a first-aid kit should also go into the bag. And one last, but very basic item: the field notebook. No one should squander original observations in the dime store of the memory. Only careful, accurate notes made at or just after the time of observation will suffice. If any long-lasting knowledge is to come from the exercise, as well as pleasure, the field notebook is among the most important tools. Just what should go into it is discussed in Chapter 8.

Entomologists have always loved their equipage. It seems the size of the subjects has been more than made up for by the bulk of the materials employed in their study. Butterfly watching affords the freedom to indulge in gadgetry as much as you desire. But one of its great charms is that none of it is absolutely necessary. Just watch and see.

7

Names and Identification

Afield with a group, I am routinely expected to name each butterfly in turn. Most people seem to have an innate wish to know the
name applied to a creature, a tag that distinguishes it from all
others. Occasionally someone objects. He or she will ask, "Why
bother with names? They're just a human invention and mean
nothing to the butterfly. Its beauty does not depend on a label."
For such people, names and the attention we pay them can actually
get in the way of enjoyment.

A good friend of mine used to regard wildflowers in this way.
My every attempt to share recognition of a plant with him evoked
a negative reaction, until I realized that he resented the naming.
It impinged somehow on his unspoken, existential rapport with
the flower. Another friend takes a dramatically different approach.
He is a super-lister after the fashion of the most aggressive birders.
To him, the ID—and the list check it authorizes—counts for
everything. He enjoys butterflies well enough, but for him their
charm and beauty take a backseat to their variety and the gaming
involved in their identification.

Naturalists need to be able to approach nature on their own
terms. Who is to say that the nature-gaming of a lister is better or
worse than the strictly aesthetic approach or than amateur or professional study, where naming is a necessity? Names are tools,
seldom ends in themselves. To appreciate their usefulness and the

pleasures involved in identification, you need to arrive at them yourself. No one should attempt to challenge another's natural inclination in this respect.

Yet I return to the conclusion that most people seem to want a tag to tie onto their observations. In this chapter I will outline the manner in which we go about giving the right name to an organism. That phrase "the right name" is itself problematic. It might be best to begin with a consideration of names themselves.

Every plant or animal has a two-part scientific name (assuming it has been given one by a describing scientist). Some have vernacular, or common, names as well. The scientific name, usually comprised of Greek or Latin words, includes the generic and the specific epithets. The generic name designates the genus to which an organism belongs—its closely related affinity group, all with common and relatively recent ancestry. The specific name signifies the species—the actual, unambiguous kind of plant or animal it is. There may also be a third name, the subspecies, which signifies a distinctive geographic race of the species. These names may be followed by that of the scientist—known as the author—who applied the species or subspecies name. The scientific name is underlined or italicized; that of the author is not. The genus (plural genera) and author are capitalized; the species and subspecies are not. So *Limenitis archippus lahontani* Herlan is the complete scientific name of the Great Basin race of the Viceroy.

These are the basic points, and they are governed by the International Code of Zoological Nomenclature. Unfortunately, there is a lot of disagreement among specialists about names. For one thing, the oldest known name is generally supposed to be used, and authorities keep coming up with older and more obscure ones. Then, too, genera are frequently revised, with the result that an accepted generic name gets tossed out ("sunk into the synonymy") in favor of one considered to be more precise by the revisionists. A recent catalog of North American butterflies (L. D. Miller, p. 252) contained many such changes. So the tiger swallowtails have actually been shifted from the venerable genus *Papilio* to *Pterourus*. (*Papilio* was the great eighteenth-century biologist Linnaeus's original genus for all butterflies; he devised the system. Later it was restricted to swallowtails, and now to one narrow group of

Family Hesperiidae (skippers):
Two-banded Checkered Skipper.
(Pyrgus ruralis)

swallowtails.) What we have always called *Lycaena thoe,* the Bronze Copper, becomes *Hyllolycaena hyllus.* White Admirals, long ago shifted from *Basilarchia* to *Limenitis,* are back in *Basilarchia* again. And the beloved Spring Azure is now called *Celastrina ladon* instead of *C. argiolus.* Even the less beloved Cabbage White has suffered change, from *Pieris* to *Artogeia.*

All of this taxonomic folderol is highly irritating and frustrating to amateurs, who cannot understand why the pros can't make up their minds. Their chagrin is somewhat warranted, and it is commonly shared by professional lepidopterists themselves. We all like stability.

Aside from their vulnerability to change, scientific names are really not the horrors one imagines when first confronting them. Most are not so polysyllabic as cartoonists portray them, and while

Family Papilionidae (swallowtails): Anise Swallowtail. (Papilio zelicaon)

Family Pieridae (whites, marbles, and sulphurs): Western White.
(Pontia occidentalis)

Family Lycaenidae (blues, coppers, and hairstreaks): American Copper.
(Lycaena phlaeas)

some are grating to the ear (*Glaucopsyche*) others are euphonious (*Celastrina*). Often the names come from mythology, as in the case of the small fritillaries (*selene, titania, astarte, freija, frigga*), or as in the case of many swallowtails (*paris, jason, helena, marcellus*) and parnassians (*apollo, phoebus, clodius*). The names may make good sense (*Phyciodes campestris* is the Field Crescentspot, whose specific epithet means "of the field" in Latin) or tell you something, such as the butterfly's host plant (*Pieris brassicae*) or distribution (*Papilio oregonius*).

Don't be afraid to try to learn them. Pronunciation needn't intimidate: There is a correct pronunciation of classical terms, but church Latin and science Latin are often not the same, and biologists differ among themselves. So feel free to be phonetic. Learning the scientific names will give you an advantage in communication, especially on an international basis: The Mourning Cloak is commonly called the Camberwell Beauty in England and Trauermantel in Germany, Le Morio in France and Antiopa in Spain, but everywhere it is *Nymphalis antiopa*.

Even in English, the common or vernacular names have never been standardized for butterflies as they have for birds. *Vanessa virginiensis* has been known as the American Painted Lady, the

Virginia Lady, and Hunter's Butterfly; whereas some species have had no common name at all. Unlike scientific names, vernaculars have no rules governing their application or usage. The Xerces Society and the Lepidopterists' Society decided to do something about this by convening a Joint Committee on Common Names in 1981. The committee was chartered to provide a set of suggested standard common names for North American butterflies, such as the American Ornithologists' Union does for birds (see Appendix II). By attempting to standardize the common names, lepidopterists hope to reduce confusion and make it generally simpler for people to become acquainted with butterflies. Of course, everyone will ultimately use the name he or she prefers. (Just occasionally, the English name has proved more stable than the scientific one. The Monarch has had dozens of versions of its scientific name, finally settling on *Danaus plexippus*. But throughout all the debate and all the scholarly aliases, it has remained the Monarch.)

Some English names of butterflies possess charm or mystique, such as the Mourning Cloak and the Painted Lady. Others, like the Comma and the Question Mark, point out distinctive features. Famous lepidopterists have been commemorated by Edward's Fritillary and Scudder's Sulphur, while the significance of Magdalena Alpine and Edith's Checkerspot is best known to their namers. As with scientific names, host plants (Hackberry Butterfly) and habitat (Rockslide Checkerspot) may be connoted by the English name. The question of "what's in a name" may be as interesting to pursue as the butterflies themselves.

There are several advantages, in my experience, to pinning names on butterflies. For one thing, a creature once named ceases to be just another anonymous part of the chaotic and bewildering diversity of nature, and becomes instead a personality to be known for its individual qualities. For another, a correct name allows one to compare a creature with its congeners (its near relatives) and other organisms. This leads over time to a sense of appreciation for evolutionary process and continuity. Furthermore, the fascinating aspects of behavior, host- and nectar-plant selection, inter- and intraspecies interactions, predation and ecological adaptation cannot fully be appreciated without knowing what specific animals are under scrutiny. Then, too, only with names can one communicate one's observations and findings to others, and

Family Lycaenidae, subfamily Riodininae (metalmarks): Little Metalmark. (Calephelis virginiensis)

hear their accounts in return. Both Thoreau and Gilbert White, in writing about their respective parishes of Concord, Massachusetts, and Selborne, Hampshire, suffered from a lack of access to standardized names for the flora and fauna they surveyed. Fortunately, in nearly all cases their observations were so astute as to leave no doubt about the species they had in mind. We, by contrast, have access to handy guides and checklists, so that our watching need not start from the ground up, as it were.

The interesting patterns of animal distribution cannot be understood or elaborated without reliable identification, and of course we cannot conserve a scarce resource if we know neither what nor where it is. So identification has many more utilities than simply adorning lists, although listing itself is a pleasure for many and should not be discounted as a recreation. For me, the main reason for attaching a name to a feature of the landscape is that it enables me to get to know it as a unique expression of the organic world, to make the acquaintance of a new face of nature, and to ask what I hope are intelligent questions.

Placing a name on a creature means nothing, however, unless the identification is correct. How difficult is identifying butterflies? That depends upon where you are and what butterflies you are looking at. In some parts of the world—the American tropics, for

Family Nymphalidae (brush-footed butterflies): Milbert's Tortoiseshell. (Aglais milberti)

example—the fauna is so large or poorly documented that no one but an expert can hope to identify many of the species encountered. Certain groups of butterflies, notably skippers, are considered a challenge to identify properly wherever they occur prolifically. Our task in North America is more demanding than in England, where fewer than 70 species of butterflies occur; much less so than in Costa Rica, where some 2,000 species fly. We have something under 700 species, about the same number as North American birds. Wildflowers are considerably more trying; moths very much more so. On the whole, butterfly identification is a reasonable undertaking. You can expect with practice and care to come to know three-quarters or so of our butterflies in the field. If this is a poorer record than for birds, it is because some of our skippers, hairstreaks, checkerspots, and others require dissection or other lab techniques for certain identification. Furthermore, variation is rampant among other groups, such as western fritillaries, making comparison in series necessary.

How should you go about identification? First, study all the books you can find in order to get a feel for the general types of butterflies, and for the sorts of characters, or field marks, important in their identification. Field guides generally give for each species both a description and a discussion of similar species as well as an illustration. From the text and pictures you will be able to see the kinds of features that help you to discriminate among the various species. At first, checkerspots, crescentspots, and small fritillaries may all look the same. Then as you begin to know their unique marks, they sort out into very different groups.

You can see at the outset that color, pattern, shape, and size are the main components of a butterfly's appearance. Everyone notices color first (except the color-blind, who must pay more attention to pattern). Lots of people confuse swallowtails with Monarchs in their minds, but the simple distinction between yellow and orange tells them apart. If a butterfly is orange, though, there are many things it could be besides a Monarch. Californians often tell me of the Monarch migrations they have seen high on Sierran summits, much as Oregonians do in the Cascades. In fact, these are usually the California Tortoiseshell—a smaller, emigratory butterfly that has little in common with the Monarch. Blue offers fewer options than orange, yet there are blue coppers and hairstreaks as well as blue blues. Green narrows the field still further, but with white you are once again in broad waters. That's when pattern comes in. Among orange butterflies, Monarchs have black veins on orange background, tortoiseshells black splotches, and fritillaries black dots on orange. The placement and heaviness of black spots and veins or the presence of green marbling and orange tips becomes important in sorting out whites. The blues are like warblers: They all look alike at first, but each species has a very distinctive pattern if seen up close. Blues can't change their spots, and their identity lies in their underside spots.

Shape matters, too. Is a ragged butterfly really torn, or is it an anglewing? Does it have tails, or are the forewings hooked? Does that skipper have rounded or triangular forewings? Size also plays a major part. The Monarch, after all, is larger than any other orange butterfly in North America, the Pygmy Blue half the size of a Common Blue. Remember that butterflies never grow in the adult stage; growth stops with the caterpillar. So, while there is variation in adult size, wingspan is a fixed characteristic with a relatively standard range for each species.

It is important early on to acquire a sense of gestalt for the various natural groupings of butterflies. Once you can say at a glance, "That's a sulphur," or "This one surely is a copper," you

Family Nymphalidae, subfamily
Satyrinae (satyrs, browns, and
ringlets): Large Wood Nymph.
(Cercyonis pegala)

Family Nymphalidae, subfamily Heliconinae (longwings): Crimson-
patched Longwing. (Heliconius erato)

will have come a long way. Examine the field marks, as far as the butterfly will allow. (Here is where binoculars or a net come in handy, even if you intend to release the butterfly later.) Watch as closely and carefully as you can, from all angles, and take notes. Note the appearance of all four wing surfaces (primaries and secondaries, above and below), the antennae, the legs, and the body scales.

Appearance alone does not guarantee a correct ID. A number of other factors should be taken into account to corroborate or complement field marks. As young collectors, my friend and I came up with what we thought was a Sooty Hairstreak in a suburban park. The butterfly, actually a pale Solitary Blue, was fairly close in gross appearance to the other. Yet, had we studied our bible, F. M. Brown's *Colorado Butterflies,* more closely, we would have realized at once that (1) we were on the wrong side of the Rocky Mountains; (2) we were nowhere near the correct elevation; (3) the requisite host plant, lupine, was entirely absent; and (4) the habitat was all wrong. Probably the date was too, for that matter. In fairness to ourselves, we probably had read all this information but decided to discount it in favor of the adventure of catching a great rarity. After all, it looked like "the picture in the book." Many false identifications enter the literature this way.

Of course, parameters do vary, and butterflies do move about, so field guide formulae are not to be construed as absolute gospel. Nonetheless, when factors such as range, habitat, elevation, host plant, and flight season are taken into account, they help to settle identification problems and eliminate incorrect analyses based on appearance alone. If your specimen's characteristics disagree with those in the books, consult a local expert.

Family Nymphalidae, subfamily Danaiinae (milkweed butterflies): Queen. (Danaus gilippus)

Let's take a butterfly through the process of identification. Say you live in Idaho and you spot an orange butterfly in the foothills of the Sawtooth Range in June. The pattern of black is in patches rather than veins or dots, and the insect is of medium size. Its outline is regular, so it isn't an anglewing, and the salmon-pink shade of orange rules out fritillaries. You correctly determine that it is a Painted Lady, but there are three species it could be. The habitat, range, and season do not determine identification, since the West Coast Lady, American Painted Lady, and regular Painted Lady are all wide-ranging (had you been in the East, at least the first one could have been eliminated). From the upperside you are able to rule out the West Coast Lady because the bar outside the cell of the forewing is white, not orange. To make a final determination you must see the underside (until you get to know the butterflies better, and learn subtler clues). Finally a shadow comes across the thistle on which the lady is nectaring, and it closes its wings. You get a glimpse of the underside. The butterfly has a row of several blue eyespots on the ventral hindwing, rather than two big ones. What you have seen is a regular Painted Lady, *Vanessa cardui*.

Often geography alone will give it away. A black swallowtail in the western mountains will probably be the Short-tailed Black Swallowtail, or maybe the Western Black Swallowtail. In Denver, it will almost certainly be the Eastern Black Swallowtail, while such a butterfly spotted in Newfoundland must be a Maritime (i.e., Short-tailed) Swallowtail. In Virginia, it could be a Pipevine, a Spicebush, an Eastern Black, or even the black form of the female Eastern Tiger Swallowtail. In Florida several more contenders appear. Obviously, care is needed in watching for the fine points.

The books and range maps are not absolutely authoritative in all cases. The time will come when you see something—you *know* you see it—that should not be there, according to the conventional wisdom. I once spotted, then netted, a tiny yellow butterfly on the Grand Ronde River in southeasternmost Washington. I knew it was the Dwarf Yellow, never before found in Washington nor nearer than Utah. My party found six more, so it was no fluke. It was a state record, one the books wouldn't have predicted. Perhaps not so very surprising, however, for the minute and fragile Dainty Sulphur, as it is also known, is a famous long-distance migrant.

A stranger thing occurred half a century earlier in another basalt canyon not far away, when a shepherd caught a Zebra Butterfly. That tropical species normally occurs no farther north than Texas and Florida, yet the Washington specimen sits today in the Smithsonian Institution. Of course, hurricanes or a railroad car may have brought it to the Snake River. Consider also the experience of a friend who, while sampling a remote part of the Colorado Rockies, found a well-established colony of Albertan butterflies. It turned out to be a new species altogether, most closely related to an Alberta type but probably isolated from it thousands of years earlier. So be guided by the books, but don't believe everything you read.

And what if you do find something unusual and are thus in a position to contribute new knowledge? That is the province of the next chapter. But new knowledge cannot be contributed without proper identification. So if you are a "no names please" aesthete who loves butterflies just as they are, unlabeled and unrecognized, let me not discourage you. Just ignore this chapter and the next. Your rewards will be as great in their simplicity as those of the most learned lepidopterist. But if you have an itch to learn something more about butterflies as you are reveling in their beauty, you will want to start getting straight on names. You'll find it fun, challenging but not daunting, and ultimately satisfying.

So that you can relate to the families of butterflies when they are mentioned in the text, here are brief descriptions of the ones you are likely to encounter in North America:

Hesperiidae, the skippers. Once thought to be links to the moths, skippers resemble them in some ways with their thick, often hairy bodies and frequently dull colors. Their antennae are clubbed, however, and usually slightly hooked; their wings, short and triangular as a rule. Skippers get their name from their fleet, darting flight. The many tawny little species are grass-feeders as larvae.

Megathymidae, the giant skippers. Southern and desert butterflies whose larvae burrow in yucca and agave roots, these 2–8 centimeters skippers fly at great speed, sometimes faster than autos are allowed to go. Rarely spotted, they present a great challenge to butterfly watchers.

Snout Butterfly visiting dogwood (Libythea bachmanii). *This butter-fly illustrates the debate surrounding butterfly names. Some specialists place it in its own family, the Libytheidae, while others consider the snouts to be a subfamily of the brush-foots. Their extremely long palpi give them the name "snouts" and separate them from others.*

Papilionidae, the swallowtails and parnassans. The family con-tains some of our largest, most spectacular, and familiar butter-flies, the swallowtails. The closely related but very different parnassans belong here too. Most of our swallowtails are some combination of yellow and black, while the mountain-loving parnassans are waxy white with ruby-red and black spots.

Pieridae, the whites, sulphurs and marbles. Everyone should be familiar with the whites, whose caterpillars feed on crucifers, and the legume-feeding sulphurs, since they are so prominent in both rural and urban landscapes. They include the pestiferous European Cabbage Butterfly, and the Orange Sulphur of alfalfa fields. Marblewings are so called because of the delicate green mottling on their hindwings below, and some have bright orange forewing tips.

Lycaenidae, the gossamer-wings. Most of our bright, small but-terflies that are not skippers belong to this family. It allies the blues and coppers, many of which are brilliantly colored with metallic or iridescent hues, with the hairstreaks, many of which bear hair-like tails on their hindwings. Also included are the suitably named metalmarks of the subfamily Riodininae. All of these small streakers require concentration and sharp eyes, to keep track of them.

Nymphalidae, the brush-footed butterflies. This large, highly evolved family includes a number of groups often considered families in their own right, but properly subfamilies. All of them share the trait of having forelegs reduced to useless brushes. The true nymphs (Nymphalinae) comprise the anglewings, ladies, admirals, fritillaries, checkers and crescents among others. They are strong and colorful and some overwinter as adults. The milkweed butterflies (Danaiinae) consist in North America of the famous migratory Monarch, the Queen and the Tropic Queen. They tend toward distastefulness acquired from their toxic milkweed host plants. The longwings (Heliconinae), also known as passionflower butterflies, have long, rounded wings colored in oranges, yellows, reds and black. Most species occur in the New World tropics, where they form complex mimicry rings. The subfamily Satyrinae are the satyrs, wood nymphs, arctics and alpines, ringlets and browns. Their larvae consume grasses, and the adults are often brown or gray with pretty textures and distinct eyespots. We have just two snout butterflies of the subfamily Libytheinae. Their palpi are elongated and joined into a prominent, rather comical "snout." Mostly southern they feed on hackberry foliage and may emigrate in vast numbers.

8

Records and Field Notes

Such is the nature of insect study that one cannot go about it for long without finding out something worth recording. Those entomologists who work on wasps or weevils are fond of saying that all the fields have been ploughed and depths plumbed when it comes to butterflies, that the challenges remain with less popular groups. Indeed, Lepidoptera—particularly butterflies—are probably the best known insects. But our knowledge is far from complete. In fact, only two or three species of butterflies have recently come to be known with real breadth, depth, and exactitude in many of their characteristics.

Even in England where lots of lepidopterists have studied a handful of butterflies for a very long time, far from all the facts are in. A friend of mine, one of the most exacting butterfly scientists anywhere, works at a lab in Dorset; he estimates that only a small fraction of the natural history of British butterflies is contained in the pages of the scores of books published on the subject. If such is the case in England, think how much we still have to learn in North America, with ten times the number of species and a tenth as many butterfly enthusiasts. The fact is that butterflies are just well enough known to allow access to them without lengthy preparation and tedious background work or arcane techniques; yet sufficiently anonymous to ensure new discoveries for the careful observer. This, I find, is a propitious balance.

Years of observation and experiments on the English Meadow Brown by W. H. Dowdeswell, E. B. Ford, and others have led to one of our best and fullest pictures of butterfly life. Few species are so well known, and much is to be learned by careful watchers.

One can hear doctrinaire entomologists say that little can be learned without a collection. It is true that many facets of entomological science require specimens, often in series, for comparison and study. For example, one would be hard pressed to understand the variation within western fritillaries or anything of their evolution without examining scores of specimens. But a butterfly in the hand is not always the only one that counts scientifically. Butterflies in the bush can tell us eloquently of matters about which pinned specimens are mute. You cannot conjecture courtship behavior from a cabinet specimen. Nor can dead butterflies elucidate questions such as host plant choice, flight pattern, territoriality, or thermoregulatory activity. And yet these are the very sorts of things that have traditionally been neglected in favor of taxonomy. So not only are there things to be learned that do not necessitate collecting, but it also seems that the odds of uncovering something fresh favor the watcher over the catcher.

A caveat here, however: Observations mean little if the species to which they refer cannot be ascertained as to identity, so voucher specimens remain important. In their absence, photographs or very careful descriptions accompanied by drawings may suffice. We are about half a century behind the birders, who have accepted sight records for about that long. With butterflies, most experts still want to see the specimen to verify a finding. This may never change for difficult groups such as skippers, where ambiguity is endemic. But overall, careful notetaking and rigorous record-keeping will help bring respectability to sight records of butter-flies.

What constitutes a record? To many people, conditioned by *The Guinness Book of Records* and the like, the word implies the best, the biggest, farthest, or fastest—it is a standard of superla-tive. This is not at all the scientific meaning. A record is simply a set of observed facts, a body of information. It corresponds in science to a datum, and records make up field data. If a record presents new information, such as the first occurrence of a butter-fly in a geographic unit, it may be so designated: state record, county record, and so on.

The basic constituents of natural history records are date, place, and source (the source is usually the name of the recorder). Be-yond this, the record can be expanded to include weather condi-tions, animal and plant associations, or any other facts relevant to the observation. Let's look at each component of a good record.

The date seems unequivocal enough, yet several systems used in the past have led to confusion. 1-11-76 might mean January 11, 1976, to an American or 1 November to a European, while 76 could refer to 1976, 1876, or even 1776. Roman numerals came into fashion to circumvent this problem, but they still can be con-fused, and they are clumsy. Therefore the major museums have reverted to the best designations for the months—their own names. Even abbreviated they are unambiguous. 11 Jan 1976 and 01 Nov 1876 are absolutely clear. Another system employs the Carolinian day, so that 001 is 1 January and 365 is 31 December, but does day 209 mean anything to you without consulting a cal-endar? And what about leap years? I always make a point of using the names of the months whenever I record dates as my own per-sonal campaign against month numbers.

Beyond the date, time can be very important to a record. For example, I was asked by a specialist on ghost moths (Hepialidae) to watch for a species known from my area. I'd sent him one I found dead in the road, but he was especially concerned to know the time of day or night it flies in nature—something the specimen couldn't tell him. It seems that each species of ghost moth flies only, and precisely, during a set brief period each night or day of its flight period. Happily, the moth came to my porch light a few nights after I began looking—at 7:45 P.M. The record would have been of interest in any case, but it was much more valuable with that snippet. The twelve-hour designation can be ambiguous if an A or a P is smudged, left off, or scribbled. So scientists normally employ the twenty-four-hour clock designation, in this case 1945 hours.

Place recording is a trickier matter, with much more room for vague, misleading, or incorrect records. Collectors and observers are seldom precise enough in their designation of place. The fashion for many years was to be extremely general: a designation such as Rocky Mtns, Oregon Territory, or the name of the nearest major town, so that a record for "Seattle" might well refer to a locality many miles distant. Especially because many new species were described from type specimens thus designated, modern-day biologists have had ample cause to curse their forebears' lackadaisical ways.

At least they had the excuses of poor maps and few named landmarks, alibis we cannot employ. The situation has improved, but many naturalists still give only the name of the nearest town or road. This is not only imprecise and perhaps miles off course, but it can also be confusing: Does "5 mi N of Rose City" mean due north? By the most north-south running road? As the crow flies? Or by the odometer? And have you ever considered how many Johnsonvilles and Deer Creeks there may be, even within a given state or province?

The British have the benefit of a National Grid, whose referencing system is so well known that many schoolchildren are perfectly capable of pinpointing a site within 100 meters' accuracy on the face of the earth. Our U.S.G.S. maps are beginning to demarcate the similar Universal Transmercator Grid on newer editions, but it will be a long time until it becomes well known and used by the public. In the western states we have the township and range survey, whereby lands were divided into square-mile sections, thirty-six to a Township. Use of township, range, and section designations is simple and straightforward, but the system does not apply to Canada, eastern states, and unsurveyed parts of the wilder West. Latitude/longitude furnishes a reliable measure of situation when designated carefully, and it can always be converted to other systems. I highly recommend that you become familiar with latitude/longitude use as well as township and range, and use one or the other in concert with the clearest description you can give for a locality. Altitude is a helpful and biologically meaningful unit as well.

A good record, therefore, might include all of these criteria—in fact, anything that will pinpoint the locale for you or anyone else who might wish to revisit it in the future. The touchstone is to be as particular as possible. "Hwy #30 N roadside 3.6 mi W of I-5 Exit 224" is to be preferred over "3½ mi W of freeway nr Shelton." Always ask yourself whether you would appreciate receiving the directions you are giving in your field records. Examples of acceptable locality records are given in the butterfly count reports on pages 116, 117 and in the sample field notes on pages 94, 95.

The final obligatory element of a record is the source. This is simply your name, if the record originates with you. If you get it from someone else, his or her name should be given. *Fide* J. Ellsworth means that J. Ellsworth conveyed the information to you and you consider it reliable. On a pin label (which should incorporate the full record), *Leg.* Martha Anderson means that Martha collected the specimen so designated. Use full surnames, since no set of three initials is unique.

I want to emphasize the importance of *writing your records down as soon as possible*, preferably at the time of the observation. *Never* trust your memory for long. It always seems at the time that you could not possibly forget or confuse a new piece of information, that it will remain as crystal clear as the exciting moment when you first acquired it. Invariably it happens that one's recollection comes under suspicion after a surprisingly short interval, shorter yet as one ages. So write it down—*now*! The consequences of not doing so can be discouraging.

I knew a boy who returned from a family trip with a butterfly that would have been a Colorado state record. His notes were written after the fact, but he was quite sure of the specimen's provenance. The record entered the literature with my help. Years later it emerged that he had been to Yellowstone on the same trip, where that particular butterfly abounds. Over time, his confidence in his memory had diminished, and it seemed more and more likely that a Wyoming butterfly had accidentally been slipped in with his Colorado catch. The record had to be suppressed.

Last fall I met a young man with two butterflies in his cabinet that would have been state records for Oregon. He claimed that they came from southern Oregon, and I am sure that he was sure. Yet the specimens bore no labels whatever, and the box contained others he had caught in the Midwest, where both of the "state records" occur abundantly. Needless to say, the local experts would not accept those records.

Yet, in another friend's collection I spied a butterfly certainly new to Oregon, and it was accepted and published without qualm, in spite of its having been collected under peculiar circumstances and lodged with its owner in New Guinea! The butterfly, a Pipevine Swallowtail, bore a precise pin label accompanied by careful notes in a field log. Subsequently, additional specimens were found in the area, confirming the record.

It is unlikely that authorities would accept a new state record that you presented on the basis of a sighting, unless two or more experienced observers saw it—and their notes or photos independently corroborated the identity beyond question. Yet county or local distributional records, nectaring records, ovipositional records, and a host of other kinds of observations are perfectly admissible fom sightings—*if* they are backed up by a carefully executed set of notes and a description, drawing, or photo that removes any reasonable doubt from the determination of identity.

Let's turn to the field log or notebook and see what it should contain. Even more than binoculars or forceps, the notebook is an essential item for the serious observer who wants to learn as well as enjoy. Any sort of notebook will do—I've tried dozens of species, from little spiral memos to weatherproof professional models. The paper should be of good quality so that it will not deteriorate in a few years from its own acid; and the pages should be bound in firmly, so that a gust of wind will not swipe a whole week's writing in an instant. You want a book that will be easy to carry and handy to use but not so small that it gets overlooked or easily misplaced.

What to write with is a more critical issue. Many people like to use felt-tip pens these days, but their ink is seldom waterproof: A healthy raindrop can splatter an incisive observation all over the page, and a puddle can be calamitous. Some field biologists opt for fine-pointed Rapidograph drafting pens with indelible ink. They make attractive, permanent notes, but they tend to clog and drip maddeningly. Ball points blot and fail to write on greasy surfaces such as a notebook dampened by perspiration. One of the best implements remains the good old lead pencil. It will write on nearly any paper, never runs out until it's too short to hold, can be sharpened with a jackknife, and doesn't run in the rain or river. You may want to type up or rewrite field notes taken down in pencil to prevent their eventual loss as a result of fading. In any case, carry several of whatever you use and save yourself from having to write in blood with a cactus quill.

We have already considered the minimal elements of a specimen sighting or record—date, place, and source. It is well to record other pertinent facts as well. The conditions, to begin with, should be reflected in your notes as accurately as possible. Temperature, wind speed and direction, cloud cover, precipitation, humidity, and barometric pressure are among the climatic features that may prove worth recording. (No one gets them all, always.) I prefer to use Fahrenheit, which is more precise because the degrees are smaller, but Centigrade seems to be the coming thing. Much of the scientific world already uses the metric system and we should probably not hold up the process. The main thing is to get the data down.

Then of course you will want to record the details of what you see happening. Records of occurrence alone are worthwhile, and they have long been the bread-and-butter of collectors interested in butterfly distribution. Biogeography is my own chief interest, and I find patterns of distribution fascinating in their own right. Yet the mere occurrence of an organism in time and space only begins to tell us about it. What it *does* is of much greater overall significance, once presence has been established. So you will be concerned with recording all the memorable features of your subject's behavior: Virtually anything a butterfly does may be worth recording. Remember that since collectors have traditionally neglected behavior in favor of capture, you have an excellent chance of spotting something new.

Anything that interests you is fair game. Does the butterfly look as if it is investigating a plant for egg-laying? How did it behave when a dragonfly took a pass at it? Is it easy to approach or wary, and does your shadow affect it? Watch for patterns, and don't be afraid to pose questions the answers to which may require a return visit. In this way you involve yourself in the process. If eggs were laid, what became of them? How many hatched? How many caterpillars were left after two weeks? Four? At what point did pupation take place, and how long did it last?

If you do not plan to collect voucher specimens or take photographs, your field notebook is a fit place for sketches and clear descriptions of the butterflies themselves. There is no need to do this with every species you encounter, most of which you will soon come to recognize in your own area with the help of field guides. But for butterflies you do not recognize, or those that may have very similar species in the vicinity, or butterflies that seem confusing in pattern or color or habitat, nothing beats a clear set of notes for a later, leisure-time determination. Taking down a description is a better use of field time than flipping through pictures in a guidebook while the butterfly flies away.

Then there are the plants in the community (especially those in which the butterfly shows any interest), other animals sharing the habitat, insects with which the butterfly interacts, landforms, soils, signs of human disturbance. Also there are the very important qualities of sex, abundance, and condition of the butterflies observed. A dot on a map indicates none of these things, not even whether there was one individual of a species present or a thousand. You will seldom be able to actually count the members of the population but you can specify carefully whether the butterfly was a singleton, rare, moderately common, or abundant. Try to establish a standard for these or other terms of abundance you employ and stick to it. The same goes for terms describing the condition of the animals. Collectors' slang terms such as "rubbed" or "a rag" mean less than fresh, slightly worn, and so on. Try to indicate the range of condition of individuals present, also whether males, females, or both are on the wing. Sex ratio is normally 1:1 in nature, but different proportions fly at different times and behavior differs so you may see more of one sex (usually males) than the other. Except for markedly sexually dimorphic species, sex determination requires netting unless you can get very near. If you find you want to try to estimate the actual numbers present, consult the following chapter.

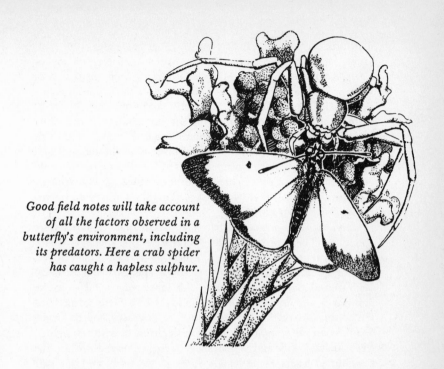

*Good field notes will take account
of all the factors observed in a
butterfly's environment, including
its predators. Here a crab spider
has caught a hapless sulphur.*

You can see that there is scarcely an observable fact unworthy of mention in your notes, and yet you could easily spend more time scribbling than watching, and that would defeat the purpose. So be selective, don't be compulsive, and enjoy your note-taking. If it becomes a chore it isn't worth it. Your own interests and the imposed realities of time and weather will no doubt suggest natural limits to the amount of time you devote to record-keeping. But this is definitely a case when a job worth doing is worth doing right. And when it comes to the contents, too much is better than too little.

Here is a sample set of field notes from my own log of 1983. Beyond certain minimum standards, style and content in field notes are largely personal matters. It is important to be as objective as possible. There is no need to leave out aesthetic perceptions altogether, for these will help you to remember the pleasure of the experience. Do not, however, allow such subjective impressions to take the place of precise description.

30 July 1983. Washington: Thurston County
Township 61N Range 3W Section 3
Mima Mounds State Natural Area, Mima Prairie, 2 mi. W of
Little Rock Observer: R. M. Pyle, leading a joint field trip of
Willapa Hills and Black Hills Audubon Societies; approximately
35 participants. 10 am–2 pm; clear, still, and warm day, 80–90° F.
Third warm, sunny day following an extended cool and rainy
period. Mima Mounds less dry than normal for this period, with
Viola adunca (blue violet) notably abundant on the mounds and
still in prolific bloom, a very late date for this to be the case.
Nectar sources prolific, chiefly exotics including *Hypochaeris
radicata* (hawkbit), *Hypericum* spp. (St. John's wort), and *Senecio jacobeae* (tansy ragwort).

Upon arrival it was immediately apparent that fritillaries were
abundant. These proved to be *Speyeria zerene bremneri* (valley
race of Zerene Fritillary) and *S. cybele pugetensis* (Puget Sound
race of Great Spangled Fritillary). Both species flying in numbers around parking lot, among the forest edge, and over the
mounds. *S. zerene* seemed more abundant by a factor of perhaps
ten to one. A rough estimate would be at least 5,000 to 10,000
S. zerene on the wing, likely many more. Most individuals sighted
were males, fresh and apparently having emerged within the
previous 48 hours. Some female *S. zerene* were out, and one pair
were found *in copulo*, permitting close observation as they clung
to low grass. A single female *S. cybele* was found drying her wings
by the trail edge, so fresh that she was unable to fly. Her dark
scaling was so dense, dark, and shiny that the distance to the
blue-black female *S. diana* (Pipevine Swallowtail mimic) did not
seem great.

Fritillaries flew low among the mound herbiage, the males apparently in search of females, the females likely seeking violets
for oviposition. Some hilltopping on mounds was taking place
and numerous intraspecific encounters were observed. Inter-
specific encounters also occurred between *S. zerene* and *Cercyonis
pegala*.

Additional species present were *Cercyonis pegala* (Large Wood
Nymph), *Nymphalis antiopa* (Mourning Cloak), *Pieris* species
(probably *P. napi*, Veined White), and *Ochlodes sylvanoides*
(Woodland Skipper). *C. pegala* was common (numbers in excess
of 1–200), flitting among mound grasses including *Festuca* spp.
No female wood nymphs were seen. As with the fritillaries, female emergence follows that of males and they may be expected

94

to be abundant if the weather holds within one to two weeks. Male wood nymphs frequently and energetically engaged fritillaries in hilltopping encounters on the mounds. Only a few whites were seen, one Mourning Cloak (another in Little Rock), and a single Woodland Skipper in a woodland glade along the nature trail. Very abundant in late summer, this species is apparently just beginning its emergence. *Tyria jacobeae* (Cinnabar Moth) larvae were abundant on tansy ragwort.

Species expected but not sighted include *Speyeria hydaspe* (Hydaspe Fritillary), *Limenitis lorquini* (Lorquin's Admiral), *Vanessa cardui* (Painted Lady, abundant in the region following large-scale immigration in 1983), *Phyciodes mylitta* (Mylitta Crescent), second generation *Coenonympha ampelos* (Northwest Ringlet), and *Epidemia helloides* (Purplish Copper).

Both Zerene Fritillaries and Large Wood Nymphs nectared repeatedly on hawkbit and St. John's wort, as well as on tansy ragwort.

Although diversity of species was low (six butterfly species sighted), abundance was remarkably high for *Speyeria zerene bremneri* and notable for *Speyeria cybele pugetensis*. This was the greatest density of *S. zerene* ever observed by this recorder. The fact is especially notable in light of the diminution of the valley race of this butterfly to the point of suspected extinction in Oregon, and its growing rarity in Washington as well. The high numbers of fritillaries and the boom year for violets may be closely related, since *Viola adunca* is the host plant for both butterflies.

Finally, there arises the question of what to do with your notes. First of all, *do not* discard them. The same goes for any collection. To the extent that they are kept for your own pleasure, they may serve that purpose and then seem superfluous. But there will almost certainly be a person, club, or museum that would find your notes and records and specimens of value long after you may have lost interest in them. Make sure they get to such a repository eventually, and keep them in a safe spot, away from moisture, in the meantime. Too many valuable sets of data have been lost to mildew, negligence, or conscientious spring cleaning! The same collector who asked me to watch out for ghost moths also informed me of a woman who collected butterflies and moths in my region in the 1930's. After a concerted search and interviews with family members, another friend managed to locate a portion of her field notes. They have proved to be very valuable to my work and that of the Washington Butterfly Survey.

In the meantime, while you are actively using your notebooks, should their contents remain your secret? Not at all. You'll probably want to know where, if you find something noteworthy, you should "send it in." As a child I found a fossil clam, and I would not rest until my father found some museum to take it. Sharing our finds and our data enhances their value to ourselves.

Happily, most areas now have a butterfly and moth, insect, or natural history society. These often maintain files of local information and may be glad to receive a periodic report of your findings. Here in Washington, we have a survey that actively solicits the records of butterfly enthusiasts throughout the state. I have given the names and addresses of a number of state and regional butterfly societies in the Appendix. The international Lepidopterists' Society, also listed there, publishes an annual season's summary of significant records as well as a membership list of lepidopterists in every state and province and many countries. If you cannot find where to "send in" your observations, start your own butterfly data bank and collect it for others in your area as well as yourself. Don't be surprised if your material is eventually cited in some erudite publication. After all, the first Mourning Cloak recorded for Cook County and thus reported is a fresh quantum of human knowledge, and deserves to be acknowledged as such.

Watch intently, take notes liberally, make records conscientiously, and you will find it difficult to avoid discovery. Even on a modest scale, that is exciting. There may be few more opportunities in the world tantamount to Darwin's voyage on the *Beagle* or Alfred Russel Wallace's survey of the Malay Archipelago. But there is probably a marsh, wood, or valley near your home whose butterflies have never been intimately charted. Certainly there are dozens of common species whose biology we know but poorly, though they live and fly in our midst.

Better known than beetles but less than birds, butterflies offer bounty as well as beauty. The bounty is knowledge. In the next chapter we will see how to take the pursuit of knowledge about butterflies a few steps further.

9

Listing and Mapping

When I began my studies of Washington State butterflies some twenty years ago, we had a basic checklist of the state's fauna as it was known in 1946, no maps of distribution, and little idea of how Washington's butterflies as a whole related to those of surrounding areas. There were more holes in our knowledge than solid fabric. Along with several others, I went to work to fill in the picture. A survey of known distributional records showed that several counties were very poorly known, while others had been fairly well explored by pioneer collectors. One county had yielded no butterfly records at all. Years later, I moved into that county— Wahkiakum, the state's smallest. I had a whole field of discovery open to me. It has been a challenge since then to decide how to array what I have learned here, as well as our findings throughout the state, so that they might fit into the growing body of butterfly facts from throughout the continent and the world.

As we saw in the previous chapter, some of the greatest pleasures of butterfly study arise from the uncovering of new facts, no matter how modest they might be. You have seen how to make a proper recording of a butterfly's occurrence somewhere. Now read on to see how records may be strung together and arranged so as to convey their content in the most informative ways.

The questions most likely to receive answers from your careful field exploration are what, when, where, and (to some extent) how many, for these are qualities open to empirical observation. The basic techniques for displaying these facts are listing, mapping, and counting. The first two are the province of this chapter, counting that of the next.

It is obvious that a list is a starting point. Naturalists have always taken keen pleasure in constructing local lists of fauna and flora. A list of species encountered is a means of understanding more fully the organisms under study, while at the same time presenting one's findings for examination and use by others. It also provides a schematic for comparing existing data with those still required: "So far I have accounted for most of the summer nymphs likely to be encountered in my area; next year I must make an effort to seek out the spring hairstreaks."

The first step in making a list is to arrange the names of species encountered in taxonomic order. The next step might be to list all the species likely to be found in the area under study, so that they may be checked off when eventually found and watched for in the meantime (such a list can be gathered from books or published state and regional faunas). When enough such local lists have been made, enthusiasts may wish to collaborate to create a state or regional checklist comprising all the taxa known to occur within the boundaries of the area considered. These have been compiled for most of the states and provinces by now, but they are constantly being updated. From these come national or continental checklists, state-of-the-art compilations that have been produced for North America every twenty or thirty years this century. The top-of-the-line checklist is known as a catalog. It contains not only the currently accepted names of all species recorded within the continental bounds (in the view of the editors) but also the synonyms for those entities (former scientific names applied to each species), the source and date of original descriptions, the location of the type specimens (those upon which the description was based), and other historical notes. We have a very up-to-date catalog for North America, a marvelous tool for all those interested in butterflies even though it is rather controversial in its nomenclature.

But to return from the big picture to a more suitable scale for most of us to relate to: Just what sort of area comprises an appropriate listing territory? I recommend a unit that will meet three criteria. (1) It should be small enough so that you can survey it fairly thoroughly in a few seasons; this way you will not become overwhelmed or daunted or lose interest. (2) It should be large and diverse enough to furnish an ongoing challenge. The law of diminishing returns will eventually set in for any perimeter, but it shouldn't happen in the very first season. (3) It should be not too well documented already by previous workers. This is easier to achieve in the West than in the East—as of 1982, there were still entire counties of Montana without a single butterfly record. But even in New York and New England, where lepidopterology has been thriving for two centuries, some areas are still less well known than others. One of the most incisive and far-reaching local lists published in recent years was that produced by Arthur and Adrienne Shapiro for Staten Island.

The county has long been considered the most convenient land category for faunal and floral lists and hundreds of U.S. counties still lack butterfly checklists. Counties are artificial constructs and they vary a great deal in size and shape (ten of my county would fit in several single large ones in Washington and Oregon). Counties have little to do with biology, except when one or more of their boundaries happens to coincide with a major river or mountain crest or other natural feature. Counties are a uniquely American unit of jurisdiction (the British counties are more akin to our states); and people, especially rural Americans, tend to think in terms of counties. In Canada, compartments fill this role but tend to be very large in the western provinces. Watchers may prefer to select a township, although this word means very different things in the East and the West.

Sometimes a topographic rather than a political feature suggests itself as a listing unit. This might be a mountain, a canyon, a woodland, or a watercourse. I selected one of the latter as my first listing project, and I have stuck with it ever since. As a young boy, I took my first butterfly treks along the Highline Canal, a ninety-year-old, 90-mile-long irrigation ditch running from the foothills of the Rockies out onto the plains east of Denver. Emerging from the Front Range in the Platte River Canyon mouth, the Highline was cut sinuously through tens of thousands of acres of farmland before returning its much diminished load to a tributary of the Platte. Most of that farmland has since become subdivisions, and its butterfly fauna has lost 40 percent of its species over the past quarter-century. I reached that conclusion during my studies of the canal's butterflies over the same time period. On that first walk, I found Painted Ladies and watched my first Mourning Cloak sail enticingly over the plains cottonwoods. I began that very day to list the canal's butterflies and I still sample portions of the watercourse annually.

Serving as it does as a biological corridor between the mountains and the plains, the ditch is a constant source of surprises. Even in its diminished condition, I still find a good deal to interest me, the more so because my ever-growing body of knowledge provides a backdrop against which to assess new findings and changes. The Highline Canal was certainly my birthplace as a butterfly person. I have collected over one-tenth of all North American butterfly species along its verdant banks, and a careful watcher could have built much the same list.

The Highline Canal was virtually in my backyard. Many people literally choose their backyards for list-making—what better place to come to know intimately? You can also manage your own plot so as to enhance butterfly abundance and diversity; this is described in Chapter 12 on butterfly gardening. There is a special mystique about one's immediate environ, having not a little to do with ego, but harmlessly enough. I have engaged in yard birding and yard butterflying on a gently competitive basis with fellow watchers of equivalent domicile, and the listing grew to an exciting pitch indeed. We cannot help but identify each new species on the list as a personal success, and the yard list itself is a ratification of our choice of abode. Some notable records and observations have been turned in by yard listers, and of course this is an excellent pursuit for the disabled or not very mobile person.

Whatever your bailiwick, be it patio or province, you will soon find it necessary to collate your list in a meaningful and useful fashion. There is no universally "best" approach, and indeed the usually accepted form is a matter of common sense. As I said earlier, list your finds according to the taxonomic order adopted by some recognized text, checklist, or field guide. If you use English names, also give the scientific name as well for precision. It's a good idea to name the author, so that you become

Spring Azures fluttering around bloodroot. Even common, widespread butterflies such as these can tell us much about the landscape when their distribution has been mapped and properly understood.

familiar with the giants of the science. If you have the slightest doubt as to the correct determination of a species, indicate this with a question mark. Follow this with an indication of whether voucher specimens were taken or whether a sight record was netted for examination or not. For sight records, list the names of others who saw it with you. Then, depending on the number of records for a species, you may want to give the full data or a summary. If you have seen quite a few Large Wood Nymphs in your area, it would not be practical to give full data for each occurrence in the list. You can divide the territory into segments, number them, and give these code numbers in the list

(I did this for the canal). You can do the same with segments of the flight season, giving numerals for the periods during which a butterfly appeared. The units should be small enough to suggest the coming and going of successive generations, information not conveyed by the simple listing of earliest and latest dates for a species.

You will want to give some indication of numbers, sex, and condition of individuals you have spotted in your area. Have you found fresh individuals of both sexes, and watched them age? If you have seen only worn males or females, perhaps the species is an immigrant, straying into your territory but not breeding there. If you have seen eggs, larvae, or pupae, this should be indicated as well.

A basic list, as you can see, is a capsule form of your field notes organized in such a way that their facts may readily be extracted. Soon you build up a literal profile of the butterfly fauna of the area you have under study. The publication of such lists has passed out of vogue lately, which is a pity because when well done they are of genuine and lasting value. It may be that a local or regional group will jump at the chance to make your list available in print, even if the learned journals show no interest.

The next step is to represent the data graphically. Maps, time lines, and charts enable one to grasp the status of knowledge instantly. They can also be analyzed in such a way as to point out or elucidate biogeographical and ecological patterns that may not be clear from the raw data themselves.

Some years ago I had the opportunity under a Fulbright scholarship to pursue studies in butterfly conservation with a consortium of English experts. My base was the Biological Records Centre of the Nature Conservancy, for a branch of government responsible for surveying and conserving Britain's flora and fauna. The BRC undertook to map the plants and then the groups of animals on a 10-kilometer-square dot-distribution map basis throughout the British Isles. At the Monks Woods Experimental Station, under the supervision of John Heath, I was able to see for myself how immensely useful such maps were, both scientifically and ecologically. The scheme was very ambitious. It was made possible through a vast network of amateur naturalists—many of them watchers rather than catchers—and through the application of computer technology. The data were updated from time to time. In examining the maps, one could see clearly whether the range of an organism was contracting or expanding, which probably hinted at something in nature that bore looking into.

So it was that when I undertook a survey of the endangered Heath Fritillary I was able to go right to the former sites to investigate what changes might have brought about a local extinction. Or for those species that the maps showed to be expanding their ranges, like the Comma throughout the 1960s and 1970s, climatic or other patterns could be sought to explain the reasons.

John Heath built up the British Butterfly Mapping Scheme and went on to develop a European Invertebrate Survey based on the same principles. Out of EIS grew the International Commission for Invertebrate Survey—of which our Washington State and even my Wahkiakum County efforts are now components. This shows the universal flow of information that, once begun by earnest searchers, becomes inexorable.

Few parts of the world match Great Britain in the completeness with which its natural history has been documented or in the number of people available to help with the job. Of course, most lands are larger and possess more butterflies and fewer lepidopterists. No wonder their mapping scheme got off the ground first. We can look at this as either a discouragement or as an exciting challenge. I prefer the latter.

The British, venturing out to fill in dots on the map (unrecorded squares become ever more scarce), call the process "square bashing." It is a rewarding game for it takes place out-of-doors among the butterflies, and every square bashed is a new iota of understanding. We, after all, have almost unlimited squares to bash if we are talking about 10-km squares, and a great many even if the units are counties.

What sort of map and map symbols are best for this purpose? Traditionally, butterfly mappers have illustrated their regions with maps showing county lines and a dot in each county where the butterfly is known to occur. This is still a common method. Ray Stanford is compiling such maps for the western butterflies, while Paul Opler is mapping the east. Because of their variability in size and shape, counties are not the ideal recording units. But county-dot maps are more precise than the alternatives in which whole

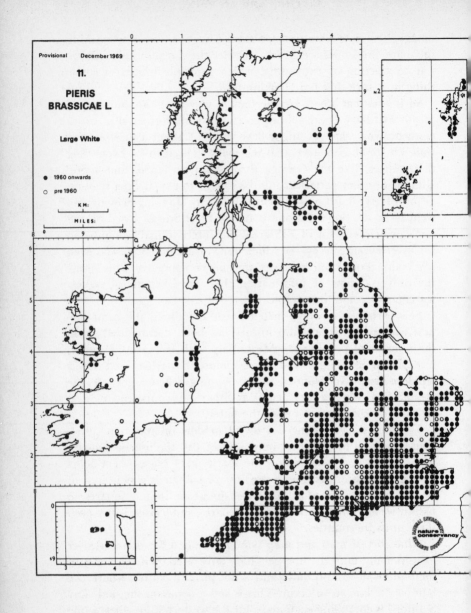

An example of a British dot-distribution map for the Large White, from the provisional atlas of 1969 (courtesy Biological Records Centre, Institute of Terrestrial Ecology).

regions are shaded or crosshatched. Animals seldom display anything like the continuous distribution implied by shaded maps. Except in the broadest sense, these are rather crude and unhelpful. County dot maps at least suggest the more confined nature of a creature's range, even if they leave plenty of room for error.

An improvement can be made by placing the dot fairly accurately instead of simply in the center of the county. If the scale permits, all records or at least a proportional sample of them may be plotted in this way, giving a truer picture. The important thing is to preserve in some other form, in an archive of data kept safely in at least two places, the full records. These can always be replotted on more precise maps as the sophistication of the mapping scheme grows.

What one ultimately wishes for is a system with the greatest possible resolution of graphic data. If you map butterfly distribution on your own small acreage, you are likely to subdivide it into some sort of grid. Such small-scale grids turn out to be the objective for many mapping programs. As I mentioned, the British system uses the U.K. National Grid. This is equivalent to the Universal Transmercator Grid employed by the International Commission for Invertebrate Survey. The kind of map possible under this regime appears on page 104. Until UTM use becomes better understood and more prevalent in the United States, most of us will continue to use counties, township and range sections, or latitude-longitude coordinates for map symbol placement. Again, so long as the basic data are sufficiently detailed, one system can always be converted to another, better one later.

If it seems all this is getting away from basic butterfly watching, keep in mind that many of the dots on those elegant British maps arise from the contributed records of butterfly watchers. There is great satisfaction to be had in taking part in such a scheme; to see a square you visited carrying its dot on the printed page gives a special thrill. More important, maps such as these enable you to better understand the greater patterns of which your local fauna is a component. The ultimate evolution of such a program would be to have every unit of local measure mapped to a high degree of resolution. We may never reach this goal in reality, and it might be quite boring if we did; but there is no reason why you cannot map your own neighborhood or nature center on a 1 km or closer basis, and thus really begin to see what's going on.

My colleagues and I in the Washington Lepidoptera Survey have built an up-to-date checklist, county- and date-occurrence charts, and a database of some 50,000 records that have been entered into the Department of Wildlife's computer files. With the assistance of the Nongame Wildlife Program we plan to publish a state-wide butterfly atlas. In my own county I have recorded over forty species, most of them new county records, and I am still finding novelties.

Our butterfly mapping program for Washington has contributed to the realization of concrete conservation goals for the state. Other practical applications of butterfly maps include comparison of the modern range of a species with the likely historical origins, to theoretically reconstruct geological, ecological, and human events that may have exerted influence; illustration of the impact of climate upon the flora and fauna; and pointing out portions of the region where field sampling has been neglected. Bridging such gaps offers some of the most challenging goals for field trips, where new records may spice the already rich pleasures in store.

The corollary of *where* a butterfly flies is *when*. To show this, a butterfly calendar works well. This can be a time line divided into days, weeks, ten-day periods, or months—the smaller the unit, the better. Or a year can be shown as a pie, with the flight period shaded. A kind of butterfly calendar appeared in the 1775 classic volume by Moses Harris, *The English Lepidoptera: or, the Aurelian's Pocket Companion*. Harris listed in one column the average date of change into the chrysalis; in the next the usual date of emergence of the adult. This is fine for single-brooded species, but those with more than one generation in a year would require additional columns. To give a butterfly calendar another dimension, make it a bar-graph with the bar indicating the number of records or individuals sighted during each period shown. This way you can see graphically the waxing and waning of the separate generations. A straight time line tends to run them together and give you no idea of periodicity except the times of the year one or more representatives of the species were to be found. Earliest and latest dates are of interest to be sure, but the number,

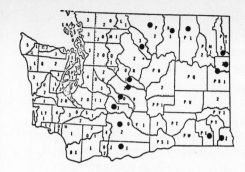

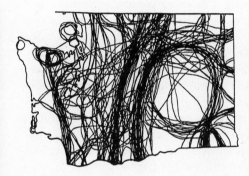

How butterfly mapping can help in countryside interpretation: The top map indicates the range of the Common Alpine (Erebia episodea) in Washington State; the middle map, known as a "spaghetti map," illustrates the ranges of 116 species of Washington butterflies, superimposed; and the bottom map shows the butterfly provinces for the state, as derived from the comparison of their distributions. These provinces were then contrasted for their nature reserve coverage and needs (from R. M. Pyle, "Eco-geography of Washington Butterflies," Atala 8:1 [1982 (covering the year 1980)].

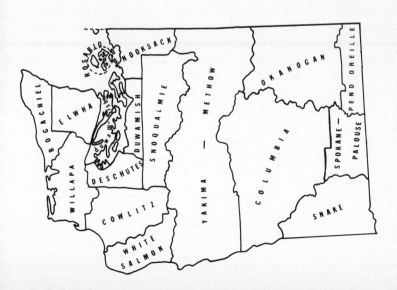

condition, and sex of butterflies on the wing at a given time are equally interesting or more so.

And so we come to counting, the subject of the next chapter. Before leaving listing, however, a few words of recapitulation are in order. I have tried to show that making lists and maps of butterfly occurrence has scientific application and function. But do not forget that it is fun as well.

Filling in the missing bits of knowledge in the butterfly map becomes something of a treasure hunt. This being a year in which the peripatetic Painted Lady arrived north in large numbers, our chances were good of finding it in every county. Otherwise, we might have to wait some six or seven years hence, until the Ladies were back. With time on her hands during a family visit, my wife set out to record it in little-visited Douglas County. She did so, and on her way back kept her eyes open for milkweed. Thus she not only plugged the last gap in the state's Painted Lady picture, but also discovered a new Monarch colony in a region where Monarchs are not common. The big rusty insects, preparing for migration, represented another county record—in rich Chelan County, well sampled for most of a century, where new dots are hard to come by. These experiences greatly enriched her trip.

There is pleasure in the simple making of a list—be it a state list, yard list, year list, day list, or life list. The birders are way ahead at this game, and for many of them listing, ticking, or "twitching," as the English call the more rabid brand, becomes an end in itself. There is no harm in such nature-gaming if it is done considerately, with respect for the birds and butterflies and for the people out to enjoy them. It is well to remember that one can lose sight of the animals in the game. To help avoid this, remember to put the butterflies before the numbers. Listing can actually help you do this. You may find it rewarding to keep a life list, which tells at a glance all the butterflies whose acquaintance it has been your pleasure to gain. A season's list, to be compared from year to year, can be useful and enlightening. A day-listing experience might be quite intense, as followers of the Fourth of July Butterfly Counts (see next chapter) can attest. But in all your listing, I hope you will take time and care to watch and really see as well.

10

Counting Butterflies

"Why aren't there as many butterflies as there used to be?" It seems that whenever I speak to a group about butterflies, it isn't long before someone asks that question. Almost everyone who notices butterflies expresses the belief that there were more butterflies when he or she was younger than there are today.

It is true that many butterfly populations have diminished, some to the point of extinction (see Chapter 15). However, by no means have butterflies declined everywhere, nor have all species gone downhill. A few species have even benefited from human activities. It is also a fact that things do seem bigger, more plentiful, and often better to the unjaded, innocent eyes of children than to more sophisticated adults. We also tend to magnify things and events in hindsight. Then, too, children have more time and leisure to take account of butterflies. When adults tell me there are no more butterflies around I have to wonder whether they have taken time to really look lately.

In order to do something for real butterfly conservation problems, we need to be able to discriminate between impressions and facts. For this and other reasons it is desirable to be able to gain a clear idea of the number of butterflies in a given place and time. What might seem a simple matter at first is fraught with difficulty. Imagine trying to count accurately all the rapidly flitting fritillaries of one species in a field aflutter with three or four other kinds of *Speyeria* and half a dozen other orange butterflies.

The very challenge of butterfly counting has caused many a field worker to give up before starting and instead to merely report abundance in general estimates: very common, fairly few, rare, and so on. Obviously such terms have no objective meaning. The other common practice has been to report butterfly "bags"; that is, the number caught by a collector at a given time and locality. This is moderately helpful in a relative way but is subject to all sorts of bias such as selection for perfectness or sex, collector satiety and efficiency, and weather.

To meet the need for a better idea of butterfly numbers, lepidopterists have developed several techniques and activities. They all give some measure of abundance, with varying levels of reliability. There simply is no way to learn the absolute number of insects in a wild population, unless it is very small and the members highly conspicuous. The better mathematical estimates probably come impressively close to reality when carried out skillfully under optimal conditions. Simply speaking, there are four basic ways to count butterflies:

1. You can attempt to count every individual you see of a species. This is rough-and-ready and open to error, but if you know the fauna and have a quick eye you can come up with a fairly useful idea of relative abundance this way. The Fourth of July Counts discussed below are usually conducted in this manner.

2. You can walk a regular transect through a set habitat, counting individuals within a predetermined distance from the path; then use the totals as relative indicators of numbers present over the habitat as a whole.

3. You can carefully count the individuals in a restricted area, then extrapolate for a larger area whose butterfly density should be about the same. Investigators use this method in dealing with the daunting problem of estimating numbers of overwintering Monarchs in Mexico and California.

4. You can conduct more or less ecologically sophisticated experiments involving the capture, marking, release, and recapture of individuals. By manipulating the results mathematically, you get an estimate of the population size. We will look at examples of these methods in reverse order.

The mark-release-recapture method is frequently employed by scientists seeking the best possible measure of abundance in a population. As a standard tool of population biologists, it has spawned many variations whereby increasingly sophisticated calculations are applied in order to achieve better statistical significance for the figures obtained. While some readers may be disappointed, most will agree that this is not the place to go into the mathematics in any detail. The bibliography in the Appendix includes technical papers on the subject for those wishing to pursue it in earnest. Among these is Paul Ehrlich's paper on the essential method, which he and his colleagues have refined for use in their intensive studies of Edith's Checkerspot at Stanford University. Essentially, by comparing the number of individuals captured, marked, and released with the number recaptured, you get an estimate of the number in the population. The simplest formula for estimating a population by this method is $P = N \times M/R$, where P is the population size, M is the number of individuals marked and then released, N the number of unmarked individuals captured on a second occasion, and R the number of marked individuals recaptured on the second occasion.

Such an experiment is certainly within the capability of a determined amateur, and it can be very revealing. Little if any harm is done to the butterflies if they are handled carefully. The marks are generally made with felt-tip markers in a pattern that distinguishes a particular individual from any other. Carrying out a mark-release-recapture study will give you an inkling of the sort of rigor demanded by science as well as the satisfaction of knowing rather than just guessing about how many butterflies are around. If you are mathematically inclined, you may want to move on to the kinds of multivariate analyses and more complex experimental models the professionals use.

Supposing the number of butterflies you encounter is too large for you even to consider a mark-release experiment. Such is certainly the case with winter-clustered Monarchs. Monarch researchers employ mass estimation techniques to arrive at an idea of their numbers. This involves taking a sample from one portion of a cluster, counting it, and extrapolating to the whole. By no means can such a measure be considered perfect, but it does give a more reliable figure than sheer guesswork and is probably accurate to the proper order of magnitude if carried out properly. I am referring to counting of the stationary clusters, but a similar manner of estimating may be used for migrating masses of butterflies. By physically counting every individual passing a given point, then multiplying the number achieved by the period of the flight and the breadth of its front, you can relate your sample unit to the flight as a whole. Malaise trap stations—large, tentlike nets that insects find easy to enter and difficult to escape from—set up along the flight front can provide useful estimates as well. Using such traps, Florida researchers have shown that annual migrations of Long-tailed Skippers, Cloudless Sulphurs, and Buckeyes involve a great many more individual butterflies than ever before thought.

Aside from visits to the overwintering Monarchs, I have on only two occasions encountered butterflies so numerous that informal mass estimates were in order. One instance involved an enormous hatch of Pine Whites in Idaho. These conifer-feeding, primitive pierids erupt in certain years, and this was the first such eruption I had witnessed. Clearly there were hundreds of thousands in a few miles of canyon, probably an order of magnitude more. I did not have sufficient time to attempt an orderly estimate, but every goldenrod, spider web, and puddle was plastered with the rice-paper wings of those butterflies. Getting a meaningful sample would have been difficult, since the sky and trees were full of Pine Whites too. At such times one is reduced to rougher quantitative statements such as "one heck of a lot of bugs."

On the other occasion, I was butterflying in the Black Canyon of the Gunnison in Colorado. Suddenly near sunset my party came upon a small arroyo with milkweed in bloom, whence a blue haze arose. There on the milkweed and in the air were vast numbers of blues. Anxious to be able to say something more intelligent about them than "vast numbers," I attempted (according to my very limited high school math, for I was a teenager at the time) to make a simple estimate. Netting all the blues on one milkweed, I counted species (six, of which more than half belonged to one, the aptly named Common Blue) and individuals (around a hundred). Then I sampled several other clumps in the same way. All the disturbed butterflies were eventually settling back to nectar, so the flower heads made a convenient sampling unit. Next I tried to determine how many milkweeds were blooming in the arroyo. From that a rough extrapolation was possible. However, in the fading sun many individuals were settling to bask and so were missed by the sample, and we continually bestirred others. I was rather overcome by the wonderment of the spectacle as well, and in the end I felt little confidence in my estimate. In a paper I wrote on the event I finally hedged, "At least ten thousand, and perhaps a hundred." But I shouldn't doubt that I was far too conservative.

The estimating methods discussed so far apply to one or a very few species present at one place or time. Sometimes we wish to get a reading on the abundance of all the butterflies in a given district. For this purpose we have two models, one prevalent in Great Britain and the other in the United States.

In the late seventies, British scientists instituted a scheme for monitoring changes in butterfly numbers. This came about when they realized that they had no reliable way of assessing effectiveness of habitat management on nature reserves, even when the reserves had been set aside largely for the rare butterflies they contained and were supposedly managed for them. The plan evolved on one such reserve, Monks Wood National Nature Reserve, a famous spot for butterflies such as the rare Black Hairstreak, but where some species were thought to have declined. This counting program was first set up by Dr. Ernest Pollard and several of his colleagues, and he still monitors the scheme nationwide, so the counts themselves have come to be known in butterfly parlance as Pollard Walks.

Pollard Walks consist of transects walked by the same observer weekly over a standard route. All butterflies seen within a specified distance of the walking recorder are counted. Such transects take place throughout the spring and summer on a wide variety of reserves and other sites, with eighty schemes operating as of 1981. The routes are chosen so as to be representative of habitats in the area, and are divided into sections for recording purposes. "The weekly counts for each brood are used to give an index of abundance for each species, and this is used to show changes in relative abundance from year to year," explains Dr. Pollard. As page 115 shows, the counts for the Large White (compiled from all over the country) demonstrate a dramatic drop in numbers in 1976, and this correlated with a severe drought.

Transects average about 2 miles in length and take an hour or so to complete. The same recorder works the transect whenever possible. All count results are collated at Monks Wood, where indices of abundance are computed and regional and national trends spotted. With continuity at recording sites, and in concert with the BRC mapping scheme discussed in the previous chapter, Dr. Pollard believes that this kind of counting provides valuable background information for conservation. "Monitoring itself," he explains, "that is, the acquisition of data on population fluctuations and longer-term trends, is valuable for highlighting areas in which detailed research studies are required. However it is the interpretation of the recorded changes which is of most interest and value." These should, after several years, begin to show correlations with climate and land use, and such results are the major goal of the program. Only a limited number of serious butterfly watchers, many of them nature reserve wardens, have taken part so far. As the transect scheme develops, opportunities to participate will expand around the country.

In North America, we have a counting scheme that is not as scientific to date but that involves many more ordinary butterfly watchers (if there is such a thing). This is the annual Fourth of July Butterfly Count of the Xerces Society. In 1974, it occurred to Sally Hughes, a Xerces member and this book's illustrator, that the Xerces Society might well sponsor a butterfly event similar to the Audubon Society Christmas Bird Count. The Fourth of July Butterfly Count has been operating ever since, with a growing number of counters taking part in many U.S. states and Canadian provinces and several other countries. Sally first conceived of the Count as a social and fun-filled event as much as a learning experience and monitoring device, and such it has become. It offers all butterfly enthusiasts a chance to get out together, see a lot of butterflies, gather for an enjoyable tally (usually involving a group dinner), and have the satisfaction of taking part in a worthwhile project.

The Fourth Counts are modeled closely on the famous Yuletime avian census. A 15-mile diameter circle is demarcated so as to take in the widest variety of habitats, and the center remains the same from year to year. Annually, groups disperse over the circle's area to count the butterflies they encounter. By no means

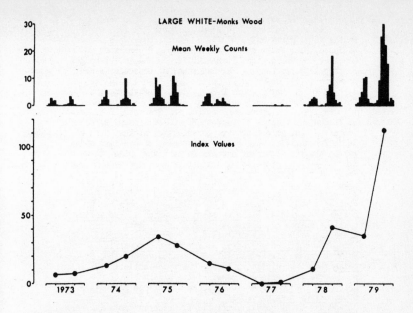

Butterfly transect data for the British Large White butterfly: mean weekly counts and index of abundance values at Monks Wood National Nature Reserve (from E. Pollard, "Monitoring changes in butterfly numbers," Atala 7:2 [1981 (1979)].

Large White (Pieris brassicae)

Eagle Summit, AK. 65°31'N, 145°22'W, includes vicinity of Eagle Summit, 100 km SW Circle, Miller House and Berry Camp. Elev. 600-1650 m; habitat coverage: Alpine tundra and swales (90%), alpine rockslides (10%). 2 July 1979; 1030-1700. Clear, 15-20°C (estimate), wind 0-5 km/hr. Thirty-seven observers in 22 parties. Total party-hours 121 (121 on foot); total party-miles 44 (44 on foot). Observers: K. Bagdonas, D.L. Bauer party (4), U. Caspi, D. Faulkner, G. Gorelick, M. Harrington, J. Hinchliff, E. Hodges, R. Hodges, F. Karpuleon, B. Landing, R. Langston, R. Leuschner & son, J. Merritt (2), J. Mori, P. Opler (U.S. Fish & Wildlife Service (OES), Washington, D.C. 20240), W. Patterson, K. Philip, J. Powell, K. Stanford, L. Stanford, R. Stanford, (720 Fairfax St., Denver, CO 80220), S. Stanford, D. Tilden, H. Tilden, W. Tilden, R. Vanderhoff, C. Wilkinson, B. Zeligs, J. Zeligs & daughter. Conservation status: Uses of land: Presently in wild state. Uniqueness of habitat: Widespread arctic. Imminent threats to habitats: None. Changes since last year: Species with adult flights every other year were all in flight. Parnassius eversmanni thor 13, Papilio glaucus arcticus 9, P. machaon aliaska 45, Pieris napi 104, P. occidentalis nelsoni 36, Euchloe creusa 1, Colias hecla glacialis 119, C. gigantea 4, C. palaeno chippewa 67, C. nastes aliaska 174, Plebejus saepiolus amica 1, Vacciniina optilete yukona 17, Agriades glandon nr. bryanti 32, Limenitis arthemis rubrofasciata 2, Polygonia gracilis 1, Nymphalis antiopa hyperborea 2, Phyciodes campestris 1, Boloria napaea alaskensis 117, B. improba youngi 150, B. polaris 137, B. distincta 10, B. chariclea butleri 289, B. eunomia triclaris 20, Oeneis jutta alaskensis 3, O. polixenes yukonensis 49, O. melissa 12, Erebia fasciata 9, E. magdalena mackinleyensis 43, E. youngi 413, E. theano canadensis 6, E. rossii gabrieli? 1, Hesperia comma manitoba 3. Total 32 spp., about 1884 individuals.

Big Black Mountain, KY/VA. 37° N, 83° W, includes Cumberland, Benham, Lynch, all Harlan Co., KY; Big Black Mtn; along creek 4 road miles S of Big Black Mtn, Wise Co., VA. Elev. 1070-1260 m. Habitat coverage: Forest and clearings at summit of Kentucky's highest peak. 10 July 1978; 0900-1500. A.M.: Clear. P.M.: Mostly clear. 21-27°C, wind variable, 0-10 km/hr. Nineteen observers in 8 parties. Total party-hours 48 (40 on foot, 8 by car); total party-miles 120 (16 on foot, 104 by car). Observers: Richard Henderson, David Hess, Leroy Koehn, McInnis (2 in party), Paul Opler (2 in party), Floyd and June Preston, Steve and Grayson Spomer, Ray, Kit, Linda, and Scott Stanford (720 Fairfax St., Denver, CO 80220), Bill and Hazel Tilden, party of two from Ohio. Conservation status: Uses of land: Mostly second-growth forest; some urban and rural areas. Uniqueness of habitats: Classic and unusually good habitats for Erora laeta and Speyeria diana. Imminent threats to habitats: Strip-mining. Changes since last year: none noted. Battus philenor 92(C), Papilio polyxenes asterius 1(N), P. troilus 8(S), P. glaucus 8(N), Graphium marcellus 9(C), Pieris rapae 11(N), Colias philodice 16(N), C. eurytheme 18(N), P. sennae eubule 1(C), Satyrium falacer 3(C), S. edwardsii 1(C), Danaus plexippus 8(N), Limenitis archippus 1(S), L. astyanax 1(C), Polygonia interrogationis 8(C), P. comma 3(N), Nymphalis antiopa 2(S), V.a. rubria 10(S), V. virginiensis 1(S), V. cardui 1(S), Phyciodes tharos 17(C), Chlosyne nycteis 2(C), Boloria toddi ammiralis 15(C), Speyeria diana 19(C), S. cybele 88(C), S. aphrodite 17(C), Erora laeta 22(C), Strymon melinus 1(C), Everes comyntas 22 (C), Celastrina argiolus pseudargiolus 8(C), Asterocampa celtis 2(S), Epargyreus clarus 76(C), Pholisora catullus 3(C), Amblyscirtes vialis 3(C), Pompeius verna 2(C), Wallengrenia egeremet 6(C), Euphyes vestris metacomet 2(C), Ancyloxypha numitor 2(S). Total 38 spp., about 510 individuals.

Hall Valley, CO. 39°28'N, 105°48'W, center Hall Valley
Campground, Pike National Forest, includes general area
of campground on N and S limits, W 1 km, E 3 km from
center along road in narrow Hall Valley. Elev. 2928-
2952 m. Habitat coverage: 50% montane meadow, 30% spruce
and aspen forest, 20% willow bog. 31 July 1979; 0830-
1200. Mostly clear, 13-29°C, wind NW, 5-15 km/hr. Six
observers in 5-6 parties. Total party-hours 17.5 (17.5
on foot); total party-miles 10 (10 on foot). Observers:
Karūlis Bagdonas (Dept. of Zoology and Physiology,
Univ. of Wyoming, Laramie, WY 82071), William Bagdonas,
John Carlisle, Teresa Clifford, Alice Houston, Mike
Rehg. Conservation status: uses of land and uniqueness of habitat: see 1978 report. Imminent threats
to habitats: Overgrazing in 1978 was heavy. In 1979,
even with heavier rainfall and lusher growth, habitat
destruction was even greater than in 1978. Changes
since last year: Botanical growth averaged two weeks
below 1978. At time of 1979 count the flora was in full
bloom for a montain habitat at this elevation. Clearly
it was 3-4 weeks behind the norm. In 1979 38 species
were recorded compared to 32 species in 1978. Parnassius
phoebus 20(C,S), Papilio rutulus 3(C,S), P. multicaudata
1(C), P. zelicaon 1(C), Pieris occidentalis 5(C,S), P.
protodice 1(C), P. rapae 2(C), P. napi 52(C,S), Colias
eurytheme 7(C,S), C. philodice 2(C), C. scudderi 3(C),
C. alexandra 26(C,S), Euchloe ausonides 4(C,S), Glaucopsyche lygdamus 22(C,S), Plebejus saepiolus 59(C,S),
P. glandon rustica 8(C,S), Lycaeides melissa 3(C),
Lycaena rubidus 16(C,S), L. dorcas 31(C,S), Oeneis
chryxus 2(C,S), Erebia epipsodea 15(C,S), Coenonympha
tullia 27(C,S), Vanessa cardui 24(C,S), Limenitis
weidemeyeri 16(C,S), Polygonia zephyrus 4(C,S), Boloria
titania helena 2(C), Speyeria atlantis 3(C,S), S. mor-
monia 57(C,S), S. zerene 8(C,S), Phyciodes campestris
36(C,S), P. mylitta 1(C), P. tharos 2(C), Erynnis persius
4(C,S), Orisma garita 4(C,S), Polites draco 15(C,S),
P. sonora utahensis 3(C), Pyrgus centaureae loki 4(C,S).
Total 38 spp., about 695 individuals. Larvae seen:
Nymphalis milberti 57 (on Urtica dioica).

*Three sample reports for a Xerces Society Fourth of July Butterfly
Count (from J. A. Powell and J. T. Sorenson, eds., "1979 Butterfly
Count Results," Atala 7 Supplement [1979]).*

does the event always take place on Independence Day. A Count Period of three weeks is allotted, and variance may be permitted for areas whose latitude or other conditions render the official period highly unfavorable. The idea is not so much to get the highest number of species—although such a competition is inevitable: Gilpin County, Colorado, long claimed the highest North American total, nearly a hundred species, now approached by the Arizonans—but to gain an impression of butterfly numbers and fluctuations year to year.

Parties take account of each individual they see or, in the case of extraordinarily abundant species, make best-guestimates. The method is fairly crude and by no means statistically sound, yet it serves to generate a rough sense of abundance within the area counted. Since techniques are standardized as much as possible and counters tend to take part from year to year, a picture of some reliability begins to build up. Three sample count reports are on pages 116, 117.

The results have been computerized for the first fifteen-plus years of the 4JBC, and patterns are already emerging. As of 1991, nearly 150 counts were taking place annually. The more there are, the clearer the picture they will generate. If nothing else resulted from them, the counts will have raised butterfly awareness and enjoyment for thousands of people. Yet they are already yielding conservation results as well.

Ever since the first year of the count in 1974, I have met with good friends, including Ray Stanford, Jan Chu, Ron Wahl, Mary Jane Foley, and Paul Opler, in Aurora, Colorado, for the High Line Canal 4JBC. We count hard in the July sun, pause for a picnic in a canalside park, and end up with a tally beneath the hackberry trees in Fairmount Cemetery. These outings have confirmed the extinction of certain species in the count area while recording the arrival of new colonists. When rapidly expanding Aurora decided to set aside some open space before it was too late, their choices coincided with our recommendations based on surviving butterfly diversity.

Fourth Counters are urged to take careful note of habitat alterations within their count circles, along with any other observations of biological or management significance. A number of nature centers already have come to rely on the counts to furnish such information. To get involved in the butterfly counts, write to the Xerces Society, whose address appears in the Appendix.

Dr. Karölis Bagdonas, former President of the Xerces Society, for years led a group of his students on a twelve-mountain-pass high country trip each summer in Colorado. Six counts were conducted on this marathon alpine excursion (one reason for the group's nickname: Bagdonas's Flying Circus). Similarly, cadres of university lepidopterists scour the Berkeley, California, region in one of the most complete counts each year. Such scientists might be forgiven an urge to carry out their studies unperturbed by the demands imposed by butterfly counts. They can be fatiguing and the report for one count, let alone many, involves much labor. But their efforts, and those of hundreds of people at nature centers, parks, forests, and fields all over the continent, are helping us to form an idea of fluctuating butterfly numbers. All these people seem to have a memorable time in the process, since most come back for more. And if such counts continue, we may at last be able to respond intelligently when someone asks, "Why aren't there as many butterflies as there used to be?"

11

Butterfly Behavior

The mildest winter on record had dripped its way into the early verdure of spring long before the equinox. Pacific Northwest seasons may be subtle compared to those of the Northeast, but to make up for their understatement they are long and drawn-out— except some winters. Fall and spring are in no hurry to get past, often stretching for months in and out of a winter marked mostly by more rain. That year, winter was an almost imperceptible extension of autumn or precursor to spring, the two of which almost met through the moister middle time. And the butterflies responded.

The heavy rainfall in this region, 116 inches annually on the average, combines with cold to kill many insects through sheer rot, I suspect, as they try to pass the winter in one stage or another. Cold or wet alone do not seem to have the same effect, as the butterfly-populous arctic and tropical rain forest attest. So when the winter is mild here, the result can be a spring more full of butterflies than usual.

On a recent April outing I was returning over the hills from the Columbia River, where many more Spring Azures than I had seen all together in the county before were clustering and sipping at wet sawdust. One bore a crisp bird's billmark across its wings. Winding down an old logging road through emerald alders newly in leaf, I noted the great number of Veined Whites flitting and basking among the afternoon sunbeams. Every clump of shamrock oxalis seemed to have its white, spreading its linen wings toward the southwest.

Farther along I rounded a bend and came in view of a great salmonberry bush standing full in the sunshine. The tall cinnamon-stick canes held aloft a screen of unfurling leaves of the freshest spring green, decorated by deep pink flowers and nearly as many pale white butterflies. One of the reasons the Veined White is so successful in many woodlands of the Northern Hemisphere is its willingness to utilize almost any available nectar source. Already this spring I'd watched them drink from a progression of early flowers as they bloomed, including spring beauty, yellow violet, dandelion, wild cherry, and dewberry. But in many years of watching I had never seen them use the conspicuous magenta flowers of salmonberry. Now, at this big bush, half a dozen or more were doing so with avidity. Others were simply basking on the reflective leaves. And on the very top, a pair of whites were mating. The male faced upward and clung to the rough edge of the leaf with his tarsi, his gray-smudged white wings held open. The French-vanilla female faced downward and held her wings tightly closed between his, so I could see the olive-scaled veins of her underside. After a time their peaceful interlude finished and she fluttered down to the roadside vegetation. A male, the same or another, immediately flashed down beside her, then another. Agitated, they crawled and fluttered around the already-mated female, but she thrust her abdomen high in the air, repelling their advances and indicating that she was no longer receptive. Eventually they left her in peace. Elsewhere, males flew high from basking posts to investigate others of their kind passing by. From time to time, two males circled high in the air until they ascertained that neither was a female.

Here in this glade, only a single species of butterfly was on the wing. The only others I'd seen all day were the drinking Spring Azures and a pair of actively courting Satyr Anglewings. Yet in this limited setting, I was able to witness courtship and mating, territoriality, basking, nectaring, puddling, and evidence of predator evasion (the billmark)—many of the activities and actions that make butterfly watching so rewarding—not to mention a goodly portion of sheer beauty. If there is so much to see in such a simple

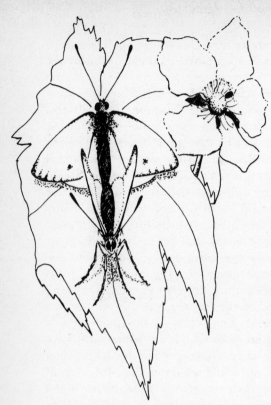

Veined Whites mating on thimbleberry. The female spreads her wings above, while the male, with wings folded, faces away and links with her. Mating may last from several minutes to all day and overnight.

butterfly scenario, imagine the action in a meadow, garden, or glade teeming with butterflies on a summer's day.

As we have seen, the identity, distribution, numbers, and appearance of butterflies are qualities of great interest. Their behavioral activities hold at least as much fascination. Even were they gray creatures, nameless and scattered randomly over the landscape, butterflies would still be wholly worth attending to for their behavior alone. Far from being little automatons with limited programs ruled exclusively by a narrow range of instincts, butterflies turn out to have startling variation in their behavior and the clear ability to modify their actions to suit the circumstances. Indeed, it is certain that at least some butterflies are capable of learning new behavior within their adult lifespans.

While behavior falls within a relatively constant set of parameters for given species, allowing for some generalization on our parts and for predictable success and survivability on theirs, it is not so tightly stereotyped as once was supposed. The demands faced by butterflies in their style of existence make it imperative that they be able to perform their jobs with precision, yet respond to new situations with some flexibility. As quite highly evolved insects, they have acquired the ability to perform elegantly both fixed and adaptive tasks. Watching them do so will enhance your butterfly outings immeasurably. Behavioral notes can also be a great aid to identification. In fact, among species terribly difficult to separate, behavioral traits may furnish the clues by which to distinguish them in the field. Perhaps you will discover some of these "activity field marks." There is a great deal to see as butterflies feed, evade predators, respond to weather and climate, defend territories, court, mate, and oviposit (lay eggs). Most behavior fits into one of three major realms of activity: sustenance, survival, and reproduction. For purposes of discussion it is useful to break these down into subcategories such as the ones that follow.

Essential to life is the intake of nutrients. We have seen that butterflies, like other insects, take in oxygen through spiracles in their abdomens and that they refer the molecules to all cells via minute tracheae. That leaves food, minerals, and water. Butterflies inherit a good deal of energy from their larvae, who made it their business mostly to eat. For some butterflies that seem to nectar little if at all, their caterpillar fat seems to be almost sufficient to sustain adult life. Indeed, for many moths it must suffice, since they have no functional mouthparts as adults. Most butterflies, however, actively engage in feeding as adults and this occupies much of their time and effort.

The chief food of adult butterflies is flower nectar, a nutrient high in sugar starches, low in protein and fats. We learned something of nectar preferences in Chapter 4 on finding butterflies, and we will learn more in the next chapter on butterfly gardening. While they are much less choosy about nectar than about larval host plants, butterflies still clearly exercise preferences. The Veined Whites I spoke of seem to use most early spring nectar sources, yet apparently eschew two conspicuous and abundant early flowering shrubs—Indian plum and red currant. I watched Mardon Skippers recently visiting a variety of prairie flowers sparingly, but without a doubt preferentially sipping from blue violets. There is some evidence that certain insects may have actual biochemical requirements that restrict them to certain kinds of nectars. An element of taste, both inherited and acquired, may be involved, and of course the visibility of the flowers and their ultraviolet reflectivity matter very much.

Before you can choose your sweets you must find the candy shop. Butterflies lack the sophisticated dances by which honeybees convey directions among one another to the flower fields. They seem to rely on random search, quartering the ground until they spot a likely source, then alighting or hovering to investigate closely. Sight, I feel, must be the operative sense here. It is possible that fragrance plays a role, though I suspect flower scents were evolved more to attract night-flying moths and poets. Clearly no one who watches can miss the fact that butterflies investigate a great many colored objects in their search for flowers and mates. Yet I am impressed by how quickly they espy and zero in on the correct color patches. It is said that butterflies prefer whites, purples, and yellows to reds and blues, but I know of nectarers on all colors of flowers: Birdwings love red hibiscus and Pine Whites go mad for blue lobelias. In any case, it is the ultraviolet reflection in concert with the color rather than merely the wavelengths visible to us that butterflies will recognize. Remember that their range of wavelengths extends far past deep purple.

Your own observations will help you build a hypothesis of nectaring choice. Equally interesting is the drinkers' behavior once among the posies. A butterfly will flirt with a dozen inflorescences before settling on one to actually probe. Can it somehow assess nectar load from without? Or it will skirt flower after fresh flower, only to return again and again to the same blossom whence it sipped before. A nectar stop may last a millisecond or a minute, or more. Recently I watched a ringlet nectaring on a buttercup for several minutes before a fly bestirred it. This was a surprise in itself, for in twenty years I had never seen any butterfly utilize the ubiquitous summer buttercup blossoms. On other occasions I have seen individuals, that lobelia-loving white for instance, remain at the bar for twenty minutes or more. Much of this variation must depend upon how much nectar has been left behind by bees, butterflies, hummingbirds, and other drinkers. Fermented nectar has been known to intoxicate butterflies, rendering them loath to leave.

Bees, of course, visit flowers for their pollen as well as nectar, the raw material for honey. It was long thought that Lepidoptera took only nectar from flowers, except for one group of primitive micromoths known as Micropterygidae. These minute, metallic purple-and-gold creatures have chewing rather than sucking mouthparts with which they masticate the pollen grains of sedges and other plants. This trait makes them very primitive and links them to caddisflies in a remote way. Most moths, and all butterflies, possess the sucking mouthparts described in Chapter 2. In many cases the very length of these drinking straws determines just what juices are available: A blue at a long-necked lily would find it a case of nectar, nectar everywhere but not a drop to drink. Small butterflies sometimes find ways of getting around this problem. Diminutive blues have been noted scrunching down inside flowers with deep corollas to reach their nectar; and I have seen a Silver-bordered Fritillary approaching irises at the base of the petals, forcing its tongue between them, so as to avoid the normal, circuitous route to the nectaries.

In any case, butterflies limit their feeding to liquids or to dried solutions that they can wet, then take up. That is, except for one special case. It has long been known that when the longwing butterflies (genus *Heliconius*) of the American tropics withdraw their proboscis from flowers they often bear a thick coating of pollen. This was thought to be incidental. Working in Costa Rica during the 1970s, Dr. Larry Gilbert of the University of Texas demonstrated that these butterflies indeed absorb the pollen grains and metabolize them, thus gaining a rich source of pure protein denied other butterflies. This sophisticated and surprising adaptation allows the longwings to produce eggs over a much longer time than other butterflies that, limited to the protein they inherit from their larvae, never make more than the batch of gametes they are "born" with. So longwings may live over periods of six or eight months, and create new germ plasm all the while. These longwings exhibit another dramatic butterfly behavioral trait vis à vis flowers. They trapline; that is, they visit circuits of flowers on a regular daily basis. As the pattern of resource availability changes through natural blooming sequence or the manipulations of researchers, the longwings modify their traplines. This information, also contributed by Gilbert and his associates, furnishes one of the most convincing demonstrations of butterfly learning.

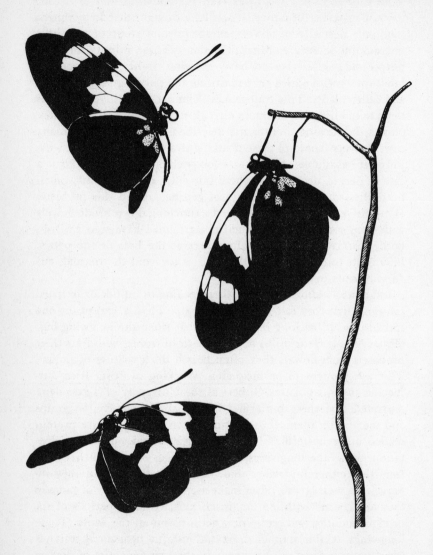

Crimson-banded Longwings flying in to their nocturnal roost. These butterflies are known to consume pollen as well as nectar, prolonging their lives and reproductive ability.

If butterflies can live by flowers alone, they do not in all cases choose to do so. Many other sources of nutrients lure adult butterflies, and you will do well to examine such substances for visitors. Still in the category of sugars, tree sap and rotting fruit attract butterflies like the finest flowers. Knowledge of such attractants in the neighborhood can lead to memorable encounters. The sight of a dozen or more tortoiseshells and anglewings crowding about a willow trunk dripping its rising sap makes a fine introduction to the new butterfly season. In Hawaii, I spied sixty or more gorgeous salmon-red and black Kamehameha butterflies climbing over one another to reach the oozing sap of rat-damaged trees. In an English town garden, Red Admirals besotted on fallen pears served up a similar spectacle. These two butterflies are closely related; they and their cohorts, the brush foots, visit sweet sources more assiduously than most. I have watched big black-and-white Weidemeyer's Admirals drawn to aphid honeydew in Colorado. Another nymphalid, the southeastern Tawny Emperor, patronizes rotting persimmons with a passion. And another, the California Sister, hangs about Napa Valley wineries where it imbibes spillage from oaken wine casks. In truth, these Sisters are not the only butterflies to become tipsy on their drink: Fruit sap and other sugary liquids fermenting in the sun produce strong brews, often inebriating to their butterfly visitors. Their flight under the influence of alcohol can be amusing to see, like the well-known offbeat works of orb-weavers under the experimental influence of LSD.

Items not nearly so nice as sugar and plums attract butterflies just as effectively. Mammal scat, particularly that of carnivores, also draws their avid attention. The fresher the better, but I have watched scores of beautiful blues gathered about dried dog droppings. Apparently they can exude moisture to dissolve the desired substances, then reingest it. Another choice repast for butterflies comes in the form of carrion. Rotting carcasses seem odd fare for imagined lotus-eaters, but butterflies visit their excrescent flesh avidly. If scat and carrion strike you as not very salubrious backgrounds on which to view ethereal butterflies, try to consider the situation biologically. Flowers may offer greater aesthetic appeal but they cannot provide all the minerals present in decomposing animal material. Amino acids, as well as minerals, have been suggested as likely nutrients derived from such substrates.

What do butterflies gain from one of their most common targets—the mud puddle? "Mud-puddle clubs" are a very well-known phenomenon among butterfly enthusiasts. Not always mud, but frequently damp sand, silt, gravel, or even dry earth may attract hundreds of individuals. Urine patches attract butterflies, a fact taken advantage of by collectors. But here I am speaking of pure water and particles of soil or sand. Swallowtails, skippers, blues, and sulphurs make themselves particularly evident at these gatherings. They become so preoccupied that one can approach carefully and take a blue onto one's sweaty finger—perspiration is another favorite indulgence. And this gives a clue. Recent research suggests that butterflies puddle primarily for the salts they may thus obtain. This would explain why some spots are favored over others just as wet, and why some butterflies are seen to squirt liquids from their abdomens after puddling. Some then reimbibe the excreted fluid (giant skippers have been noted doing so); others "spit" onto dry soil in order to dissolve what they desire to drink. Whether puddles serve the function of butterfly salt-licks—as seems likely—or merely as sources of moisture, they accommodate the watcher wonderfully. I relish the memory of Queen Alexandra's Sulphurs, their lime-green and yellow shapes wedged by the dozen into Colorado canyon dust after fragrant summer showers, and five species of swallowtails amassed at spring seeps nearby. Travelers in the tropics tell of truly fabulous aggregations of kite swallowtails, giant sulphurs, and others along Amazonian riverbanks and Congolese shores.

Note the places where you see butterflies drinking, for some of them will be novel. I mentioned the Azures at sawdust. A relative, the Common Blue, surprised me by sucking moisture from the porous broken end of a cattail stalk in a Wyoming marsh. What can you add to our knowledge of butterfly diet and drink?

The subject of larval feeding behavior reads entirely differently. I will treat it in more detail in Chapter 13 on rearing butterflies. Most larvae feed on the foliage, buds, or flowers of green plants. One in North America, the Harvester, nourishes itself solely on a certain kind of woolly aphid. Carnivory occurs among some other lycaenid butterflies elsewhere, and among many species in the form of cannibalism among siblings. Perhaps the most fascinating instances of this take place among certain blues, whose larvae change from herbivores to carnivores in mid-development.

Many species of blues have evolved symbiotic (occurring in the same range) relationships with ants. This usually consists of the caterpillars exuding a sweet substance known as honeydew, which is then taken up eagerly by the ants. The ants are thought to provide some protection from arthropod predators such as beetles to the sweet-bestowing larvae. If you would like to find the chiton-shaped caterpillars of blues among their host plants, watch for concentrations of ants. Often their more obvious presence will lead your gaze to the larvae in their care. This sort of ant–blue cooperative evolution has occurred many times. But only a few species have taken the relationship to the lengths of the Large Blues (genus *Maculinea*) of Europe and Asia. These uncommon butterflies lay their eggs on specific host plants, wild thyme in the case of the English Large Blue. The young caterpillar feeds for a while on the host plant, molting its skin a couple of times and growing. Then it drops to the ground. An ant happens along and, perhaps mistaking it for ant brood, seizes the blue larva with its mandibles and carries it below ground to the ants' nest. Thereafter the larva lives a subterranean existence, feeding on ant brood. The ants tolerate this behavior and continue to gather honeydew from the newly carnivorous caterpillar. Pupation takes place in the nest. The following spring, the adult butterfly emerges underground, crawls to the surface, and spreads its wings. (This kind of extreme specialization has its price. Land-use changes in Britain favored the wrong kind of ant, ultimately leading to the extinction of the British Large Blue. This was demonstrated by Dr. Jeremy Thomas of the British Institute of Terrestrial Ecology. Now all the other *Maculinea* are endangered worldwide due to habitat alterations affecting their delicately balanced life-style.)

Only the most persistent researchers, such as Dr. Thomas of Great Britain, have observed much of this remarkable life history. Anyone, however, can watch blue larvae being tended by ants, and many other feeding behaviors. "To survive I need a meal ticket," wrote Elton John, and that is certainly true of butterflies and their caterpillars. But the meal ticket itself is not as much of a problem as avoiding many other threats to survival as they go about their activities.

Survival behavior offers many remarkable and obvious subjects for observation. Birds, spiders, robber- and dragonflies, ambush and assassin bugs, lizards, and many other small predators catch and consume butterflies whenever they have the opportunity. As a result, butterflies have evolved many impressive means of defense. Books have been written about these adaptations and their implications, and space here allows only a brief glimpse. As canvases for the creativity of evolution, butterfly wings have no match. They openly display a dazzling array of tricks, guises, and deflections to confound would-be predators. These include mimicry, whereby palatable butterflies come to resemble distasteful ones that birds have learned to avoid; false targets—eyespots and red-spotted tails "designed" to deflect bird strikes away from the head and body; camouflage, or crypsis—coloration that helps the insect to blend into its background.

Such visual tricks would confer little protection without the appropriate behavior. In order to get the most survival value from their looks, butterflies must make the right moves. A tortoiseshell alights on a tree trunk—not a white birch, but a brown oak or elm whose bark matches the dun color of its underside. It becomes nearly invisible. But should an insect-hunting bird peck too closely, the tortoiseshell flashes its bright orange upperside, startling the color-conscious bird long enough to get a head start in flight. An arctic alights on a boulder; chances are good that the mineral speckling and lichened patterns of the rock will match the mottled lower surface of the arctic's wings. (It has long been supposed that the purpose of these butterflies' habit of tilting their closed wings upon landing is to reduce their shadow so as to further enhance their crypsis, and so it may be; but the prevailing modern theory assumes that the wing tilts in order to better catch the sun's warming rays, i.e., photo-orientation.) Hairstreaks and blues consistently rub their hindwings back and forth while at rest. Is this done to draw attention to the false heads and billboards created by their trailing tails and marginal bright spots, the better to target attacks away from their vitals?

Behavior clearly can enhance survival in many ways. Yet much more observation and experimentation is needed, for it is all too easy to hypothesize a cause to match the effect with no real evidence. For example, do the silver spots of fritillaries really serve

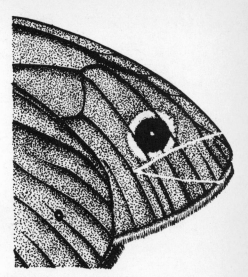

Eyespots enable butterflies to escape bird predation by directing attack away from their bodies. Here the "bull's eye" has been struck and the butterfly, a Great Basin Wood Nymph, released unharmed. The attacking bird's bill left a crisp impression of its bill etched into the scales of the wings.

to resemble dewdrops in a morning meadow, thus camouflaging them; or is this just a pretty idea? Or could the metallic orbs serve just the opposite purpose—that of warning birds as they flash that "here goes a perfectly foul-tasting butterfly"? We may never know all these answers, but your careful observation may very well help to illuminate the questions.

Which butterflies play possum when you pick them up? How often do you find eyespots and wingtails torn away by bird attack? In the wood nymphs I studied in Colorado, more than 10 percent had bird tears around their eyespots—a figure that seems about average for such bull's-eye butterflies. That indicates a wide margin or survivorship thanks to the eyespots, and therefore a powerful evolutionary incentive for their development and maintenance.

The extravagant display of bright colors to signify distastefulness is one of the most effective and widespread butterfly defenses, as demonstrated so famously by the Monarch. Poisonous milkweed host plants render Monarchs highly untasty, and birds learn this in one try, later avoiding Monarchs and all butterflies that resemble them. The Viceroy, quite a close lookalike to the Monarch, evolved from butterflies similar to banded white admirals. Al-

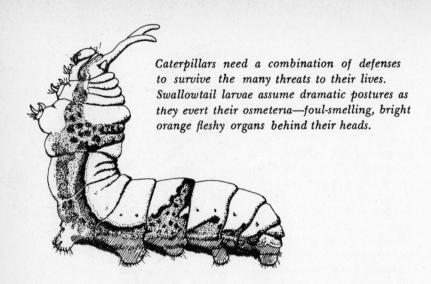

Caterpillars need a combination of defenses to survive the many threats to their lives. Swallowtail larvae assume dramatic postures as they evert their osmeteria—foul-smelling, bright orange fleshy organs behind their heads.

though long thought to be palatable to birds, the Viceroy turns out to be distasteful too. Birds educated on one or the other will avoid both Monarchs and Viceroys. Some lepidopterists are coming to believe that butterflies on the whole are relatively untasty and that this fact is what allows butterflies to survive flying by day (unlike more palatable moths, which escape birds under the cloak of darkness), and that they operate as one vast Muellerian mimicry complex. Muellerian mimics are distasteful lookalikes, who double the trouble and lessons for hungry birds; tasty creatures mocking distasteful ones are called Batesian mimics.

A force more powerful even than predators in molding butterfly behavior has been climate, and its daily expression, weather. The elements probably account for as much butterfly mortality as predators, parasites, and disease together. How does the frail butterfly survive the pounding maelstrom? The harsh winter? The drought or flood? Each species has developed its own style of coping with winter, dry and rainy seasons, and other more-or-less regular climatic stresses. They may hibernate in one stage or another to get through the cold, estivate to pass the hottest, driest period, or even migrate. As for day-to-day weather threats, special behaviors for surviving these have similarly arisen.

New England naturalist Noble Proctor reported to me a sighting of Compton Tortoiseshells circling and entering a radio transmitter structure on a mountaintop. They were seeking, and probably found, a safe nook in which to pass the long, cold winter. Walking to work in Portland, Oregon, one day, I spotted a West Coast Lady as it flew directly into a cherry tree and took up a protected posture, wings held tightly together and pulled snugly in toward the body, beneath the natural umbrella of the cherry leaf. Seconds later the first big raindrops fell from what had seemed an unthreatening sky.

Some miles to the east, in the Oregon Cascades, several people I know have been fortunate enough to observe mass movements of California Tortoiseshells. These periodic emigrations center on the Cascade volcanoes and sometimes close down highways by their magnitude. They do not seem to relate directly to climate or weather, but to host plant overexploitation and resultant population dispersal. However, these mass movements appear to have a long-term, four-to-seven-year periodicity that may involve sunspots or geoclimatic influences. The still more dramatic migrations of Monarchs (see Chapter 19) represent direct response to the northern winter: in order to exploit temperate milkweeds yet survive the freezing months, these essentially tropical butterflies actually migrate out of the territory. By overwintering in cool Californian and Mexican climes, they preserve their energy to journey part way back and reproduce on the way, come springtime.

Temperature affects butterflies in a fundamental way, since they remain about the same temperature as their surroundings. Flight muscles need to be warm to work, and ovaries require warmth to incubate their precious load of eggs. So butterflies have evolved definite relationships with the sun. Basking is a very common activity among butterflies, and it provides some of the very best watching shots. Some butterflies, like the arctics, bask with their wings closed and tilted to the sun. I have watched Nelson's Hairstreaks tip right over against a maple leaf perch. These butterflies are called vertical (or lateral) baskers. Horizontal baskers, such as Painted Ladies, spread their wings wide to catch the rays. Others may choose a method halfway between the two, or open and close their wings slowly as they bask. Baskers may be sluggish as well as spread, so they give great photography opportunities. But once they attain their flight temperature they may be off like a shot. Color, of course, aids heat absorption. All-black Magdalena Alpines are living solar cells. Female sulphurs and parnassians at high altitudes tend to have blackish scaling on the parts of their wings that surround their abdomens. On the other hand, many desert and Great Basin butterflies possess a pallor that may enhance camouflage in alkaline surroundings, or may serve to reflect away excess heat.

A butterfly's appearance and modifications came about to ensure its survival. But a butterfly is first and foremost a flier, and flight is its most basic element of defense. At all times butterflies must be prepared to be evasive on the wing. Even noncollectors should chase butterflies for a while to get a sense of this. Every collector knows that butterflies recognize them as a threat and behave accordingly. From the bullet-shot of giant skippers to the persistent fluttering of parnassians, from the maddening darting about of hairstreaks to the powerful sailing of swallowtails and flapping of sulphurs, the grass-blade weaving of satyrs, and the hill-climbing of whites, butterflies exhibit many types of evasive flight. Just face down a few Mourning Cloaks as they approach you along a streambed or track, and try to net them head-on. Almost invariably they will sail effortlessly over the rim of the net. Or pursue Magdalena Alpines on the high talus above timberline, where active chase is out of the question. It is very difficult not to believe that the black coursers are having their own sport with you, as they sail up or down the boulderfalls directly toward you, only to swing wide or high at the last second. Of course, collectors have not been the selective force leading to such behavior; birds have. Or does Magdalena recognize in a poised butterfly net the same threat that lies in the great inter-boulder spiderwebs in which I sometimes find them, bound in silk? One of the great things about netlessness is that you can become an unthreatening part of the landscape, just another rock or log. And by moving slowly enough, you can approach even the most wary and evasive butterflies without giving them cause for alarm.

Flight and beauty are the special hallmarks of butterflies: Beauty is incidental to the animals, while flight determines how they are able to live. It gets from place to place by flying. Some species,

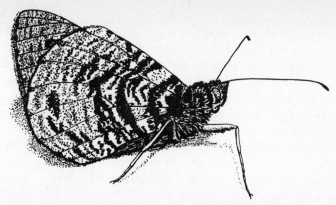

By lying flat against the ground, this Uhler's Arctic maximizes heat collection by the wings, which act as solar panels. An earlier theory suggested that this tilting behavior improved camouflage by reducing the butterfly's shadow.

such as certain checkerspots, remain within the meadow of their birth for their entire lifetime. Others, notably sulphurs and large fritillaries, may wander wide distances—not migrating, just wandering—especially the males after mating. The home range of butterflies differs dramatically between the nomads and the stay-at-homes and the many species that are neither. Since collectors necessarily intercept flight, watchers have much to contribute to an understanding of where butterflies go and what they do when

Tawny skippers (Hesperiinae) *tend to bask in a manner unlike other butterflies. This Whirlabout, still for a change, demonstrates the typical posture with hindwings held almost perpendicular to the angle of the forewings.*

they get there. Endurance and fleetness of foot are helpful here. Be aware also of the manner in which butterflies fly. Each has its own strokes, speed, and style. I find I can tell the different whites apart, when too far away to see pattern, by their flight modes. With practice, you will gain the ability to identify many moving targets by their color, profile, and flight pattern.

There are two other kinds of flight behavior you will find hard to overlook: territoriality and courtship. But noticing them and telling them apart is another matter. One school of thought maintains that insects are too primitive to exhibit actual territorial behavior, and that all instances of one butterfly chasing another should be considered potential courtship forays. Most lepidopterists, however, believe that butterflies certainly exhibit territoriality. In that case, it becomes challenging to determine the motive for a particular flight.

It is a fact that butterflies frequently fly out at passing objects. Pearl Crescents, American Coppers, and anglewings elicit the terms "pugnacious" and "investigative" for their striking behavior of this kind. The object of such sorties may be another butterfly of the same or a different species, a different insect, a bird, an amber light on a vehicle, or even a person. I have watched whites pursue snowy flecks of foam from a waterfall, Tiger Swallowtails follow a frisbee, Brown Elfins dart at chips of bark—a great way to find them in their extensive palaces of salal. Perhaps the most dramatic challenge I remember involved a Lorquin's Admiral and a Glaucous-winged Gull. Posted on a rose in a public garden, the admiral perceived the gull flying by some 20 feet overhead and flew up to meet it. Each time the gull passed over, the admiral engaged it, battering the big bird until it left, oblivious to the tiny attacker. This occurred time and time again, each encounter ending with the handsome admiral resuming its perch in the sunny rose garden. Such adventures may not always finish so felicitously. My observant friend Noble Proctor spotted a Spicebush Swallowtail in pursuit of a crow, which proceeded to nab the importunate insect and consume it in mid-air.

Such examples of sallying forth can be interpreted either as misguided territoriality or as deluded courtship flights. Butterfly vision first attracts males to potential females of their own species, while pheromones (chemical perfumes) determine species recog-

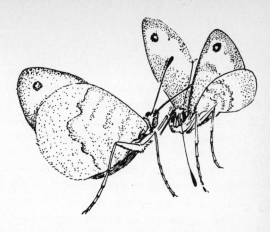

Courtship of Grayling butterflies. Classic experiments have shown that these European satyrs possess highly ritualistic courtship behavior. Here the female strokes the male's forewings with her antennae, smelling his pheromones.

nition at close quarters. It is quite conceivable that these butterflies could have been simply having a look at anything going their way on the off chance that it might be a receptive female. In fact, a set of experiments by the great Dutch ethologist Niko Tinbergen demonstrated that oversized female models may elicit stronger courtship advances from males than normal females. He demonstrated this with Grayling males and large paper superfemales. I carried out a similar test in Colorado with the black Magdalena Alpines of the timberline rockslides. My great (20-inch wingspan) female model of black cardboard, named Maggie May, flew down the talus slopes on clear fishline. Obligingly, she bobbed and soared over the granite field as a newly hatched virgin female might on her maiden flight. And how the males reacted! They flew at Maggie May with the greatest vigor each time she passed over. Since male Magdalenas do not maintain territories, but course up and down the rockslides in search of females or perch randomly to watch for them, I interpret these exaggerated shows of interest as courtship pursuits rather than attempts to drive other males away.

Other experiments in England, however, seem to demonstrate the authenticity of territoriality among butterflies of another satyrine species. Dr. Nick Davis of Oxford studied Speckled Wood butterflies in Wytham Wood; the males were holding posts in the sun-dappled glades. Each time another male entered its field of vision, a perching male would strike out to drive it away. Mock combats ensued, with little actual contact, until the interloper retreated. In virtually every instance, the holder of a territory retained it. When two males were fooled into thinking they were both in possession of the post, their battle went on. Perhaps the sitting male scent-marks the site, registering priority that intruders respect.

Territorial encounters usually involve little real combat, since their purpose is to repel rather than injure the rival. In this, butterflies as well as many other creatures are well ahead of humans: Their intraspecific conflicts tend to be stylized and seldom involve real bodily harm to antagonists—and almost never to whole populations. Only one butterfly in my acquaintance, a Colorado canyonland subspecies of the Short-tailed Black Swallowtail, engages in real physical contact to an impressive degree. Collectors have great difficulty obtaining fresh males; so violent are their cliff-hanging duels that all individuals soon become tatty.

Most butterflies that utilize a "territory," either to find mates or to drive off other males, seem to approximate one of two strategies. Dr. James Scott, a knowledgeable lepidopterist and skilled observer, has designated these styles "perching" and "patrolling." He believes their sole function is to enable males to contact potential mates. Perchers select a post from which they investigate passing objects. Patrollers move up and down a set course, often a gully, hedge, or path, seeking contacts. In a third common tactic, believed by many to serve as a method of courtship rendezvous, butterflies fly to the summits of prominences and mill about. Most hilltoppers are males, and a female flying up into their midst will soon be attended to. Dr. Oakley Shields, a veteran buterfly investigator, studied hilltopping and found that many species engage in the practice at one time or another. Anise Swallowtails, Spring Whites, and several checkerspots are among the more noted hilltoppers. Many species combine elements of all three patterns.

If territoriality does occur among butterflies, as I believe it does, just what is the male defending? Most likely, good places to meet females, so that his genes might be passed on. This squares with my belief that perching butterflies both defend territories and approach potential mates during these pursuit flights, and that a given pursuit may serve either to repel a male or engage a female, whichever turns out to be appropriate upon closer examination. If the flying object turns out to be a gull or a frisbee, neither behavior is appropriate, but nothing is lost except a spurt of energy unless the target turns out to be hungry.

Be this as it may, the ultimate purpose of butterflies is to make more of the same and the ultimate in butterfly behavior, from both the watcher's and the butterfly's perspectives, is courtship and coupling. Such a large and glorious array of behaviors has arisen to ensure that the right partners get together at the right time that I can only touch on the subject. Stand in any alfalfa field or clover meadow in July. Within seconds, if it is sunny, you should see yellow and orange flags rising, flapping, spinning, and spiraling on the breeze. These are courting pairs (and eager males) of Common and Orange Sulphurs. If two males come into contact, they will likely orbit one another upward for a time, then, realizing their error, disengage and plummet in opposite directions. An encounter between a male and an unreceptive female may eventuate similarly. But if a male and a receptive female engage, the spiral flight goes on and on. Eventually the pair drops to the ground where they begin a terrestrial dance in the aftermath of the aerial minuet already performed.

These two sulphurs, the Common and Orange (or Alfalfa Butterfly), frequently hybridize because of their artificial abundance in alfalfa fields. But this is unusual. They are closely related and most of their offspring survive. For most animals, cross-breeding of species leads to death or a loss of viability or fertility among the offspring. This is a waste of genes, a loss that nature will not tolerate. So barriers have arisen to prevent hybridization and conserve genes. These may be anatomical, chronological, or ecological —or they may be behavioral. In other words, two different species of butterflies may not fit together; they may fly at different times of day or year, or occupy different habitats; or their special form of courtship behavior may keep them apart. For this reason, butterflies have evolved their distinctive courtship choreographies in order to ensure recognition between suitable mates.

For many species, this dance expresses itself in complex movements. It may involve encircling flights, such as sulphurs take, as well as ground pirouettes. The early stages tend to be more spectacular and consist of visual recognition of potential partners.

The later steps usually involve chemical communication at close quarters. By smelling one another's pheromones, courtiers determine to their satisfaction that they are indeed right for one another. Male Queen butterflies flutter, slow and low, before the females, and extrude paintbrushlike organs known as hair-pencils from the tips of their adbomens. With these they waft clouds of invisible, powerful pheromones on the air in their wake. Females follow, sniffing the magic stuff with their antennae, becoming more and more receptive. Such enticement-in-flight is part of the courting repertoires of many of the Monarch's relatives, although the Monarch itself lacks hair-pencils. Instead, it carries its pheromones in scent-pads on the hindwings. More common among butterflies, and always exquisite, are the circling, stroking, fluttering dances on the ground or among the foliage. I once watched a pair of Purplish Coppers as they did an allemane-left, then faced off and began to stroke one another's wings with their antennae. Often it is the wings, and special scales on them known as androconia, that carry the key to consummation.

You may begin to wonder whether the conclusion ever occurs, and indeed, why there are any butterflies at all, so often does the encounter end in sweet parting. Recently I observed Silvery Blues courting at sundown in a swale of lupine, a very nice sight. One male pursued a female for some time, both fluttering almost in place, until she finally settled. Then as he continued to hover, she batted him over and over by flicking her closed wings rapidly. This finally changed to stationary fluttering on her part, but it was equally effective in keeping him at bay, if less abrupt. Two other males butted in and both times the ardent suitor left to drive them away, then returned to the still unreceptive female. Finally, after twenty minutes of this, a third interloper arrived, a very small male, and the weary original simply gave up and flew away. But the female wasn't having any from the newcomer either. Perhaps she had already mated and was interested only in laying her eggs.

There is little room for improvising in these acts. Instinct has choreographed these gentle contacts so precisely that a false step can shatter them. Then, too, female receptivity is a brief and fragile thing, and many a courtship is broken up by the wind, a bird, a fly, or another male horning in. Courtships often begin as

*Courtship at close range
involves sexual and species
recognition through the use
of chemical pheromones.
This male* Prepona *broadcasts
his perfume from the elaborate
patches of androconial scales
near the base of the hindwings.*

ménages à trois, or with a whole train of males on the tail of a
female, until one succeeds or she evades them all. So eager are the
males, having emerged earlier and the weaker ones already per-
ished, that few females remain virgin past their first morning of
emergence. Certain tropical longwing males actually couple with
the pupal female just prior to her emergence, gaining access by
cutting through the pupal shell with a genital file. The females
must already be emitting pheromones; in any case, they are in no
position to resist.

In twenty-five years I have observed hundreds of courtships
and found many pairs of butterflies *in copulo,* but I have very
seldom observed them getting into that state—in one instance a
pair of Eyed Browns, a satyr and a dryad, coupled instantly upon
meeting. Your persistence, patience, and unobtrusiveness will
eventually allow you to see the entire lock-and-key, stimulus-
response sequence, even to smell the pheromones, and to witness
one of the most elegant, delicate scenes in nature: butterfly love.

If this portrayal seems anthropomorphic, even to the repeated
use of the verb "to dance," consider the parallel: humans dance
to steps as rigidly laid out; they come together and part a thousand times for every dance that leads to marriage, constantly
probing for suitability and receptivity; their attraction is ruled
at least in part by pheromones, as we now know; and, while we
seem to exercise will, we nonetheless follow the same romantic

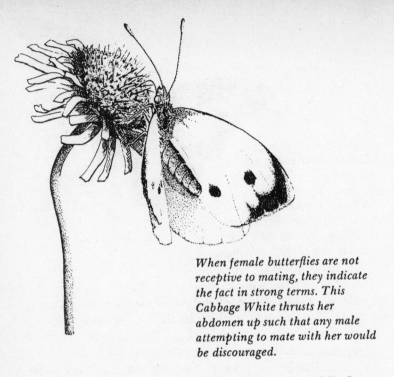

When female butterflies are not receptive to mating, they indicate the fact in strong terms. This Cabbage White thrusts her abdomen up such that any male attempting to mate with her would be discouraged.

patterns over and over through the generations. So while I may take some license, I do not think the comparison is so very overdrawn. The chief difference as I see it is that butterflies probably worry a great deal less about it all than we do.

On the first warm day of spring, I stood on a bluff watching courting pairs of Anise Swallowtails and Veined Whites circle out over the bay. Perhaps along with nectaring on beautiful flowers courtship is the loveliest aspect of butterfly behavior. But everything a butterfly spends time at is compellingly worth watching. I can offer no better advice than to seek butterflies in action. As the courtship/territoriality debate shows, our knowledge is far from complete. There is much to learn about social evolution, inter- and intraspecies relationships, intelligence, instinct, and many other subjects through the careful observation of behavior. Ethology, the science of behavior, is even less settled than ecology. So consider butterflies as actors. You will be surprised at the breadth of their roles, and pleased as they reveal themselves to be so much more than beautiful objects.

12

Butterfly Gardening

A memorable article in *National Geographic* from the 1930s contains a most evocative illustration. Delicately painted, it depicts a spray of lilacs attended by nectaring swallowtails—a Zebra, a Tiger, and a Spicebush, if I recall correctly. That picture made a strong impression on me many years ago. Yet I did not see such a sight myself until just last summer. It was in a northern Washington town, where lilacs had spread by suckers throughout an all-but-abandoned pioneer cemetery. Through the fragrant purple haze (for the blooming lilacs filled the place) I could see flashes of yellow. When I got closer I spied three species of swallowtails nectaring on the lilacs—the Western Tiger, Two-tailed Tiger, and Pale Tiger—a spectacular sight.

Clearly it is a good thing to have lilacs around if you want to attract swallowtails in spring. But lilacs bloom briefly. Should you desire the company of the bright nymphs of late summer, the fragrant flowers of that other purple-spiked plant, the butterfly bush, will do nicely. As a boy I sought Black Swallowtails on farmhouse lilacs, but frequented my neighbors' butterfly bushes for Painted Ladies. Add a patch of annuals—sweet William, zinnias, and marigolds for starters, and some phlox and aster—and you have a basic butterfly garden good from April through August. If you garden anyway, you can pay a little attention to butterflies' needs with very little extra effort. There will be more of them around, you will notice them more, and your garden will be a richer place. That's not all there is to butterfly gardening, but it is a start.

Butterfly gardening can be as simple as letting a few dandelions and nettles go or as complex as a complete horticultural program. Whatever your efforts to accommodate butterflies in your yard, they will respond and you will be gladder for it. The hints that follow are only an introduction to a growing butterfly pastime that is winning new devotees with every planting season.

Attracting birds to one's backyard has been a popular activity for a long time. More recently, the National Wildlife Federation's Backyard Wildlife Program has promoted the idea of sustaining a wide variety of interesting animals in the garden environment. As supplementary habitat, wildlife gardens have real conservation value; the pleasure they bring is their own reward. As natural countryside diminishes, we have become more and more aware of the importance of urban and suburban green space as wildlife habitat. The more native plants and animals we can encourage around our own homes, the fewer will be displaced by our growing need for space.

Luring and keeping beneficial insects in the garden is nothing new in Great Britain. L. Hugh Newman, author of *Create a Butterfly Garden* (see Appendix), has been doing just that for decades. Members of the British Butterfly Conservation Society and many ordinary gardeners have discovered the pleasure and satisfaction to be found in butterfly gardening. Although this peaceful, pleasing activity has been less well known in North America, lately it is coming into its own. The Xerces Society has published a major book on the topic, geared to different regions of the country. This and other important titles may be found in Appendix II, Further Reading.

I know few lovelier ways of enhancing a garden than with butterflies. Far from just a form of decoration, butterflies give gardens a whole new animate dimension. Obviously, the watching opportunities afforded by a butterfly garden can be excellent. To be able to walk out your own door, or even gaze out the picture window, and watch an array of colorful butterflies in a lovely setting of your own device is to enjoy them doubly. There is pro-

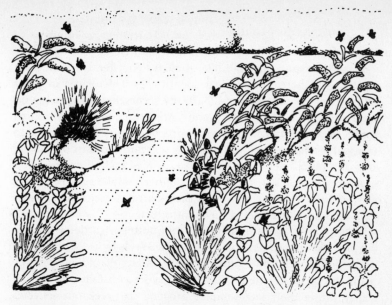

A simple butterfly garden. Plants in the foreground include Sedum, Rudbeckia, *mint, and butterfly bush. The flagstone path provides a basking space; the hedge offers protection from the wind. If conditions allow, the lawn area can be given over to meadow.*

found satisfaction in the realization of a plan for the fruiting of the earth, as any gardener will tell you. Yet, whereas plants grow where you plant them, butterflies are free to come and go. To get them to come where you want them to be, and to remain for a time or even to reproduce for generations, is a challenge and a joy.

The basic requirements for gardening butterflies are two: nectar with which to entice and nourish the butterflies, and the proper foliage for their larvae to consume. Beyond these essentials, a number of other features may be added to enhance the suitability of the garden habitat. But food, for both butterflies and caterpillars, is the first concern.

The first line of enticement is nectar. That butterflies have nectaring preferences, and differ in their nectaring abilities and behavior, we already know from Chapter 11. Due to the different shapes, depths, nectar capacity, color, and reflectance, flowers may be more or less suitable for the butterflies in your area. It is not simply a matter of planting "purple and white flowers, fewer of reds and yellows." Far and away the best strategy to follow is to become familiar with butterflies' favorite flowers in your neighborhood and surrounding habitats, then try to offer them in your garden. And here I make first mention of a principle of great importance: *Survey* the local butterfly scene. If you know something of your local butterfly fauna, what they are exploiting in nearby meadows and woods, what sorts of flowers draw them into town parks and gardens, you will have a great head start on casting your own plot. Then when you go to the seed racks, nurseries, and catalogs, you won't be shooting in the dark. Make sure you carry on your local resource survey in each season, to see what flowers work for what butterflies as the months turn.

An important factor in planning your butterfly garden is seasonality, or phenology, as biologists call it. Week by week, different butterflies emerge and find different bursts of blooms. So the spring brood of Veined Whites may visit coltsfoot and spring beauty, while their late summer progeny will seek out senecios and asters. Lack of nectar, particularly in early spring and autumn, can be a serious limiting factor on populations. In order to maximize the diversity and abundance of butterflies over as long a period as possible, you will want to provide nectar on as many days of the year as possible. Some butterflies have been able to extend their ranges by taking advantage of newly introduced nectar sources; others have lengthened their flight periods in the same way. One can actually have butterflies around the garden longer than they survive in the wild by furnishing resources unavailable outside your garden. Volunteer Douglas asters maintain our skippers into October. If this seems unnatural, it is a good deal less so than growing tomatoes in a hothouse.

Obviously, the most useful complement of nectar plants will consist of a mixture of native and exotic flowers. What about the question of native vs. non-native plants in butterfly gardening? With the rise of native plant societies a new appreciation for indigenous flora has come about. There are some native plant purists who eschew the use of any exotics in attracting wildlife. While the native plant movement is enormously important for wildland butterflies, the judicious use of exotics in the garden greatly extends our ability to draw and keep butterflies near the home. Generally, I recommend that the nearer a piece of ground is to a natural state, the greater the emphasis that should be put on native plants. My own land was planted a century ago with such an odd mixture of trees and shrubs from Europe and the American East, since taken over largely by native plants, that the ecology today is a great jumble. I have no compunction about planting a new exotic here today. Likewise, in an urban setting, I would not hesitate to advise the use of established domestics for nectar. Nonetheless, it is good not to lose sight of natives even in the city. If the butterflies are using wildlings in nature, chances are these will work well in the garden setting as well, if you can get them to grow. Always be sure to follow regulations and conservation common sense when obtaining wild plants to take home. Some gardeners I know raid sites about to be developed, saving native trees, shrubs, and herbs from the bulldozer.

What kinds of flowers attract butterflies? Different ones in different areas, of course. In general, bright single flowers with corollas that are not too deep and petals large enough for good perching platforms work out well. Among the universal best are phlox, zinnias, asters, marigolds, sweet rocket, some daisies, hyssop, Sweet William, coneflowers, black-eyed Susan, milkweeds (including butterfly weed), butterfly bush (*Buddleia*), larkspur, lavender, pink stonecrop, dandelions, thistles, mock orange, teasel, honeysuckle, and morning glories. Once again, a little observation of the butterflies themselves in your environs and in your own garden, along with a few seasons of experimentation, will point the way. The butterflies will let you know what they like and dislike. The fact that a flower is showy does not guarantee that it will attract butterflies. Peonies, gladiolas, nearly all roses, and most fancy double blossoms are all useless for the purpose. A homely dandelion is worth any number of expensive roses in the butterfly garden.

Having enticed butterflies into the garden, how can you induce them to stay? Most butterflies that wander enough to have found the garden in the first place will not be inclined to make it home, for they will be wanderers by instinct. However, if the nectar is rewarding enough, they may linger a few days before moving on. And if they should find others of their kind and the proper host plants, they may well leave behind a batch of eggs.

Nectar plants are vital to the butterfly garden. Common high summer visitors to the butterfly bush in Britain include the Comma, Red Admiral, and Peacock (bottom).

One advantage of having a generation that grows up in a garden is that some of the individuals may well remain there. In this way resident populations of butterflies begin to build, along with a rolling turnover of nomads pausing at the oasis, eventually making up together an increasingly rewarding garden fauna. So it behooves the butterfly gardener to furnish preferred larval food plants for likely visitors as well as adult food.

Here, the choices are more limited than for nectar. Field guides, such as my own to North American butterflies, will let you know the names of appropriate host plants in your area. Your task is then to establish them about your place. Obviously, rather than randomly plopping plants here and there, you should try to approximate the habitats in which they might be found outside town. Here is another point where your local survey comes in very handy. If Queen Anne's lace grows in full sun in nearby swamps, don't plant it in a shady, well-drained site. You may wish to work with your soil in order to provide microhabitats for acid-loving, sandy soil plants, for others of limey predilection, and so on. On the whole, both nectar and host plants should receive a good deal of full sun if you expect butterflies to frequent them. In fact, the sun becomes a critical factor in all your butterfly garden planning, so vital is it to the insects. Indeed, many females will choose a sunny sprig on which to oviposit over an adjacent spray in the shade. Native plants are likely to be more useful than exotics as larval hosts, so specific are butterflies in their host plant needs. Nevertheless, Mourning Cloaks and White Admirals will accept weeping willow as readily as a wild species, and Black Swallowtails do at least as well on carrots or parsley as on native umbelliferous plants.

This raises the question of the harm caterpillars might do to other garden plants. Gardeners who are used to fighting caterpillars in their gardens may be appalled at the suggestion that they should invite them into the battleground for lunch. In fact, very few butterfly species cause significant damage to garden plants. Most feed singly or in small groups, as their eggs were laid, and spread out as they grow so as to have plenty to eat. Those that lay their eggs in big clusters, such as checkerspots, include few garden visitors anyway, since they prefer wilder habitats. Exceptions occur among a few of the brush-foots. Mourning Cloaks may feed in rather robust numbers and defoliate individual boughs of willows or elms. If they become a cosmetic problem, it is a simple matter to transplant some of the insects. Cabbage Butterflies clearly wreak havoc with garden crucifers and nasturtiums, but again, the best way to deal with them is to pick off the green larvae by hand. Most butterfly gardeners are quite pleased to share their carrots and dill for the pleasure of the company of Black Swallowtails; they simply plant enough for both.

So basic is the following rule that I will only state it once and briefly: Butterfly gardeners use garden sprays extremely sparingly and with great care, if at all. Yet their gardens survive, unravaged, perhaps because they haven't sprayed all the beneficial predatory and parasitic insects along with the pests. A diverse garden is a healthy one. A heavily sprayed garden is one in which more and more poisons are needed to achieve the same effect, as predators are annihilated and pests gain resistance. It is also a boring garden, repellent to visiting butterflies, lethal to those that linger. In short, you can easily garden for yourself at the same time and place as for butterflies; the conflicts will be few.

Far from being serious plant pests, some butterflies serve as important natural predators on weeds. In its boom immigration years, the Painted Lady helps to defoliate a good deal of pasture thistle. Red Admirals, Milbert's Tortoiseshells, and Satyr Anglewings all feed on stinging nettles as larvae. Nettles are considered weeds by many because of their invasive powers and painful sting. The conscientious butterfly gardener will actually permit and encourage small stands of these "noxious" plants for the colorful butterflies they support. Planted carefully so that they are hidden behind a curtain of phlox or trimmed to look like another bed of flowers, they probably won't get you into trouble with the neighbors or the weed inspector. Winston Churchill commanded his gardeners to let nettles prosper in the great gardens at Chartwell in order to encourage the nettle-feeding butterflies. Many British gardeners know that a nettle bed spared in spring means butterflies on the Buddleia in high summer. The stakes are even higher there, because in addition to the pretty Small Tortoiseshell and the Red Admiral, the British are blessed with the gorgeous Peacock Butterfly—another nettle-eater. More and more they are beginning to tolerate a bit of nettle at the bottom of the garden,

Black Swallowtail caterpillar on carrot leaf. Many butterfly gardeners simply plant a little extra of favorite host plants, so as to have enough for the butterflies and themselves.

especially since the publicity generated by the recent, very success-ful Butterfly Year.

For the next stage of sophistication, try to anticipate some of the other needs of the butterflies you hope to host. For example, most butterflies like to bask; indeed they need to when it grows suddenly chilly. Can you provide a sunny bank, with stones, bare earth, frondy vegetation, and other sunbathing blankets for butter-flies? How about a patch of sand kept damp? If a pet uses it for the predictable purposes, all the better. For butterflies that over-winter as adults, you might wish to try placing hibernation cells about. Try coffee cans half full of leaves and bark, empty bird-houses, or one of the commercial versions (see Appendix)—any-thing that mimics a hollow tree with an inviting orifice and insula-tion. To have a tortoiseshell emerge from a shelter you had thoughtfully provided, then to nectar on your early coltsfoot on the first warm day of March, finally to mate and oviposit on your fresh green nettle leaves, would be a coup and a joy. Be sure to leave some dead, dried plant stalks and twigs around for cater-pillars to climb and pupate upon. Wooden eaves and fences

Natural predation helps to keep larvae down to modest numbers in the butterfly garden: a warbler prepares to return to its nest with a billfull of inchworms.

work better for this purpose than steel and aluminum. Last summer a friend and I were inspecting a Weidemeyer's Admiral larva on her willow for several days running. When it turned up missing, I swung around to the wooden fence and pointed to where I would have pupated if I had been that humpbacked caterpillar. Just there, to my surprise and great pleasure, hung the fresh chrysalis. A mulched part of the garden will serve for ground pupaters, while others will spin up among the last leaves on their host plants.

It would almost seem as though the butterfly gardener were trying to improve upon nature. The hobby can indeed become an intensive form of site management. Professor Herb Kulman, at the University of Minnesota, has developed the theory in detail and dubbed it "butterfly production management" (BPM). The idea is to maximize the diversity and abundance of butterflies at a given site, for whatever reason. Where BPM is applied thoughtfully, a site will respond by yielding more than nature's share. At the Drum Manor Butterfly Garden in Northern Ireland, for example, Henry Heal practiced BPM in an old, walled Irish garden under Forestry Commission ownership. With its suntrap qualities and judicious planting, Drum Manor provides visitors with many more butterflies to see than they would in the nearby countryside, from early spring into late fall. Butterfly management has also been employed at Oxen Pond Botanic Garden in St. John's, Newfoundland. Naturalist Bernard Jackson has selected plants in such a way as to offer visitors a representative array of local butterflies. One specialty of Oxen Pond, the Short-tailed Black Swallowtail, is a Maritime region endemic. The Newfoundland fisherfolk unwittingly created rich butterfly habitats in their colorful cottage gardens. These have passed largely from the scene, but Jackson tries to perpetuate the ambience at the Botanic Garden.

Drum Manor and Oxen Pond share a common objective in that they aspire to host the greatest diversity and abundance of native butterflies possible under the prevailing conditions, through selective management. Yet in both cases the butterflies are wild, free to come and go, so these gardens are not butterfly zoos. Butterfly zoos (or more often insect zoos) do exist, where the subjects are actually held in captivity for the visitor to see, enjoy, and study. Major insect zoos may be seen in San Francisco, Cincinnati, Washington, D.C., and Portland, Oregon. In Portland, Washington Park Zoo officials have found their insect zoo to be one of the most popular exhibits. Tokyo maintains one of the most ambitious insectariums at its Tama Zoo. It has five objectives: to reproduce and display each species' habitat, to illustrate its life history in progress, to show the range of insects' physical traits, to exhibit adult insects year long by artificially manipulating their environments, and to breed endangered species for liberation in the wild.

The London Butterfly House at Sion Park pioneered the tropical conservatory devoted to living butterflies. Such "butterfly houses" now occur throughout Britain and in several other countries. (See Appendix III for U.S. addresses.)

So it is that butterfly gardening actually works with nature, not to improve it (impossible conceit!) but to complement it as the best horticulture has always done. In the case of those Maritime fishing villages, the cottage gardens became a resource worth conserving in their own right. Some naturalists feel that gardening of any kind is a side issue, a distraction from the real task of preserving natural habitats. Of course, no garden could ever substitute for the original one. But since most of us dwell in places already made unnatural through our own agency, mightn't we as well take pains to have as many butterflies around as we can? Surely, seen this way, butterfly gardening is an entirely benign and even beneficial activity.

To what degree gardening actually serves to conserve butterflies is open to some debate. Some say very little, because the butterflies involved are simply vagrants. Yet their movements—and survivorship—are no doubt enhanced by the rich nectar sources they encounter as they pass through gardens. And to the degree that butterflies may be influenced to remain and breed, new habitat has been created in place of some that was altered elsewhere. Admittedly, we are speaking primarily of common species, but the day that those animals become rare is a day we should all rue, and butterfly gardening can help in its modest way to forestall it. Indeed, British biologist Professor Dennis Owen regards British gardens as perhaps the nation's "most important nature reserve," so diverse are they with respect to a mosaic of plants and the insects they support. While that may be overstating the case a bit, there is no doubt in my mind that gardens amount to quite a lot in conservation terms—and the more they are consciously managed on behalf of butterflies and other wildlife, the better.

Conservation of butterflies is the subject of Chapter 15. But before leaving it for now, there is one other point relevant to gardening. In our enthusiasm for pro-butterfly management activity, we must not be misguided into making inappropriate introductions of species. Untold harm has befallen natural systems and economies by the purposeful or inadvertent introduction of exotic species: witness our own European Cabbage Butterfly. Just as the Starling had its proponents who formed a society on behalf of its introduction into the United States (they tried a dozen times before they were successful), there are those who would endow butterfly faunas with species unnatural to their number. Conservation philosophy is firm on this point: Don't do it. You never can tell in advance what harm will be done, whether to native plants, crops, or other insects through competition, disease, or parasites. Just visit Hawaii if you have any doubts about the unwisdom of introductions. Even regionally, it can be damaging to introduce creatures from outside the home gene pool. They may bring traits ill-adapted to local conditions. Furthermore, biogeographers do not appreciate people who introduce species outside their known ranges, thereby disrupting the patterns they work so hard to assay.

In butterfly gardening, bring butterflies in by all means, but from no farther away than they might be expected to fly in their own lifetime. And never introduce a species to an area outside its historically known range of occurrence. Finally, it is irresponsible to set butterflies out unless the receiving habitat is in proper condition for them, for they will merely fly away or die. So as much as I would, in the abstract, like to have Peacock butterflies in the nettle patches of the Pacific Northwest, I shall refrain from placing them there and encourage others to do the same.

My butterfly garden, on an old homestead known as Swede Park, came ready-made with Western Tiger Swallowtails breeding on the willows and nectaring on the old rhododendrons; Pale Tigers on the alders and sweet Williams; and Clodius Parnassians ovipositing on native bleeding heart in my woods and coming out to nectar on the wild dandelions I encourage in my lawn. (The day I wrote this, I watched a parnassian female, so heavy with eggs she could hardly fly, clamber onto a bank of brambles. I could see the outline of the blackberry leaves through her clear, waxy wings; the crimson spots of her hindwings glowed against the pink bramble blossoms. For several minutes she nectared; then, replenished, she sailed off in search of bleeding heart foliage on which to lighten her load.)

The yard has a sunny south slope, as sunny as it can be in the Washington rainforest belt. It is not bad material for a butterfly garden, and we have worked with it. My first butterfly bush did badly in poor soil. The next I nourished with regular daily applications of ready nitrogen. It flourished, and high summer found its tall stalks bowed under blossom as well as skippers, ladies, admirals, and whites. Spring Azures appear in February or March, coppers and crescents patrol the summer paths, and Red Admirals tipple at fallen apples in the autumn. Anglewings appear from the woodpile on warmer winter days. Now, I cannot imagine life without a butterfly garden.

13

Rearing Butterflies

At an early age I noticed brown-spotted butterflies hanging about a tree in my suburban Denver backyard. Catching one, I found in a field guide that it was called a Hackberry Butterfly, after its larval host plant. This puzzled me, for the tree I caught it on was a Chinese elm. Each summer, it turned out, male Hackberry Butterflies perched on and flew about that elm, but I never saw any females near it. I remained confused until one day, venturing a little farther afield in the neighborhood, I spotted more of the butterflies gliding about another ornamental tree. It had similar but larger leaves, a distinctive smell, and clusters of dark, round berries: it was a hackberry tree. Here were females, too (larger and paler than the narrow-winged, caramel males), and as I watched them, they were courted by the males.

Inspecting the leaves, I found jade-green, fancy-helmeted caterpillars with twin "tails." These I took home and fed on fresh hackberry leaves. It was not long before I had all sizes of the tapered larvae, as well as pupae formed by the most advanced caterpillars. These I learned to find on the tree as well—turning over leaves to pick out the delicate green, white-lined chrysalids, plump and thorny, elegantly camouflaged against the rough and serrated foliage.

The great thrill came one day when I awoke to find adult Hackberry Butterflies fluttering within their bedroom rearing chambers.

I had missed the first hatching, but by remaining alert and rising earlier than usual after that, I was able to witness the entire process of eclosure. The essential miracle of the "birth" of a butterfly unfolded before my eyes. The green case darkened (first I thought it was dead, like some I had let get damp and hot), then got shiny, and I could begin to discern the features of the butterfly through the pupal shell: black-and-white eyespots on rich brown wings, antennae, great round eyes. At last the mummy case burst open and the long-folded legs, antennae, and proboscis sprang forth like watchsprings unloosed. I was alarmed at the sight of the wings— all wet and crumpled and tiny. But as the insect clung to the now-paled and empty case on its withered leaf, it began to wave the wings gently and pump the fluid from its swollen abdomen into their veins. The wings expanded, and in an hour or so they had assumed their true shape and the crisp condition necessary for flight. The butterfly stretched its tongue, linked the two halves together, and coiled it safely between its furry palpi. A drop of reddish fluid came out of the tip of the abdomen. It was ready to go.

This newly formed butterfly now resembled the Hackberries in my specimen box, except it bore the vibrancy of life that they had lost. Indeed I had read that one of the chief reasons for rearing butterflies was to obtain perfect cabinet specimens. This certainly works. But after watching my first home-reared Hackberry undergo all its precarious changes from minute egg to magnificent butterfly, I hadn't the heart to make it a specimen. It was a male, so I released it beside the Chinese elm, where it took up the post perhaps vacated through the agency of a hungry bird. I never did fully understand why that elm, a full block from the nearest hackberry tree, should have become regular male territory for *Asterocampa celtis*. But I was always thankful for its having led me into the wondrous arena of rearing butterflies. I was to rear many broods of Hackberries. And while searching for the early stages, I also spotted Mourning Cloak larvae on the *Celtis* trees and great dragon-eyed caterpillars of Two-tailed Tiger Swallowtails on nearby ash foliage. Just like the freshly hatched butterfly, I was ready to go.

Anyone's life can be similarly enriched by rearing butterflies. Throughout this book I have extolled the glories of butterfly

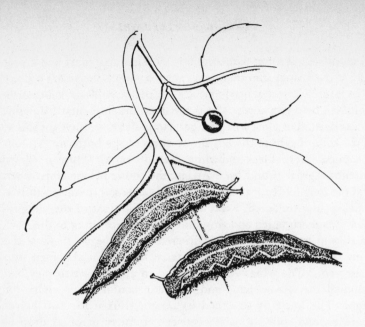

Hackberry Butterfly larvae, equipped with "horns" fore and aft, pass one another as they cross a hackberry leaf. Celtis *trees are their sole acceptable host plants.*

watching and the pleasure it brings, so that further superlatives may seem unnecessary. But the process of insect metamorphosis is truly special, and to be able to watch it in its most dramatic form—butterflies transforming—is a gift from nature not to be turned down or forgotten. That profound and radical change we call complete metamorphosis, whereby an egg, then a minute, wormlike caterpillar, finally a quiescent pupa eventually become a soaring butterfly, has few parallels in art or nature for sheer wonderment. Speaking as one who has seen two total eclipses, comets, volcanic eruptions, and birds of paradise, I feel that one can be witness to few greater things than the making of a butterfly.

Aesthetics aside, larval behavior can be interesting in its own right; certainly, watching the female seeking and using the proper egg-laying substrate makes compelling entertainment. These animals, once they leave the egg, are not just tubes of tissue eating and waiting for their big moment. The old joke has it that two caterpillars are watching a butterfly overhead and one says to the other, "You'll never get me up in one of those things." But they do get there—at least some small percentage of survivors do—and the path to becoming airborne is fascinating to watch (if dangerous to live). The rearing process is bound to teach much of plants and patience. Above all, there is enormous satisfaction to be had from following a creature all the way through its life history. Much remains to be learned about our butterflies' life histories, and the job requires little but patience and the power of keen observation. You can make the activity as simple or as painstaking as you wish. In this chapter I will describe the basics, beyond which you will no doubt elaborate as inclination or invention dictate.

First of all you need to obtain the rearing material. Since the life cycle is just that, you can come in at any point: egg, larva, pupa, or adult. There are three ways to get eggs: by hand-pairing adults, from an already mated female, or by finding them in the wild. I will discuss the first later. The second is the surest and easiest way. Most females encountered in the field have already been mated, since males hatch first and are ready to court as soon as the females emerge. In the act of copulation the male inserts a spermatophore; each egg becomes fertile as it passes by the spermatophore on its way to being laid. It is therefore a simple matter to collect a female with a net, keep her quiet and cool in an envelope, take her home, then confine her in a cage with fresh food plant. If, that is, you know what the food plant is. There is little point otherwise, unless you have a good guess, because most butterflies are quite specific in their plant requirements and the hatchlings will die without the proper food. In the absence of the right plant the female may not lay at all. But if you can cage her over the proper greens, you should soon have a batch of eggs with which to launch your rearing program.

Seeking eggs in the wild involves two techniques. The first requires you to follow females closely to see where they oviposit, then to simply recover the eggs and make off with them. Egg-laying behavior differs greatly from species to species. Recently I observed two species of elfins at a seaside locality. The female Brown Elfin flew relatively slowly, perched at length on a kinnikinnick flower, tapped around with her antennae for a few minutes, then curled her abdomen down and deposited one bluish-green, bagel-shaped egg deep in the bracts of a pink flowerbud. The entire act was very deliberate. The female Pine Elfin, in contrast, hastened about her business impatiently. She flitted rapidly, alighting in quick succession on one or another bough in a ring of small pines. I found it difficult to keep her in sight, let alone approach her closely for long, and never determined for sure whether her brief stops left eggs behind or not. If so they were wonderfully concealed in the complicated pine florets. At this writing the Brown Elfin's young has attained the prepupal stage, two months after the egg was laid. I have yet to find a Pine Elfin egg.

Some butterflies—whites, for example—are known to scratch the plants with their hind feet, tasting them for recognition. Dr. Frances Chew, a Tufts University biologist, has shown that this enables them to reject plants similar to their hosts but which would prove lethal if consumed. Others, including some skippers and satyrs, merely drop their eggs into the midst of the vegetation, leaving the baby larvae to find their own food. Since these butterflies are grass-feeders, the caterpillars' chances are good and the casting-of-the-die method of egg-laying probably saves energy for the female. Since strategies differ so, you will need to be watchful to spot the product. But if it isn't as easy as gathering eggs from a henhouse, collecting butterfly ova after they have been laid obviously may have greater rewards.

Dr. David McCorkle, an Oregon teacher and lepidopterist, is one of the rare breed of people who seem to be able to spot butterfly eggs, larvae, and pupae wherever they go. Few are the field trips with Dave when he fails to find some immature stages. Most of us are less observant. But with practice and patience, it is possible for most people to find butterfly eggs—even without resorting to Dave McCorkle's frequent practice of scaling tall Douglas firs in search of hairstreak ova on clumps of mistletoe. Of course, batch-layers like checkerspots make it easier than those whose eggs are deposited singly. A big yellow swallowtail globe on a carrot leaf will be more readily spotted than a green sulphur spindle on a leaflet of pea. Knowing the host, watching the females, and looking sharply at many, many leaves are the keys. Investigate both surfaces—some species routinely lay on top, others on the bottom. With care and experience, few kinds of eggs will continue to resist detection altogether. Japan boasts a rich fauna of beautiful hairstreaks that overwinter as eggs secreted in bark cracks and bud

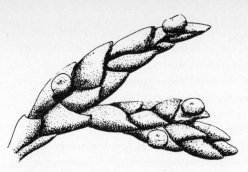

Hunting butterfly eggs in order to rear them out requires special watchfulness. These hairstreak eggs are well concealed among the scales of cedar twigs.

scars of oaks and other hosts. A special kind of lepidopterological sport has arisen there in which collectors hunt the tiny white tablets in the depth of winter. The pursuit of these delicate packets of life need not be quite so rigorous. Languorously trail a female butterfly around a summer meadow and discover what a gentle pastime it can be.

In general, the same principles apply for seeking caterpillars in the wild. Being bigger, and progressively so, they are more conspicuous than eggs. We all come across caterpillars in summertime, usually the furry, obvious sorts that are mostly moths. The visibility of larvae depends upon their strategies for defense. Monarch caterpillars taste bad and advertise the fact to birds. Bright stripes make them easy to spot on milkweed leaves. For the first few instars (stages between molts), checkerspot larvae cluster in spiny groups on sticky webs, like tent caterpillars. Such a nest is quite conspicuous on the host plantain, penstemon, or paintbrush. Tiger Swallowtail larvae match the green of the leaves they eat but show fearsome false eyes; at rest, they curl leaves into tube-tents. Unrolling such shelters as often as not reveals a brooding spider, but sometimes a *Papilio* larva stares back at you.

Certain species such as the Hackberry Butterflies I wrote of earlier possess elegant background camouflage. As you develop a search image for them their crypsis will cease to fool you. The caterpillar of a Viceroy may look like a bird dropping to a bird, but the disguise ought not to get past the dedicated caterpillar spotter for long. Be sure to note just what plants you find your larvae on; that becomes vital later. The same, of course, goes for eggs. In searching for larvae, it helps to know the host in advance for species you are likely to encounter. Failing this, keep your eyes open as you move through the vegetation; become a leaf-turner by nature, and watch for damage to leaves and petals—the agent may be lurking nearby. In such a way one finds many caterpillars and fresh food plant records as well.

When larvae have had their fill, reach their full growth, and get ready to "spin up" (a term more appropriate to cocoon-making moths), instinct tells them to wander in search of the perfect pupation site. The extent of the walkabout varies according to species and location. For this reason, you may not find the pupae directly on or near the host plant. Conversely, one encounters caterpillars on walkabout far from their source of sustenance. The Hackberry Butterfly larvae all seemed to pupate on the underside of hackberry leaves, virtually where they had fed. But I learned to seek Mourning Cloak and Cabbage White chrysalids under the eaves of my house, some distance from the willows and crucifers on which they had dined. Swallowtails like branches, tree trunks, poles, posts, fences, dried plant stalks, and stones. Checkers and crescents in my experience prefer to hang from rock edges and ledges. I recall coming across a fresh chrysalis of a small fritillary suspended from the overhang of a mountain boulder, hard beside a brilliant patch of Parry primrose—and a Field Crescent chrysalis on a stone in the middle of a hot gravel road, where it surely would have been crushed or cooked.

The search for chrysalids and cocoons becomes one of the most exciting parts of the rearing hobby, because it is a real treasure hunt with living jewels as the reward. Nor is it a pleasure reserved for winter. We associate cocoons and chrysalids with the harsh winter months, think of them as sarcophagi for the dead season. But many butterflies overwinter in another stage and pupate in spring or summer. The winter waiters may be easier to find due to the absence of foliage, especially the big cocoons of some moths (see Chapter 17). Whatever the season, be on the lookout for any object that seems in disconformity with its background. Our three-dimensional color vision gives us a great advantage in spotting such incongruities. Birds share this advantage and put it to use as important predators of developing Lepidoptera: intelligent jays

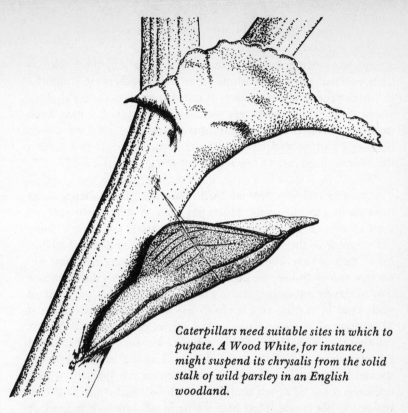

Caterpillars need suitable sites in which to pupate. A Wood White, for instance, might suspend its chrysalis from the solid stalk of wild parsley in an English woodland.

are not always fooled by the ploy of looking like a sliver of bark when you are really a plump and tasty pupa.

While poking about willows in search of swallowtail chrysalids after the leaves fall, be watchful for another kind of hidden hibernator. This is the caterpillar of the Viceroy and other admirals of the genus *Limenitis*. While still small, they consume most of a willow leaf, then roll the tip into a snug sleeping bag. These they knit to the twig in advance with a silken thread so as not to fall into the oblivion of the leaf litter. You can clip off these hibernaculi, as they are called, take them home, and watch the young larvae crawl out in spring when the willow buds burst. Be sure to give them plenty of fresh, tender leaves, and you will have adult admirals by June or July.

Anyone harboring ambitions to find and rear immatures should be prepared to transport them whenever they may be encountered. Film canisters, small vials, and baby food jars make handy receptacles for eggs, caterpillars, and pupae. Protect the latter with a bit of cotton or dry grass. To take home a supply of host plant as well, you will need a vasculum—a moisture-conserving container in which vegetative materials will not wilt at once. Or try zip-lock plastic bags, which work very well. More than once I have been unable to safely transport a found treasure, or else I have lost it, because I had no adequate container at the time. It just takes a little foresight to carry a few whenever you go into the field.

Once you arrive at the "lab" with livestock, the challenge shifts from finding to nurturing. Much has been written on the subject, with reports of the results of numberless trials and errors. Some titles appear in the Appendix to lead you to more detailed advice. Many factors bear upon successful rearing. Among the most important things to keep in mind are fresh food, fresh air, adequate but moderate moisture, and suitable surfaces. The question of what kind of rearing receptacle to use is an important one, as it bears upon all these conditions. Any sort of container will do that confines the animals, permits free flow of air, furnishes shade, and accommodates the plant material as well as the insects. The old standard, a large jar with holes punched in the lid, still works; but keep it out of direct sunlight, which will make any glass container too hot inside. Host plants wilt rapidly in such holders. A better choice is one that permits air to flow freely, such as a screen cylinder with netting over the top. It is essential, of course, that the holes in the screen be too small for young larvae to escape through or predators to enter by. I want to point out that the oxygen flow is not for the benefit of the larvae's respiration, but to prevent the growth of mold and bacteria that may kill them under stagnant conditions. Caterpillars require very little air for breathing.

The ideal rearing cage allows the roots or stems of the fresh host plant to rest in water. Caterpillars easily drown, so there should be a sleeve to let the stems out but keep the beasts in. A friend of mine, an accomplished Seattle butterfly breeder named Jonathan Pelham, uses free ice-cream cylinders from a chain shop, with netting over the top. These roomy tubs sit on bowls of water into which the plant stems protrude through small holes in the bottom cardboard lid. He has found this cheap and easy setup to be very satisfactory, and it keeps the host plant fresh for days.

This is an important point, especially if the nearest stand of it grows some distance from home.

Fresh food is absolutely essential. Wilted leaves promote mold and may become unpalatable. Caterpillars obtain most of their water from leaves they consume, so dried-out foliage means dessication or simply starvation. If your system does not keep the food plant fresh and full of turgor, make sure you change the leaves or flowers often—probably daily. Keep the containers in a fairly cool location that receives sunlight but not direct, sustained beams— fresh air but not a cold draft. If you follow these simple pointers your livestock should thrive.

Some breeders, especially those who rear in volume—such as butterfly farmers—sleeve larvae in bags of netting tied so as to enclose growing sprays of the hostplant out-of-doors. Still another method involves placing potted plants within the rearing chamber and watering them normally. This may be ideal if the amount of foliage produced is sufficient for the number and appetite of larvae and to keep the plant healthy as well. No matter how you contain caterpillars, be sure to clean out their pellet-like droppings (known as frass) at least daily. They can encourage mold and disease. Some rearers go so far as to boil all containers prior to placing larvae in them in order to minimize viral and bacterial attacks; others simply wash them out with soap and water, then dry them.

How about handling larvae? Big, robust caterpillars may be handled with care and suffer no ill effects (although *you* may, if you pick up some of the moth larvae bearing urticating hairs); but you should not squeeze, for caterpillars are all soft parts inside with little outer protection. Tiny larvae are more difficult to handle without harming them. A fine camel's-hair brush barely moistened usually works very well for transferring little ones to fresh food. If you haven't one, or simply cannot see the tyke, you can just put new food in and take the old out after a reasonable interval, when feeding damage should be visible on the fresh supply. Always check old host carefully for hiders before discarding it. And never let it accumulate.

I prefer keeping younger larvae, say, the first three instars, in separate vials or boxes with bits of fresh food proffered daily. When they grow larger I let them mingle over potted or drinking plants. This does not apply to colonial species, of course, which normally stay together when very small. One reason for separating small solitary larvae, aside from the possibility for closer care, is the relatively high incidence of sibling cannibalism among them.

If you have found a caterpillar on its host, or recognize the species and know its recorded hosts, you will have no problems at mealtime. With larvae of unknown provenance or preference, the best you can do is to treat them as you might a hungry but mute niece or nephew left in your care: that is, offer them a selection of available foods from the "pantry" (the surrounding habitat) and hope that one or more will be accepted. The only way to know if they've been eating is to watch for telltale nibbles or frass. Once they get down to it they consume plant tissue prodigiously, and feeding evidence is very apparent. Never assume that the oviposition substrate is necessarily the correct host. Were that the case, Sierra Skippers would eat lichened fenceposts, which is where Dr. Don MacNeill discovered their eggs are laid. They do not. They crawl down after hatching and feed on grasses. Female butterflies also make mistakes, or approximations.

Do not hesitate to experiment with foods. Suppose you know that your insect prefers penstemon, but you have exhausted your supply. Try snapdragon, or any other plant in the penstemon family, Scrophulariaceae. As I have said before, the butterfly lover cannot resist becoming something of a botanist. Common sense takes over in emergencies. Not long ago I obtained the egg of a white laid on a weedy crucifer by my mailbox and that of the Brown Elfin mentioned above on kinnikinnick. The crucifers were bulldozed and the kinnikinnick was miles away. The white's caterpillar did well on bits of cabbage and broccoli that stay succulent for ages, while the elfin munched its way through several flowerbuds from a garden rhododendron, another heath. Fritillaries generally accept pansies, which are just cultivated violets anyway, and most grass-feeding skippers and satyrs will graze contentedly on Kentucky bluegrass or other lawn grasses. Host plant specificity extends to the family and often the genus level, and sometimes only a particular species of plant will do. So try your luck, without sacrificing larvae to wild whims. I always feel that the butterfly breeder has a responsibility to try to get as many larvae through as possible and to provide conscientious care for the creatures he or she has removed from nature.

Most butterflies have specific host plant needs in wood or garden.
Here a Baltimore Checkerspot oviposits on turtlehead.

No matter how excellent the care, however, there will always be
heartbreaking failures. On my first visit to the Pacific Northwest,
my mother took me by rail through the Columbia Gorge. I desper-
ately wanted to find an Oregon Swallowtail, described in that same
old *National Geographic* article referred to in the previous chapter.
During a side trip I recovered one plump and healthy caterpillar
of the coveted insect. The porter on our train smuggled me parsley
from the dining car with which to feed it (a tarragon feeder in
nature, it will accept umbels—the food of its near relatives—in
captivity). In due course the treasured animal pupated, and I kept
it safe all through the winter. One spring day the resplendent
Papilio oregonius emerged while I was off in the field. Upon returning, all I found were bits of freshly spread wings: my cat had
eaten the Oregon Swallowtail.

Then there were the Valerata Arctic larvae I took back to Yale
following a summer's research in the Olympic Mountains, the sole
home of this butterfly, which had never before been reared. I fed
each test-tube larva bits of fresh grass in fast-food joints all across
the country; took them through one winter's diapause in a refrigerator (they probably pass two in nature before becoming adults);
then got them into Yale's specially equipped controlled climate

chambers. Another winter passed, this the real one, and most of the larvae came through. Then, as they resumed feeding, the third and fourth instar larvae began to die of a mold. All the care I could take, all the sophisticated equipment at my disposal, could not save the last caterpillar: it died just prior to what would have been pupation. I might have done better with jam jars.

Keeping larvae through the winter is always rather tricky. Eggs and pupae are simpler: keep them out-of-doors under normal temperatures, spray with a fine water mist occasionally, keep mice and spiders away, and most will probably come through all right. Larvae are another matter. Even with all their antifreeze and other winterizing adaptations, they are more vulnerable. Cold exposure seems to be necessary for many species. Fooling the larvae with a refrigerator winter of eight weeks or so, then resuming feeding if you can get the plants, is often more successful than placing the larvae out for the whole of natural winter.

Perhaps the greatest source of losses to butterfly breeders (and frustration) is insect parasitism. Insect parasites (properly called parasitoids because they kill, rather than accommodate their hosts) account for much of the mortality among early stages in nature and in captivity. Wasps and flies, from minute to fairly bulky, insert their eggs into the eggs or larvae of Lepidoptera. These then hatch and consume the caterpillars from within. It is dispiriting to have a fine larva wilt and die, then to see a big tachinid fly emerge from its discolored skin. An even ruder surprise lies waiting when the doomed caterpillar manages to pupate, then instead of a butterfly emerging, scores of tiny ichneumonid wasps pop out instead. Not uncommonly, entire broods may be lost in this way. Such events, however, are natural. They should be regarded philosophically, and with scientific interest. Parasitoids are no more evil for their habits than is the caterpillar for devouring the plant. Watch the interaction and appreciate it in its own right, if you can. Samples of parasitoids should be collected and preserved for eventual identification by specialists, since many are unknown.

In fact, all aspects of your rearing should be recorded, for your own greater pleasure and for the facts you may disclose. It is surprising how many of our North America butterflies have not adequately been described throughout their early stages. Take notes, make drawings and measurements, shoot photographs. Try to make color descriptions precise. Record periods of instars, and save shed skins and head capsules glued to a bit of card with data copied onto it. If you have a lot of larvae you may wish to preserve examples of each instar for study. (This entails boiling for three minutes, then immersing in a solution of water and alcohol in equal parts.) Get as much information from the process as you can—if you are so inclined. But never let the recording of facts get in the way of the sheer wonderment and pleasure that rearing can bring. Any joy that becomes tedious soon ceases to be a joy.

At last, if all goes well, the new butterfly emerges. This is the magic moment: eclosure, rebirth, the genesis of beauty and vibrancy, a creature about to take wing, a promise fulfilled. And what to do with it? How to make it last? There are various answers. Many collectors rear butterflies in order to obtain perfect series of specimens for their trays. This certainly is the best way to get unblemished butterflies for pinning, and it reduces pressure a little bit on wild populations. So collectors kill the butterflies as close to the moment of hatching as the wings are fully spread, so as not to lose a scale. The British are keen on releasing more individuals than they keep, to ensure a positive ratio of survivorship. Indeed many more larvae survive to adulthood under the protective custody of the breeder than in the wild. But it is also true that as many animals survive in the wild as the environment can comfortably support, so mass releasing may have little real impact on the population at large. The effect may be more in the mind of the releaser; more a matter of conscience than conservation.

Other butterfly raisers just like to have the living creatures around them. They will keep the adults as long as they live, feeding them on a dilute solution of sugar- or honey-water soaked into paper toweling. (Incidentally, feeding captive females in this manner helps to ensure that they will lay eggs for you. If a butterfly seems reticent to feed, *gently* uncurl its proboscis and place it on the damp paper, or place its tasting hind tarsi on the sweet spot. It should begin to sip avidly, if it's hungry.) Keeping butterflies as pets or research subjects can be done quite readily for days, weeks, in some cases months. A brood of Carolina Satyrs sent by University of Florida zoologist Dr. Tom Emmel enlivened my

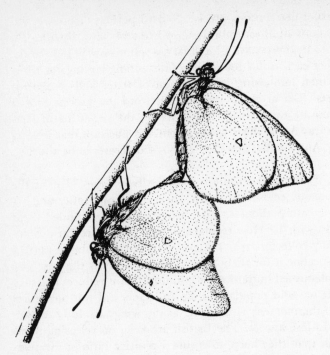

A pair of sulphurs in copulo. *Having reared butterflies all the way through from the egg, you may be able to induce them to mate—and begin all over again.*

New Haven lab all through one dark winter. Dr. Larry Gilbert maintains an impressive colony of tropical longwing butterflies in his labs and greenhouses at the University of Texas. These butterflies' ability to live for a long time in captivity has made them popular in living butterfly exhibits at various zoos and conservatories.

Butterflies kept alive in the classroom make for a wonderful ongoing biology lesson. Millions of American students have had the opportunity to watch Monarchs emerging on the classroom windowsill, but I wonder how many teachers take the lesson one step further—that is, to begin a new generation.

Many breeders consider the ultimate rearing experience to be starting over from the same stock they have brought all the way through. This may not be as easy as breeding house pets. We have seen how complicated the courtship of butterflies can be. Left together in a cage, fresh males and females of the same species *may* mate—or they may not, lacking proper environmental stimuli. In this case you can attempt to hand-pair them. Holding each partner in one hand with tweezers, place their abdomens gently together and stroke them back and forth softly. As the male's claspers spread apart, insert the female's rear with very little pressure. Swallowtails and some other butterflies couple quite readily given such an introduction. Once the female has been inseminated, you are ready to start from square one.

Butterflies I have reared have endured all these indignities and others. More and more my current attitude comes to resemble what it was when my first Hackberry Butterfly came out. There is simply nothing else like releasing a butterfly you have reared yourself, watching it fly off to whatever awaits it. In a way one is paying it back for the pleasure it gave under confinement. Such a notion clearly is sentimental and anthropomorphic, and the pleasure one feels in releasing a reared insect probably has no counterpart in the creature itself. Nonetheless, it feels good. "Butterflies are free to fly," wrote Elton John, and I for one have growing difficulty in countermanding that for those I rear. You can decide for yourself. But remember not to release butterflies outside their native areas. If you rear exotics, their best fate is to become pampered pets or marvelous photographic subjects. Photography, the subject of the next chapter, enhances both the pleasure and the learning to be had from rearing butterflies. You can even have it both ways: "Collect" your brand-new butterfly with your camera, then watch it fly away free.

14

Butterfly Photography

When in 1974 my *Watching Washington Butterflies* (Seattle Audubon Society) came out, it was the first American butterfly book to be illustrated entirely with color photographs of live butterflies in the field. Many of the species had probably not been photographed before. Indeed I knew few other people pursuing butterfly photography in more than a casual way at the time. All that changed in just a few years. When the photo call went out for my *Audubon Society Field Guide to North American Butterflies* in 1980, scores of photographers responded with slides. The editors were able to round up pictures of the majority of species taken under natural conditions. Today I have no idea how many people are taking pictures of butterflies in a serious manner, but I suspect they number in the hundreds in North America. Still, as is the case with watchers, it must be just a fraction of the number of bird photographers. The field is still relatively open, although the quality of photographs being taken has gone up dramatically in recent years. Still, there are species that have never been photographed well and naturally.

At first thought, the supposed expense and technicalities might put many people off this activity before they begin. I feel it is best to identify its virtues and values first, then look at the potential problems. Initially, there is the obvious pleasure to be found in making a portrait of a beautiful object. Few subjects satisfy more when they come out on film. Then there is the capacity for reconciling what is for many butterfly enthusiasts a painful enigma: how to collect these bright insects without killing them. For persons with this problem, photography affords the perfect answer. They can take home their "trophy" or specimen, yet leave the butterfly to fly free. Too, there is sport to be had here—good sport. Butterfly photography gets you out and about as much as any kind of hunting I know, in much more varied terrain than golf, and affords excitement on a par with the best angling. Picture-taking furthermore gives a focus for observation, makes us concentrate more carefully on our subject. Looking through a 35mm frame is certainly not the only way to see what happens in nature, but it is a way that focuses the attention. Of course there is great satisfaction to be had in sharing good shots with others who appreciate a photograph well taken. These and other rewards give plenty of cause for taking up butterfly photography.

When it comes down to it, the butterflies themselves furnish the best argument. Most people involved in this hobby never logically decide to do it; they become seduced by the possibilities. John and Norma Riggenbach, accomplished Florida butterfly portraitists, were on the lookout for new finds one day when they happened upon a great lantana patch. ". . . such lantana as we had never seen before," they wrote in the *Miami Herald's Florida Magazine* (January 16, 1983). "Brilliant scarlet and gold blossoms, shimmering with the wings of feasting swallowtails—more than an acre of them!" They saw eight species of swallowtails in all, and photographed a new one for them, the Gold Rim—number forty-six on their photographic checklist of about ninety Florida butterflies. "This little untended garden was so rich in different butterflies," they went on, "black ones, white ones, huge swallowtails, tiny blues—that anyone who spent a few minutes simply looking might well have gotten the 'bug.'" The Riggenbachs have certainly caught that bug, resulting in a series of very beautiful pictures indeed.

So much for the argument in favor. How about the expense and technical difficulty? Certainly one can spend a great deal of money and get highly technical pursuing complex and sophisticated methods of snapping butterflies. Stephen Dalton achieved his goal of getting perfect, stop-action photographs of insects in flight only after creating whole new photographic systems. The results—magnificent and amazing freeze-motion portraits—appear in the (1975) book *Borne on the Wind*. Considerable expense and enormous technical mastery were involved, but few among us will seek such heights. In fact, gratifying results and perfectly satisfactory photographs may be achieved with moderate expenditure and a beginning photographic aptitude near zero. I proved that to my own satisfaction, starting from scratch with little knowledge and cheap optics. In this chapter I will assume the aspiring butterfly photographer to be both uninformed and impecunious. As expertise grows and fortunes permit, there are few limits to what can be achieved with the current state of photographic technology and art.

Both the costs and complexities of photography arise from the equipment and film necessary to achieve the desired outcome. The subject matter is a simpler concern of taste and experience. All three depend entirely on reflected light, the raw material of pictures. How one deals with light and the images it carries will determine the success of the enterprise. Much of the challenge comes in understanding how light behaves and how the equipment, film, and subject all respond to it. So let us look first, in an introductory way, at cameras, lenses, film, and other light-catching equipment. I will only skim the basics of this broad and evolving field as they apply to butterfly photography in particular.

The choice of camera is the starting point. For nearly all insect photography in the field a 35mm SLR (single-lens reflex) camera is essential. Such a camera focuses closely directly through the lens, which is interchangeable. Attempts with other cameras, such as box, instant, and view-finder, will prove frustrating for the most part. People used to instant cameras often feel intimidated by SLRs, which they regard as fancy, expensive, and complicated. Their capabilities are much greater so their workings are more complex and they do tend to cost more. But many SLRs today have automatic-electronic light metering systems that take away the guesswork. These can be overridden in case you know what you are doing and wish to experiment; otherwise, few decisions need to be made, and they are nearly as simple to use as the instants. Even the nonautomatics have through-the-lens metering that

A bright, fresh Buckeye nectaring on asters—what could make a more inviting subject for a color photograph? The right flowers will still the flightiest of butterflies.

makes correct exposure easy in most cases. It needn't take long to learn the basic operating procedure for an SLR, automatic or otherwise. As for cost, SLRs are so competitive that unit costs keep coming down, much as for home computers. Today you have a choice of perfectly acceptable SLRs for under $200; less for used ones. You can spend much more for the biggest names, but the refinements they offer are best appreciated by experienced photographers well versed in the subtleties of the craft.

Lenses must be considered next. Most SLRs come equipped with 50mm lenses. These are perfect for landscapes and portraits but seldom focus closely enough to give a satisfactory image of any but the largest butterflies. The next step up involves screwing a close-up attachment on the end of the lens or inserting a hollow device known as an extension tube between the camera body and the lens. The close-up lens provides magnification, while the tube lengthens the focal distance, permitting closer focusing. A bellows unit works like an extension tube but may be adjusted for length, accordion-style. These methods cut down available light and provide very little depth of field, which is a big liability. Depth of field means the proportion of a three-dimensional object that can be in focus at once. So with poor depth of field, you have to be sure a butterfly is spread absolutely flat or else much of it will not be in focus in the picture. Furthermore, these items of equipment require that you virtually perch on the butterfly's back to get its picture, since their region of focusability is also very narrow. It is a rare butterfly that sits still while you nudge it with a bulky piece of glass. Good pictures have been taken with both of these primitive systems, but there are better ways.

The next refinement comes with the addition of a telephoto lens or zoom-telephoto lens. Such long lenses work like telescopes and in effect bring the subject closer. Their problem is that on their own they cannot focus closely. But if you link up a telephoto lens with an extension tube or a bellows unit, you can focus on a butterfly from a few feet away and still fill a fair part of the frame with its image. Of course, the size of the butterfly and the length of the lens make a lot of difference. But this gives you much more latitude for getting the shot without scaring off the insect, as well as increased depth of field. I have taken most of my butterfly pictures this way, with 200, 300, and 400mm lenses. As they get longer they get more effective for magnification but also heavier and harder to hand-hold. I find it quite feasible to hand-hold even a 400mm lens if I use a shutter speed of 1/125th or 1/250th of a second. Such a set-up can be assembled for around $300, new camera and lens included. Interlocking light metering might cost rather more. A zoom lens, ranging from 80 to 200mm or so, greatly increases the focusing capabilities of such a system, enabling you to shoot from different distances.

Without much doubt the best lenses available for butterfly photography are macro lenses. These are finely ground optics capable of focusing from very near (an inch or so) to infinity. The ordinary 50mm macro lets you focus more closely than the normal 50mm lens but still requires the subject to be still; it is better suited to wildflowers than butterflies, which tend to stir at such close encounters. The great innovations for butterfly photography are the longer macros, from around 90 to 250mm. The longer the better, for it gives both magnification, great focusability, and good depth of field (depending upon the light)—with great simplicity of use and compact dimensions. Such lenses are pricey ($300 or more) and not easy to find. They may come down in price as their virtues become more appreciated and the market for them grows. Beware of long lenses called "macro" that are not. Many so-called "macro-zooms" focus closer than normal telephotos and out to infinity, but not nearly as close as a genuine macro lens. Such lenses, often sold at bargain prices, have limited usefulness for butterfly work.

Film comes next. First you need to decide whether you wish to have prints or slides, or both. (I make the assumption that you will be shooting in color, although some very nice black-and-white work has been done with butterflies.) Prints are easier to share one-on-one; slides are obviously better for an audience. Publishers want slides, and they are cheaper to make. Prints can easily be made from slides, not the reverse. Films vary in their receptivity to light, as expressed in the ASA number. ASA 200 film is much more light-sensitive than ASA 25. That means it takes less light to expose it, so it can be used under darker conditions. This property is called speed—a fast film is one with a high ASA number. Depth of field is determined by the size of the camera lens aperture (called the f. stop: the higher the f. stop number, the smaller the aperture and the greater the depth of field; in most cameras F.22 is the smallest aperture giving the deepest focus) and that in turn is determined by the amount of light available. And since the faster the shutter speed the sharper the picture of a moving object (and that also depends on having enough available light), it stands to reason that a faster film makes it easier to take sharp, fully focused butterfly pictures. Using ASA 200 film with available sunlight you can usually shoot butterflies at 1/125th or 1/250th of a second, with an f. stop of 16 or 22. So why even consider a slower film? Because the slower films are reputed to have better color saturation, truer color replication, and less graininess in the image. ASA 25 is the favorite of many professionals.

The use of slower films for insect photography dictates the probable need for flash equipment. Or to put it another way, if you wish to use natural light, you will need to use faster films. To flash or not to flash is one of the fundamental decisions in butterfly photography. Flashers like to do so because electronic lighting allows them to use richer film, to stop action, to shoot under suboptimal light conditions or in the dark, and to black out much of the surrounding scene or background. Nonflashers prefer available light for the more natural look it imparts to their photographs, its simplicity, and because they like to include the background rather than black it out, even though it becomes a greenish blur in many cases. It's cheaper, too. Most butterflies, after all, will be found in the sunshine. For all these reasons I prefer available light myself. But flash adherents swear by the flexibility it gives them. You may wish to borrow flash equipment to enable you to try both before you buy. Of course there is nothing to keep you from switching back and forth, changing films or perhaps camera bodies to meet different conditions.

Lighting, films, cameras, and lenses all come down to personal choice, preference, and pocketbook. A more volatile subject of debate among butterfly photographers involves manipulation of the quarry in order to get it on film. There are photographers whose lack of patience, diligence, skill, or time induces them to nature-fake their photos. This involves gassing, pinching, chilling, or (at worst) pinning the subject so as to immobilize it for the sitting. Purists (my bias is obvious) abhor or at least reject such practices. Whether or not the butterfly recovers from the experience, the photograph almost invariably gives itself away as bogus by the unnatural position of the wings, legs, or antennae. How would a person look if similarly immobilized for a portraiture sitting? I have nothing against taking such pictures if it is the only way available—and for the upperside of species that will never open their wings at rest, such as Ochre Ringlets or many sulphurs, it may be the only way—but in my view, faked pictures should not be passed off as naturals. Nor can I imagine that manipulators derive as much satisfaction from their posed snapshots as the purists do from their candid successes.

And what about success? What makes a butterfly picture successful, and how often can one expect to succeed? Although soft focus may make pretty movie scenes and greeting cards, most of us hope for clear, sharp pictures with as much of the animal in focus as possible. Proper exposure means that the colors will be neither too pale and washed out nor too dark and muddy. Butterflies tend to be highly reflective and hence easy to overexpose, especially whites and sulphurs and blues, so that a little under-exposure (according to the meter) often yields better color satura-tion. Composition is another parameter. Normally you have little to say in the matter and less time to arrange it, but try to center the butterfly and to fill from half to two-thirds of the frame with its image for the most pleasing results. Flowers and foliage make more felicitous backdrops than mud or scat, but sometimes one has no choice on that score. I could not believe my luck one day when I came upon a bright golden Western Sulphur hanging from the orange Columbia Lily on which it was ardently nectar-ing. If you pay attention to these elements of the picture—focus,

Some butterflies seldom if ever alight with their wings spread, among them the Ochre Ringlet. Photographers must be satisfied with underside shots, unless they are willing to manipulate the subject.

exposure, composition, background—your transparencies or prints will show it. Many photographers consider that they are doing well if they reach a success ratio of one or two good shots out of ten attempts. With practice and care, you may well be able to do better than that. These days I seldom snap the shutter unless I feel I have a keeper in store, but I have discarded many poor slides in the past. Every bit of raw film exposed means greater experience, so try to remember or note down what you did each time in terms of shutter speed and aperture, so that you can relate it to the results and learn thereby.

Without a doubt, as much or more of your success will depend upon your powers of stealth and patience in tracking the subject. Everything said in Chapter 5 about approaching butterflies to watch them applies equally here. If you move slowly and fluidly, make no rapid movement, and exercise great care and concentration, you should be able to approach most perched butterflies closely enough to shake your camera at them. I often find that clicking the shutter puts butterflies to flight. Is it the sound, the vibration, the sight of the diaphragm moving through the lens, or my exhalation of relief? In any case, butterflies often fly away before you get a second—or indeed a first—shot. Patience is surely the most important item in your bag of tools and tricks—patience with the butterflies, patience with the sun and the fleeting clouds, patience with yourself. Not infrequently you will give up in sheer frustration and curse your clumsiness. Later, when the actions become more natural, satisfied sighs begin to outnumber the curses.

Sometimes sheer chance can make a picture happen or not. During the summer of 1970 I was determined to photograph Vidler's Alpine, a Northwest endemic and a favorite species of mine, for inclusion in my Washington book. Its flight period was past in the Olympic Mountains and in the Okanogan Highlands. I reasoned that it might still be on the wing, at cool, northern Mount Baker on the British Columbian border. And so it was. But clouds kept the alpines down in the heather and sedges during most of my visit. Finally, nearing the trailhead late in the afternoon, I was about to pack it in when the clouds parted and the *Erebia vidleri* rose from the turf. A perfect chocolate-and-cinnamon alpine alighted on an arnica for nectar just long enough for me

Wary butterflies like this Gray Comma may prove difficult to approach. Basking in the sunshine with wings fully spread, however, they may furnish excellent photographic opportunities.

to snap two photographs. Then the clouds zippered up and it dove back into the protection of the grass. I had my pictures.

Two summers before that, I tried to photograph a number of European species of alpines in the mountains that gave them their name, with reasonable results. Toward the end of the trip I stalked a species new to me across the snowy rocks of the Italian Dolomites, which it resembled on its pallid underside. Again and again the Italian *Erebia* paused and flew before I could compose a shot. Many individuals did this, before one finally sat for me—and sat, and sat. Perhaps it was ill. Some butterflies never seem to sit still, while others of the same species seem content to pose forever. You can save a lot of time by recognizing the sitters and passing by the flirts. Sometimes the problem lies in the substrate; find the right sort of platform and the subject will become compliant. In still another instance of *Erebia* stalking, last summer saw me on the trail of little Theano Alpines in a Colorado high country meadow. They refused to perch, except exquisitely and momentarily upon a rich russet composite. Then I found that they loved to bask on the broad leaves of marsh marigolds, and I shot all my film in no time.

Once you have begun to build a collection of butterfly photographs, you will probably want to find things to do with them. If you elected to take slides, you can share them with audiences. Each fall my friends John and Vikki Neyhart share their fine new slides with an annual gathering of Oregon lepidopterists. Schools, churches, scout groups, and natural history societies cry out for well-delivered slide presentations depicting the local butterflies. Butterfly slides, carefully edited to weed out duplicates and highlight only the best, may be interspersed with habitat and host plant or nectar flower pictures to place the insects in their ecologic context. Never try to show all your slides at once: too much of a good thing invariably sabotages audience interest.

Contact with other butterfly people will keep you informed of occasions when they gather to share their favorite photos. The 1983 Annual Meeting of the Lepidopterists' Society in Columbus, Ohio, featured the First National Lepidoptera Photographic Salon. Conducted according to practices approved by the Photographic Society of America this event signifies how far butterfly photography has come.

Whatever uses you may find for your photographs, whether you publish them in articles as the Riggenbachs did or project them for groups as with the Neyharts, be sure they are ready by storing and labeling them properly. Write your name, the name of the subject, and the date and place of the exposure on each print or slide; or key them to a notebook with codes. Beware of fingerprints on the emulsion; they etch their way in and ruin slides. Try to store pictures away from dust and heat. Consider glass mounts, and make projection copies of any slides you may someday wish to publish: they should remain untouched and unprojected. Plastic sheets with windows, special slide cabinets, and combination specimen-slide cabinets and drawers are all appropriate storage units. A photograph well cared for is an image that retains its value.

Butterfly photography as a hobby is not particularly susceptible to the law of diminishing returns. No matter how many species you get on film, there are always better pictures to take—sharper, brighter, better backgrounds, the other sex, another surface. Then you can always go on to moths—or movies. Aside from Monarch biologist Lincoln Brower and British filmmaker Robin Crane, I know of few people who have made excellent motion pictures of butterflies. This activity offers even greater challenges and broader frontiers than stills. The new video and film equipment has made motion pictures much more tractable for would-be filmmakers. On a recent expedition to view the overwintering Monarchs in Mexico, Portland filmmaker Manson Kennedy used video equipment to capture the scene, with gratifying results.

If you are at all photographically inclined, I hope you will have a go at collecting butterflies on film. Much has been written in the British butterfly press about the conservation value of this alternative to specimen collecting. Whether or not it has significant conservation impact is a question for the next chapter. But this fact is indisputable: there is no better way of getting your butterfly in the hand while letting it live in the bush.

In good conscience, before closing the subject, I should say something about the dangers of butterfly photography. John and Vikki Neyhart summed them up beautifully in a leaflet prepared for Oregon friends and colleagues, and their comments apply equally well to butterfly watching as a whole:

Heat exhaustion/heat stroke (wear a hat on hot days); Rattlesnakes (always a possibility in the desert); Falling (try to keep an eye on the butterfly AND on the ground you're walking—or running—on); Addiction (there are many things in life that are more important and every bit as entertaining as the pursuit and enjoyment of butterflies. But, on a sunny day, in the middle of a flowery mountain meadow, it's sometimes difficult to remember what they are).

15

Butterfly Conservation

A butterfly watcher in San Francisco half a century ago might have gone to any number of places to observe Xerces and Mission Blues. Many changes have taken place in the city and its surroundings in the meantime. Today the Xerces Blue is extinct; it cannot be seen alive anywhere. As for the Mission Blue, it is a federally listed Endangered Species, confined to a few habitats that are still at risk. What happened?

Already in 1875, entomologists were taking note of the decline of native species in the Bay Area. In a letter to Herman Strecker written on September 26 of that year, H. H. Behr wrote, "*G. xerces* is now extinct as regards the (immediate) neighborhood of San Francisco. The locality where it used to be found is converted into building lots, and between German chickens and Irish hogs no insect can exist besides louse and flea."* In 1943, the last colony died out, apparently because of military construction. The Mission Blue, a denizen of ridges and hills whereas Xerces occupied more vulnerable dunelands, has been forced to retreat before advancing development on San Bruno Mountain. This besieged island of remnant habitat supports several endangered species.

California has all the ingredients necessary for producing endangered species: lots of plants and animals that occur nowhere

* Chicago Field Museum Archives, *fide* F. M. Brown.

else along with human overpopulation. Most butterflies have special habitat requirements, as we saw in Chapter 4. When human
activities upset these conditions, species adapted to them must
move on, adapt further, or become extinct—usually the latter.
Most of our butterflies have wider ranges than these narrowly
endemic blues, and are not yet endangered. Nonetheless, many a
local population disappears each year, causing Behr's lamentation
to be repeated (minus the chickens and hogs) over and over by
lepidopterists. These mini-extinctions add up until once-common
species become less so, eventually growing rare or even in jeopardy
of survival. Once almost entirely neglected in favor of larger,
furrier animals, butterflies and other beneficial insects under
threat have gained much attention lately. This change of attitude
is coming none too quickly, and it is not at all certain that it has
come in time. We are beginning to realize that, without great care,
we could lose much of the world's precious butterfly resource.

It should be obvious that the root of the problem lies in the
landscape and our stewardship or lack of it. Butterfly collectors,
by virtue of their own small numbers and inefficiency and in view
of insects' remarkable reproductive capacity, cause next to nothing in the way of real conservation problems. Only the greediest,
most intensive collecting practiced on the most restricted and concentrated species has a chance of exerting any lasting impact on
populations. This is not to exonerate what lepidopterists them-

*The Xerces Blue, first American
butterfly to be extirpated by
human development. Extinct since
the early 1940s, its name is
honored by the Xerces Society, an
international body concerned with
conservation of rare insects and
their habitats.*

selves refer to as "game-hog" collectors, who may very well succeed in knocking down local flights to the disappointment of others who may wish to see the butterflies in the area. Nor is there a total absence of overcollecting: I have personally known certain island and bog populations of butterflies to be seriously reduced or wiped out by unconscionable collectors. Conservative practices and common sense are called for, as Chapter 3 explains.

What about pesticides? There is no doubt that the poisoning of environments with insecticides and herbicides has a marked deleterious effect on butterflies and other non-target insects. Butterflies may vanish from intensively sprayed areas, and roadside spraying with herbicides is an outright abomination that reduces attractive communities of flora and fauna to ugly bare patches. Yet not even pesticides have been demonstrated to cause actual butterfly extinctions, and their ill effects do not cause as much harm as the main problem: habitat alteration.

When we change habitats through building, bulldozing, paving, landscaping, plowing, grazing, inundating, or other activities, we destroy them for many of their prior occupants. Their specialized native plants and animals tend to give way to generalist, often exotic weedy species that can live under disturbed conditions. Dams, freeways, jetports, and shopping malls all displace what was there before. In fact, it is difficult for humans to occupy a landscape for any intensive purposes without displacing wildlife. This becomes a cumulative process leading to the loss of natural diversity, one symptom of which is endangered species.

You may wonder about the consequences of extinction and the loss of diversity. Many more species have become extinct than are living today, after all. Is it not a natural process? It is, but the difference lies in the rate of extinction. Over millions of years, the rate has generally been slow except for cataclysmic interludes such as ice ages. During the present millennium, and especially since the Industrial Revolution, the extinction rate has risen drastically. We are killing off our ecological base, spending our living capital.

Species are the raw stuff of medicine, agriculture, and many other enterprises. They are also the source of infinite intellectual and spiritual satisfaction. Ecologists believe that more diverse ecosystems are stabler ecosystems, yet we are undermining that stability with every extinction. Paul and Anne Ehrlich, noted population biologists and writers, liken wanton species throwaways to popping rivets on an airplane. You cannot measure the impact of each lost rivet easily, but eventually the wing falls off. And species are certainly dropping out much faster than they are arising. So when we speak of butterflies as candidates for extinction through human agency, we are discussing potentially serious losses. Butterflies and moths pollinate flowers, furnish songbird diet with their larvae, contribute extremely useful scientific study subjects and a rich aesthetic treasure. Clearly we should do all we can to keep them around in the greatest abundance and diversity possible as their world and ours changes.

Besides the Xerces and Mission Blues, butterflies offer many more examples of extinct and endangered species or subspecies around the world. The planet's largest butterfly is at risk today. Queen Alexandra's Birdwing, spanning up to a foot with its outstretched wings, lives in a narrow coastal strip of rainforest in Papua New Guinea. This habitat has largely been logged off or replaced with oil palm plantations. Across the sea in South America, an evolutionarily important swallowtail has all but vanished before the expansion of Rio de Janeiro across its river delta, and the same fate has befallen an Argentine morpho as Buenos Aires grows. The speedball cutting of tropical moist forests all over the Southern Hemisphere eliminates masses of species of insects before they can even be studied or classified. European blues, coppers, and browns face extinction through the drainage of their wetland habitats for more intensive agriculture. War, recreation, and water diversion place Middle Eastern oasis endemics at severe risk. Conversion of grazed downland to plowed arable fields displaces chalk soil-adapted blues in Great Britain. Water projects in the western United States threaten great Nokomis Fritillaries and others that depend upon desert springs and seeps. Urban expansion and drainage in Florida nearly wiped out the Atala Hairstreak, an iridescent green gem, and Schaus' Swallowtail. Several specialized skippers survive only on tiny remnants of the American prairie where they and the bison nearly went the way of the Passenger Pigeon. And the greatest butterfly spectacles on earth, the winter aggregations of migratory Monarchs, stand in jeopardy from coastal development in California and logging in Mexico. I could cite many more examples, having studied these sad statistics for a quarter-century, but the point should be clear by now: Butterflies need help, along with whales, seals, tigers, and pandas.

It is important to emphasize that wholly endangered species are not the only problem. For every species in jeopardy, there are thousands of local populations threatened by asphalt or apartment houses. These are important, too. Suppose a creature dies out within your "radius of reach"—the area to which you have easy access. In some respects, it might as well be gone altogether, because you will not be able to see it as you could before. This applies particularly to the very young, the old, and the immobile, as well as to the poor. I believe this "extinction of experience," as I call it, can have a snowballing effect. As diversity fades within people's immediate environs, they become less exposed to nature, thus more apart from it, finally less caring; so that the next bit of green goes with even less notice taken or resistance offered. On the other hand, the retention of wildlife in the cities and suburbs goes a long way toward maintaining the essential bond between people and nature that breeds a sense of stewardship and responsibility for the land and its life far beyond city limits.

Here I speak from experience. As I've said, I grew up in an ordinary subdivision on the edge of Aurora, Colorado, a suburb of Denver. The foothills across the city, populous with wonderful Rocky Mountain butterflies, were out of reach on a daily basis. Instead I found my Elysian Fields (or close enough) along a prairie ditch known as the Highline Canal. This intermittent watercourse carried mountain water from the Platte River Canyon to farms on the plains. Plants and animals, including butterflies, concentrated around its moist banks. They used it as a corridor, so that I might find foothills species well onto the plains along with prairie butterflies. My early searches were lit up by encounters with Black Swallowtails, Purplish Coppers, and cream, grass-green, and rose Olympia Marblewings that astonished me with their pristine beauty. My butterfly-hunting partner, Jack Jeffers, tracked the elusive Goatweed Emperor with me in old farmyards where he finally netted it. Later we found Arrowhead Blues around clumps of lupine, chocolate Wood Nymphs and Golden Skippers in the long, overhanging bank grass, and big banded Weidemeyer's Admirals acting territorial on the willows. Mourning

Cloaks were regulars, Monarchs occasional, and Aphrodite Fritillaries great rarities. An array of crescents and skippers darted among the annuals and grasses along the weedy canal-tender's path. There was never a lack of discovery or stimulus, from the first Milbert's Tortoiseshell of March to the last Painted Lady of November; and in winter, there were cocoons and chrysalids to be found. A town kid could have had no more adequate butterfly haunt than the Highline Canal in the 1950s and early 1960s.

But as I left for college, things had already begun to change for the worse. Fields became parks, golf courses, and shopping centers. The marblewing meadow became an athletic field. Most of the land next to the canal simply disappeared under housing tracts, as the population quadrupled. Each summer I returned to find less and less that I recognized. Prairie dogs and burrowing owls vacated in favor of apartments and condominiums, mountain bluebirds abandoned the site of the new jail.

Aurora's new town center is situated eight miles from the one I knew. With its migration it swept away most of the worthwhile butterfly habitats in town. Each summer I have continued to study the canal's changing butterfly fauna, painful as this has been. I can now document that the stretch I have studied, typical of the area, has lost a full 40 percent of its butterfly diversity. Nor is this unusual. Many lepidopterists can recount similar losses in their hometowns. Needless to say, the butterfly watching opportunities flee when such changes overtake a place.

What can be done about these changes? Are they inexorable? Should we simply move onto greener fields, while they last? That is one possible response. Another is to become involved in practical conservation politics and action to try to save habitats. It was for this purpose that the Xerces Society, named for the extinct Xerces Blue, arose in 1971. Xerces has worked to raise public awareness of the positive aspects of insects and their relatives, and to help prevent further local and total extinctions. In the past ten years, through these and other efforts, some progress has been made. Reserves have been created, laws passed and defended, and developments altered to accommodate rare butterflies. The U.S. Fish and Wildlife Service has taken action to protect a number of butterflies and moths and other arthropods under the Endangered Species Act, among them the Mission Blue and several others

Queen Alexandra's Birdwing of Papua New Guinea, largest butterfly in the world, is endangered by oil palm plantations that replace its native rain forest. The male, shown here, shines with blue-green brilliance, while the larger female (up to a foot in wing-spread) is black and white. Queen Alexandra's Birdwing is one of the species to appear in IUCN's Invertebrate Red Data Book.

referred to above. Butterfly farming and habitat conservation programs have been undertaken in Papua New Guinea to help birdwings and other species, and serious negotiations are under way aimed at protecting Monarch overwintering sites in perpetuity in Mexico and California. The World Wildlife Fund spends money on butterfly projects, and many butterflies were included in the first *Invertebrate Red Data Book* published by the International Union for Conservation of Nature and Natural Resources in 1983. In Britain, Butterfly Year 1982 proved a great success in rallying public interest and involvement. And that is the key. To save butterflies and their habitats, concerned people must act together.

Xerces Society newsletters are full of examples of people doing just that. Robert Dirig, Don Rittner, and other members banded together to save portions of Albany's Pine Bush, home of the scarce Karner Blue butterfly that was described by novelist/ lepidopterist Vladimir Nabokov. Jo Brewer, well-known author, lecturer, and butterfly gardener, enlisted the aid of neighbors to defend neighborhood habitats in her Massachusetts town. Xerces members have worked personally with representatives of oil companies and the Army Corps of Engineers and many public agencies to win consideration of butterfly habitats in their plans. Dr. Karölis Bagdonas sought protection for Weist's Sphinx Moth, "missing" for half a century, when his field team rediscovered it in an eastern Colorado sand wash. Drs. Paul Ehrlich and Dennis Murphy sued to obtain federal listing for the Bay Checkerspot during the Reagan Administration. The Atala Hairstreak has become common again. Many other successes, small and large, have occurred.

What about the Highline Canal? When it began to be degraded, I tried to rally support for it as a greenway with a series of habitat preserves tucked all along its 90-mile length. There was little interest back then, before the first Earth Day. When people did come around, it was a little late; most of the good habitat was gone. In the end we got our greenway trail, some seventy miles of it, but the opportunities for wildlife watching were much diminished. Bowing before powerful economic pressures, this turned out to be a conservation victory with distinct limits. A kid prowling the canal today will still find admirals and whites, but the Goatweed Emperors, Olympia Marblewings, and much of the rest is gone forever. It's a nice place to walk or ride and escape the suburban ennui, but will there remain enough of interest to spark a young naturalist's delight?

Perhaps your own community still retains a spot where all or most of the local butterflies fly. Is there a nearby marsh, meadow, wood, or waste that meets this description? Chances are that if it exists, and has not already been protected in some way, it will be at risk of alteration now or in the near future. You can make it your business to locate such a place, investigate its status, and set about working with others to set aside its best features. Often such can be brought about through some sort of creative compromise, so that an either/or confrontation may be avoided.

Becoming a successful, effectual butterfly conservationist means gathering support and experience, as well as understanding for all sides. Always there is strength in numbers and knowledge. Avoid stridency and unsupportable allegations. Join together:

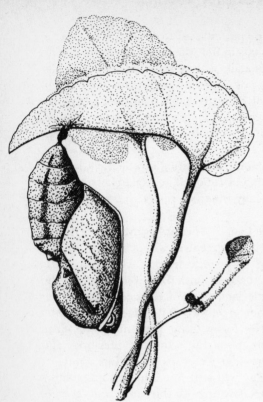

Their need for particular food plants and habitats makes butterflies vulnerable to landscape alteration. Should the violets disappear from an English woodland, the High Brown Fritillary (here in its chrysalis) would follow. Natural habitats must be conserved and managed properly if we are to retain a rich array of butterflies.

Join with other individuals of like concerns, join organizations that can channel energies to best effect. For butterflies, in addition to the Xerces Society, there is The Nature Conservancy, the primary habitat-conservation group. And the Audubon Societies, the Sierra Club, the National Wildlife Federation, the Wilderness Society, Friends of the Earth, Defenders of Wildlife, native plant societies, and many other groups concerned with maintaining natural diversity in a healthy environment for humans and others all will welcome your support. I believe that all nature-users have an obligation to help conserve nature. But you cannot join everything and remain effective, so choose according to your style. You may be better at voluntary management work on nature reserves than at organizing and debating. Perhaps you have a work skill that would facilitate some worthy group's task.

What about rearing and releasing butterflies as a conservation activity? It is a nice idea, but does little good unless habitats have been prepared to receive them. Generally, habitats will have as many butterflies as they can support from natural immigration. Sometimes reintroductions are called for following local extinction, but the cause of the dying-out must first be established and corrected. This is a job best left to professional reserve managers, although amateurs can certainly help under their guidance. The problem seems not to be so much one of replenishing butterfly populations as mitigating the environmental impact of human populations when they grow too large.

Just setting land aside is not enough. Butterflies have become extinct on reserves because not enough was known about them. This happened to the English Large Blue. So you can see that one of the most important aspects of conservation is learning about the ways and needs of butterflies and passing on the information. The next chapter deals with those topics. By studying every detail in the life of the federally threatened Oregon Silverspot, Drs. David McCorkle and Paul Hammond have greatly increased its chances for survival. And through Dr. Jeremy Thomas's research, the Large Blue was reintroduced to Britain from the Swedish subspecies. It is said to be doing well, now that its requirements have been understood and met.

It is too late to study the Xerces Blue. Nor can it be reintroduced, for it has no near living relatives. In its case, extinction truly is forever. But we can take a late, bitter lesson from the Xerces Blue and resolve to lose no more.

16

Teaching and Learning
with Butterflies

At about the same time I was first noticing butterflies out-of-doors, one or two experiences in school especially piqued my interest. While taking part in the production of a class mural celebrating spring, I decided to add a butterfly. My teacher helped me find a model, a picture of a crimson, black, and white Red Admiral. Once I'd drawn it I wanted to see one in real life. Later the school librarian steered me to the meager insect section in the library, where an Audubon Nature Study booklet leapt out at me: On the cover was the Black Swallowtail I'd already spotted (without a clue as to what it was) at the Highline Canal. The town library offered a little more. Next stop was the bookstore, where I bought my first copy of A. B. Klots' *Field Guide to the Butterflies*. Although this Peterson Field Guide was for the eastern part of the country, it covered many of the butterflies in eastern Colorado where I lived. It put me on the right path.

Dr. Klots addressed an entire section of his book "to teachers and nature leaders." He wrote that his book would not only serve to identify butterflies, "but it can also be used as a source book for building a broader program of natural history. The Nature Study taught in our schools and camps needs such broadening." This was certainly true in my case. My scout group paid so little attention to nature that I dropped out, and my schools had next to no nature study in the curriculum. One or two teachers sympathetic to my enthusiasms encouraged them but could provide little guidance. The fact is that nature study was on its way out in the Sputnik 1950s. It could have been an arid time for a would-be young lepidopterist. But I was lucky: I had Professor Klots and another great teacher, Dr. F. Martin Brown, in the form of their books. Brown's *Colorado Butterflies* became my bible. I met Denver butterfly collectors Ray Jae and Richard Buchmillar, who had infinite patience for my questions, and took me into the field. A marvelous stroke of serendipity brought me to the Rocky Mountain Biological Laboratory, where I was able to tag along with professional butterfly researchers Charles Remington and Paul Ehrlich and their students. All these stimuli cemented my interest and ensured my continued involvement with butterflies.

There was a time when all our schools offered nature study as integral parts of the syllabus. My grandmother led botany walks at a Washington mountain school in 1916, and that was not unusual. Half a century later, nature study had gone out of vogue in the face of hard science and space-race math competition. So in 1967, when I tried to offer a butterfly course in the summertime, only one student responded—my present colleague, Jonathan Pelham. Then a change came about. The wave of ecological enlightenment that began in the late 1960s carried with it a great public desire to learn more about nature. This brought a new day for nature study in schools, now called environmental education. Outside the schools, nature centers, museums, and wildlife clubs began to offer more and more educational opportunities in natural history. In 1977, a decade after my first abortive attempt, I was able to teach three butterfly classes and each was oversubscribed. Every summer since then my butterfly classes and walks have been full. The time of the butterflies has arrived, it would seem.

As elegant teaching aids and a superb interpretive resource, butterflies have few matches. They illustrate many aspects of biology as dramatically as any other organisms and are more accessible than most. The unfortunate fact is that they are not used more for these purposes. When young people with a yen for butterflies find little reinforcement in school, it can be discouraging. Together with peer pressure, this can extinguish youthful enthusiasm altogether. I encourage kids to take butterflies and their early stages to school, to enlist their teachers' and classmates' interest. No student should leave elementary school without having seen a butterfly hatch from its chrysalis; teachers should make this experience available. A cage full of Monarch larvae, munching milkweed and ready for release once they gain wings, makes a fine way to welcome students back to the classroom in the fall. Some teachers participate in Monarch tagging programs, so their students can take part in these migration studies. Tagging and releasing the butterflies in itself teaches quite a lot; recoveries are rare, but when they occur it is a fine bonus to the exercise.

Scout and camp leaders should not ignore butterflies either. As children become more sophisticated, chasing butterflies becomes less and less "cool" and therefore less acceptable as a hobby. But if an entire group can be induced to take nets in hand, such negative peer pressure disappears. Most of the kids will go back to video games afterward, but they may retain a little more tolerance for their friends who remain dedicated bug-chasers.

Many classroom and laboratory aids and other teaching materials related to butterflies are available. Film strips, slide packs, video loops, live and preserved specimens, and various observing and experimental tools can be obtained from biological supply houses and educational firms. Some years ago the Xerces Society cooperated with a major teachers' magazine to produce a fold-out poster of the Mission Blue. The elegant photographic poster and attendant information on this endangered butterfly proved very popular in classrooms and led to a great many inquiries. The amount of educational material on the Monarch alone is staggering. Teachers should be urged, by students and parents, to incorporate a butterfly unit in their life science classes. It need not involve making collections, the classic tenth-grade biology project in entomology, unless students wish to do so. There are many worthwhile alternatives, from mark-release-recapture studies to behavioral observations. Writing and visual arts activities can be incorporated with good effect. In my classes, I offer students an array of activities, each a different way of relating to and learning about butterflies.

Teachers could do much worse than to consult Professor Klots' instructions for nature leaders, published in 1951 but every bit as appropriate today (see Appendix). This tight, informed essay generates enthusiasm through its very words. The author ad-

Butterfly wings furnish canvases for genetic and developmental expression. Few are as revealing as this bilateral gynandromorph of Queen Alexandra's Sulphur. The wings show that the embryology went wrong, so the adult emerged as one-half male, one-half female.

dresses teachers' needs, group organization, advance preparation, group trips, study of material, and exhibits. He suggests an abundance of ideas upon which the thoughtful teacher or camp leader may elaborate. One of Klots' most useful sections deals with the comparison of butterflies between various habitats. He recommends sampling in cultivated areas, dry and wet meadows, woodlands and agricultural areas. "The lesson teaches itself," he concludes. Chapters 2, 4, and 11 of this book will give you more ideas along these lines. Don't overlook the value of a butterfly count as an educational activity. Many nature centers now incorporate these into their normal summer programs.

Another kind of project around which intense participation can be built is a campaign on behalf of a state insect. Several states have now designated official insects, and this is not a trivial matter. Such a symbol helps to raise appreciation and awareness of beneficial insects and their conservation, as well as to promote insect education in general. I was active in the campaign to have the Oregon Swallowtail designated that state's official insect. Eventually we succeeded, but it took a lot of lobbying to convince the legislators that it was a worthwhile bill. My own representative never came around on the issue. Now we are plotting a campaign to push the Colorado Hairstreak, a gorgeous purple imp of the scrub oak canyons, as Colorado's state insect to go alongside the Bighorn Sheep, Lark Bunting, Rainbow Trout, Blue Spruce, and

Blue Columbine. Check and see whether your state already has such a symbol. Maryland has adopted the Baltimore Checkerspot, California the California Dogface. Even if the place is taken, you could learn more about the designated insect and help to educate children about it or support the campaign to have the Monarch designated "national insect" by Congress.

A great many educational projects also take place outside the schools, and this becomes more important as budgets are cut. Butterfly and moth walks offer outstanding experiences for persons seeking outdoor lore, given decent weather, a few species on the wing, and a convivial group. I held my first butterfly walk for the Seattle Audubon Society on May Day, 1970. Now that chapter and many others include butterfly walks among their scheduled field outings, using local lepidopterists as leaders. The sample field notes on pages 94, 95 give the results of a very satisfactory outing of this kind. A few years later I began leading butterfly groups at National Wildlife Federation Conservation Summits. In fifteen years of teaching at the Estes Park, Colorado, Summit, I have found conditions and butterflies different each season. The complement of species varies with the weather, shifting the fauna toward spring species one year, summer the next, according to snowmelt in the Rockies. The students vary as well. I doubt that I shall ever tire of these walks, for they refresh me as much as they seem to invigorate the people who walk with me. The fact is that it is very hard to miss with butterflies. It takes no special talents to lead a butterfly walk, if one observes a few simple principles of good interpretation. Here are some of my recommendations for a good butterfly walk:

1. Know your habitat in advance. Always survey it ahead of time so you do not waste time and frustrate participants.
2. Pick spots with good nectar sources and puddling spots, or lay out baits, so as to guarantee some close-up watching.
3. Observe regulations or obtain necessary permits. A run-in with a landowner or ranger can be embarrassing and ruin a walk.
4. Have alternate dates in case of cloud; it is easy to be skunked by bad weather, and one's first butterfly ramble should be rewarding. A rain check is better than a wash-out.

The designation of the California Dogface as the official State Insect of California helps to bring butterflies to the attention of schoolchildren and others.

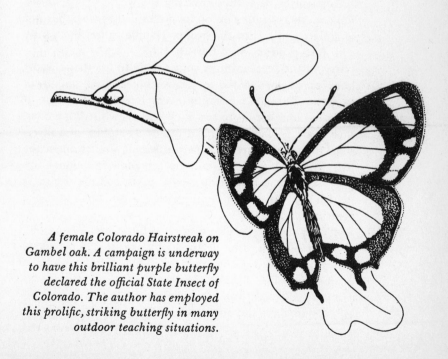

A female Colorado Hairstreak on Gambel oak. A campaign is underway to have this brilliant purple butterfly declared the official State Insect of Colorado. The author has employed this prolific, striking butterfly in many outdoor teaching situations.

5. Aim for diversity: try to show your group examples of all the major families to be found in the area.

6. Keep the size of the group down. I was offered a choice of either 17 or 47 participants for two walks I will lead this summer. I did not hesitate. Too many (more than 20) makes it difficult for everyone (or anyone) to see anything.

7. Urge walkers to get intimate and move in close. A lot of shy people will not speak up if they fail to see the object of attention. It is up to the leader to make sure that everyone sees everything, assuming that the butterflies cooperate.

8. Carrying a net and a pair of forceps will enable you to show butterflies at close range. But do not kill specimens on a butterfly walk unless you are certain that no one will be upset or offended. Most butterfly walkers want to see "their" butterflies fly free after examination. On the other hand, indicate a tolerance for insect sampling as a necessary and normally harmless part of the pursuit of entomology. I always insist that collectors should dignify their specimens with scientific data, thus ensuring the worth of specimens. I allow others to use nets on my walks if they wish, but not to collect while with the group. Handle butterflies gently with forceps so as not to hurt them.

9. Carry a hand lens and urge your people to use theirs. Show how: optic close to the eye, move object back and forth to focus. But don't examine every butterfly this way; it takes too long for all to see. Pick one or two striking ones, such as a furry-faced nymph, green-eyed sulphur, or a silver-spot, then make sure each person sees it well through the lens. With a big swallowtail you can show individual sapphire scales on a black field, sexual parts, and the proboscis (which you can unroll gently with a grass stem—always a great hit).

10. Don't try to tell the whole story of butterflies in one outing. Reveal rather than lecture; provoke instead of merely piling on the facts. Leave room for individual discovery and let the butterflies do a lot of talking.

11. Humor helps, but cuteness and anthropomorphism usually detract from the quality of a talk.

12. I prefer not to call every butterfly "him" and I don't let

my students get away with it. Examine the insects for sex, then use the correct pronoun. If you can't tell, there is nothing wrong with "it." Making them all masculine, a common habit, obscures the importance of sexuality in butterfly biology and evolution. Try to find a mating pair or to induce a hand-pairing. Remember that courtship offers some of the most rewarding observations of all.

13. Demonstrate how to approach a butterfly closely, but try to keep the group back far enough so as not to disturb the subject. With a small set of quiet people, everyone can get up close. Otherwise encourage people to try it on their own later. I try to disperse the group into the meadows for half an hour's personal butterfly communing before concluding the walk.

14. Watch for immature stages as well, and for females ovipositing. Most people have never seen butterfly eggs and react to them with pleasure and amazement.

15. If you find butterflies mud-puddling, you can try this: Place a finger with perspiration on it before a blue, gently nudging it aboard. Then transfer it onto someone's sweaty brow or nose. Probing for salts with its tongue, a butterfly so positioned may remain there for several minutes. Or it may bask at length on the surface you have selected. This tickles but delights, and makes for wonderful photographs. Or, with the blue still on your finger, pass it from person to person giving them eye-to-eye encounters. They will find it remarkable that a wild butterfly may be handled and examined in this way. The blue may remain preoccupied, sucking salts from your finger, until it is time to go and you have to send it on its way with a gentle prod. This may be a cheap trick but it certainly enchants your audience.

16. As the group breaks up to explore solo, I charge ahead collecting as many live examples as I can find, storing them safely in papers. Then in the shade of an aspen grove or around a picnic table beneath an old cottonwood, I show them one by one so as to give a good accounting for local diversity. As I finish with each butterfly I release it into the air. At the end, if time permits and it seems appropriate, I may share a reading with the group. My preferred

text is Vladimir Nabokov's marvelous essay "Butterflies" from his masterful early autobiography, *Speak, Memory*. By happy coincidence, the closing paragraphs of Nabokov's piece pertain to the very setting where I lead my Colorado walks each summer, beneath Long's Peak in Rocky Mountain National Park.

Each leader will develop his or her own style of interpreting butterflies. I tend to concentrate on natural diversity and conservation, ecology, evolution, behavior, and the sheer beauty of butterflies. But my comments are meant only as suggestions. You may find entirely different methods to suit you more comfortably. Whatever works to convey the essential nature of butterflies is right. It should be obvious whether your group is with you or not. Some people prefer not to be taught, but merely introduced to the subject, then left to explore it themselves. Others need more guidance or special help.

For me, one of the special pleasures of butterfly teaching comes when I have the opportunity of working with the blind or disabled. Wheelchair people and the elderly need surfaces, grades, and conditions they can deal with. The bedridden can have butterflies brought to them, then released at their window—an uplifting experience. The blind present an intriguing challenge to the butterfly teacher, for there is much more to a butterfly than its looks. Tarsi tickle and wings flicker, giving sensitive skin a distinct impression of the creature. And butterflies have scents. The osmeteria of swallowtail larvae smell sharp and tangy, while the adults may have a sweetish smell. My students routinely agree that male Phoebus Parnassians smell distinctly like corn chips. Imagination will meet this challenge in a dozen ways. The blind have many ways of watching. Helping to bring butterflies into their world gives me a vicarious pleasure and teaches me to appreciate them in new ways too. (Here too it might be worth reiterating that color blindness need not be a serious barrier to butterfly watching. This common genetic trait affects two of the best butterfly students and teachers I know.)

When young people show a special interest, let them help lead. I have had a succession of teenaged teaching assistants in my Colorado classes. They lightened my job, aided the process, enhanced the experience for all concerned, and learned quite a lot. As they have grown up, each has maintained her butterfly bond.

After all, the best way to learn is to teach. If you can find no butterfly classes to take, organize and teach one yourself. My friend Joan DeWind did this at a Connecticut nature center and became the local butterfly expert. Soon you will feel comfortable as a field leader. One of my summer courses was entitled "Butterflies Can Change Your Life." And I believe that; but first you need access, a point of contact. That is what teachers are for. Then the butterflies take over. For as Buddha said to the butterflies, "I thank you, you are my masters. From you I have learned more than from all the writings of the Brahmans."

17

Moths: Learning to Love Them

One late night as I was reading in bed, a great thump at the window drew my attention. Another thump, then more, as some great bat-like object tried to get in. I opened the window and in it came, eclipsing the light of the lamp and casting huge, improbable shadows as it fluttered about the room. I got to it just before the cat did, and picked it up gently so as not to rub off its tawny fur or caramel scales. It was a Polyphemus Silkmoth. The big animal struggled—stout furry legs and feathery antennae waving, strong thoracic muscles straining between my thumb and forefinger. Those robust antennae showed it to be a male. His wings were the softest tan, rimmed with delicate mauve above, big blue eyespots clear-centered so I could see through the wing. Below, chestnut bands crossed pink wings flecked with chocolate scales, the eyespots yellow-ringed. I turned out the light, released him, and he sailed out into the night in search of a female calling with her pheromones on the breeze.

In the East, several kinds of giant silkmoths come to porches and windows—Cecropia, Prometheus, and Luna in addition to Polyphemus and others. Here in the Far West we have only the Polyphemus and Ceanothus Silkmoths. Any curious, open-minded person would delight in such a night visitor. Yet I know many people who would happily forego the beauties of these moths and all others: they just don't like moths. A common prejudice. But it means these people miss out on a group of insects similar to butterflies yet much more diverse and extremely interesting in their own right.

How are moths related to butterflies? The question should really be put the other way around. Moths comprise most of the order Lepidoptera, several hundred thousand species in several suborders. Butterflies are but a diurnal, colorful offshoot of one of those suborders, some 15–20,000 in number worldwide. So moths vastly outnumber butterflies, to whom they have largely surrendered the daylight hours. Since butterflies fly by day, they evolved a great many defenses from color-sighted predators, usually expressed in their color patterns. Moths, on the whole nocturnal, generally tend to be drabber. Yet there exist moths—such as the Uranias—whose hue and brilliance rival those of any butterfly. Moths tend to have fuller, hairier bodies, but this is not always true. And while butterflies hold their wings vertically over their backs, and most moths fold them roof-like, geometrids hold them butterfly-like. The one characteristic most useful for separating butterflies and moths is the shape of the antennae. Virtually all butterflies have clubbed antennae (a thickening at the end), while those of nearly all moths, whether ferny, feathery or filamentous, taper to a sharp point. By checking the antennae first you should always be certain. Soon, with practice and watchfulness, you will be able to learn the basic groups of moths by sight: sphinxes, silkmoths, millers, micros, tigers, geometers, and so on.

If moths are so like the universally beloved butterflies, why are they so often looked upon with indifference, antagonism, fear, and loathing? As creatures of the night, like bats, moths may seem malicious to some people. Then there are clothes moths. These are tiny, nondescript members of the microlepidopteran family Tineidae. Most moths' larvae could no more subsist on woolens than you or I could. Of the others, nearly all plant-feeders, a number do compete vigorously for resources we value. The Gypsy Moth, Spruce Budworm, Tussock Moths, Peach Rollers, Tent Caterpillars, and garden cutworms of this world do not endear themselves. Even so, only a small percentage of moth species may be considered pests of food and fiber. The rest are benign or beneficial.

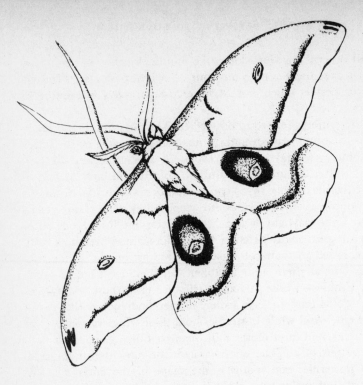

An adult male Polyphemus Moth. One of a number of species of giant silkmoths, some of which inhabit nearly every part of North America where forests grow.

Some people dislike the hairiness of moths or worry about getting them in their hair. Like bats, moths have no desire to go there. Others object to their congregating about the porchlight. When dense they can be a nuisance, it's true. I remember a Colorado cabin so full of millers that one had to douse the lights in order to be able to breathe. Nonetheless, moths are mostly misunderstood. They comprise a little-known world of variety, soft beauty, and fascination that I would hate to miss. They take butterfly watching on around the clock. Moths, approached without prejudice, offer a great deal of enjoyment. Naturally, they require their own manner of study.

Diurnal (day-flying) moths may be spotted in much the same way as butterflies. Some, such as the Cinnabar Moth, come in bright scarlets and gun-barrel blue—as bright as butterflies, they fly differently. Others look instantly mothlike, with their whirring gray wings. Many geometers (inchworm family) fly by day and some of these resemble satyrine butterflies. Often as a young collector I trailed what I thought was a new satyr, only to have it turn out to be a brown striated geometer.

The majority of moths are fly-by-nights, so they require special techniques to locate and observe. Let's begin at dusk. Go out

A Polyphemus Moth face-to-face. Moths tend to have heavier, hairier bodies than most butterflies. Their antennae lack clubs and may be full and feathery, as on this one. Their function is to catch the scent of the females on the night air.

into the garden. Spy along the rows of four o'clocks, over the tops of the lilacs, around the edges of the petunia bed. Moths suck nectar like butterflies. The sphinx moths in particular have long proboscis and prefer to visit these tubular flowers. What is that, hovering near the four o'clocks, darting from bell to bell? It looks like a hummingbird as it hangs in midair, a blur; but it is gray and has a long, yellow-spotted body. It is a sphinx moth. So named for the posture assumed by their larvae, and also known as hawk or hummingbird moths, sphinxes hover with rapid, invisible wingbeats like those birds, as they probe flowers with their long proboscis. Three or four inches is common, but one African sphinx visits an orchid with 18-inch nectar spurs— and its tongue is that long! Rare is the sultry summer dusk that fails to produce a sphinx moth or two hovering over the petunias. One of my early spring pleasures was watching the immigrant rose-winged White-lined Sphinxes coming to glistening lilacs at twilight after a rain.

Sphinxes also come to lights, and light is what you need if you hope to see many moths. Searching flowers with a flashlight may be fairly rewarding—special moths come to evening primrose, which opens just for them—but nothing beats lights for drawing an interesting assemblage of moths where they may easily be seen. In my youth I used to haunt the local shopping center spotlights and go from door to door to glean moths from neighbors' porches. I suppose this was an acceptable activity for a boy, but as I assumed a man's dimensions I began to draw the attention of patrol cars as I made my rounds. Indeed I know few moth hunters who have not had to explain themselves to the constabulary at some time.

A safer and more effective technique is to set up your own lights, in the darkest place possible. Mercury and long-wave ultra-violet (black) lights work best. The nearer to a patch of wooded habitat the better. Moth-lighting usually involves hanging a white cloth behind the light or spreading it on the ground around the source. If you happen to be merely watching moths, the sheet should be adequate. Collectors employ traps that invite the moths into an orifice but prevent their escape. These can also be used to trap moths throughout the night in advance of leisurely morning

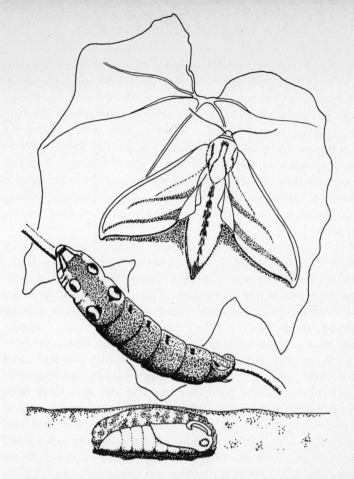

Life stages of the Elephant Hawkmoth. The pupa, with its trunklike proboscis case, lies naked without a cocoon in its earthen chamber. The larva's large eyespots may serve to intimidate potential predators. Adult hawks are also called sphinx moths, due to a posture often assumed by the caterpillar.

examination of the catch. Light traps can be fitted with killing jars, but it is better to fill them with sections of cardboard egg cartons for surface area, footing, and hidey-holes. The catch can then be looked over and unwanted specimens turned loose. This should be done some distance from the trap or birds will learn to frequent the spot for the morning pickings.

The spectacle of moths gathered around a light in the tropics can be truly astonishing—thousands of winged, scaly fliers of myriad shapes, colors, patterns, and sizes. The display at your porchlight or blacklight may not be so spectacular, but the moths of almost any locale will include a rewarding array of interesting species. Most visitors simply take up a perch where the moths may easily be examined. If the moth you wish to look at refuses to settle, catch it in a jar and plunge it into the freezer for a few moments. This will not hurt it, but will slow it down enough for a good look. Many moths possess the ability to create body heat by shivering, so they may not remain immobilized long by this treatment.

What is it about lights that attracts moths? The moth to the flame is an age-old image, but only recently have biologists begun to understand the reasons behind it. Moths, like butterflies, have vision sensitive to the ultraviolet. This alone may suggest the attractiveness of UV lights for them. But one theory gaining ground proposes that the light attracts moths less than it dazzles them. In other words, when a moth flies within visible range of the light, its brilliance disrupts the insect's ability to orient using dim natural light. This causes it to begin circling and ultimately to drift in toward the light: the moth to the flame. Far from "liking" lights, then, moths—if capable of so feeling—would be highly frustrated by bright city lights. In fact, it has been suggested that the proliferation of mercury and sodium vapor street lights has added to the pressure on giant silk moths and contributed to their decline throughout the urban Northeast. Drawn from the country to the bright lights, they spend their nights circling lampposts instead of seeking mates. According to the theory, by thus disrupting their courtships, the powerful lights reduce the big moths' reproductive success. At the same time, moths concentrated around light sources are vulnerable to bats at night and birds in the morning. Whatever the actual relationship between moths and light, the fact that moths come to lights makes it possible for us to observe them closely.

When using lights, one is forced to remain within reach of a power supply source or else pack heavy batteries around. Moth hunters desiring greater portability often fall back on the other time-honored attractant: bait. As described elsewhere in this book, rotting fruits and other substances may be used to entice butterflies. Moths will come to fruit as well, but they seem to prefer a mixture of sweet-stuffs that practitioners simply call "sugar." At least one recipe exists for each person who makes it. A typical mixture might consist of the following ingredients: a couple of pounds of sugar, a bottle or two of stale beer, mashed overripe bananas, some molasses or syrup, fruit juice, and a shot of rum. This unpleasant-sounding brew should be left to ferment in the sun for a few hours, whereupon it becomes even more cloying. I have never been clear as to whether the addition of alcohol enhances the attractiveness of the fluid to moths or merely enhances their watchability or catchability by dulling their reflexes.

The traditional method of sugaring involves painting the "sugar" on tree trunks, rocks, stumps, fence posts, or any other surfaces in or near a likely-looking moth habitat. Clearings or lanes in deciduous woodland are especially good. The sugar should be applied in the late afternoon and left to "cook" in the last sun of the day but not long enough to evaporate. A sultry, cloudy evening gives the best mothing; clear, cool, breezy and moonlit nights are not as good. When you return to the site as night falls, lantern or flashlight in hand, proceed from station to sugar station, and you should see a succession of moths coming for the bait. If you want to take some back for study or observation, quickly place a jar beneath the drinking moth. Often it will drop when disturbed right into the jar. Otherwise prod it gently in that direction. Keep the jar in the dark to prevent the moths from battering themselves to bits. Otherwise simply enjoy the moths *in situ,* as they probe the cracks in the bark for the dripping liquor, their eyes shining like fiery garnets in the beam of the lantern. Some drinkers become quite besotted and easy to approach; others sip sparingly and retain their wariness.

Experience will show that some places sugar better than others. One summer I led sugaring walks for my classes in two disparate localities. In the foothills, we tried a Ponderosa pine wood and a quaking aspen grove. Neither yielded many moths at all. But in a cluster of Plains cottonwoods a few nights later, we watched big red underwing moths flicker through the lantern beam, hover by the cottonwood trunks, then settle gingerly and extend their tongues toward the gleaming sugar. Dozens of the beautiful moths came to this bait, giving one the sense that prairie groves are better than mountain forests. Yet on another summer night years earlier, my mother and I enjoyed an excellent night's sugaring among the pines and aspens near a cabin we had taken in a foothills canyon. On that occasion we added cherry cider to our sugar bait, and it has been one of my central ingredients since then.

Lately many lepidopterists have become more aware of their impact on the environment in various ways. Sugaring the old way can leave unsightly patches on the trees and may attract many insects other than moths that can get stuck or preyed upon. A new way of sugaring that avoids these problems has gained acceptance recently. It involves soaking sponges in the sugar vat and hanging them from limbs of trees, rather than painting the woods. While less pleasing as a moth background, the sponges leave no sticky trace and make collecting easier. Use your own discretion. However it is done, I highly recommend sugaring as a uniquely rewarding nature-by-night experience.

Perhaps no author has painted a more evocative scene of a moth outing than W. J. Holland in his essay "Sugaring for Moths," which appeared in his 1904 standard, *The Moth Book*. This casual but suspenseful piece is a classic of period natural history writing. In it, Holland describes the entire event from mixing the sugar, daubing the trees, and resting for the evening's work, through mothing by lantern-light, scurrying for the protection of the old veranda as the storm comes, and anticipating the morning's labor ahead in setting the catch. He describes the moths themselves and the rising excitement of a pair of lepidopterists (the narrator and his protégé) in terms that cannot help but inspire the reader's enthusiasm. Here is a sample:

> Let us stealthily approach the next tree. It is a beech. What is there? Oho! my beauty! Just above the moistened patch upon the bark is a great *Catocala*. The gray upper wings are spread, revealing the lower wings gloriously banded with black and crimson. In the yellow light of the lantern the wings appear even more brilliant than they do in sunlight. How the eyes glow like spots of fire!

Sugaring for moths: three species of underwings come to sweet bait on a tree trunk. This traditional method attracts moths that may otherwise seldom be seen.

When I lead a moth walk, I try to find a quiet and comfortable place where I can read selections of Holland's essay to the group. It adds such flavor that it can make a success of a near-mothless night (it is available in a Dover reprint edition). On one such occasion I had just come to the part about the thunderstorm when the lightning flashed, thunder crashed, and the sky opened so that we too ran for shelter! We finished the piece in a rustic lodge, examined our catch, and set them free onto the rain-fresh night air. I cannot guarantee that the elements will play true to the script like that, but I can assure you of a worthwhile night out.

Still another method of attracting may bring spectacular results. If you can obtain a living female of any of the saturnine (giant silk) moths, such as Cecropia or Luna or Polyphemus, fresh from the cocoon and therefore virginal, you can employ her to attract males. Of course, this works only if these moths live within a certain radius of the female's position. Males have been known to track calling females from ten miles away, but one or two miles is probably much more common. Place the female moth in a room with screened, open windows, or better yet, in a screened cage outdoors. (Specialists construct dainty harnesses of thread with which to tether their moths.) She will release pheromones, which the males pick up with their great feathery antennae. Like Argonauts to a siren, they sail out of the night to surround her. The spectacle of the ardent silkmoths flapping their great wings around the object of their desire is not to be forgotten. Gene Stratton Porter, whose 1912 book *Moths of the Limberlost* captures the charm of moths better than any others for me, described such an experience:

In connection with Cecropia there came to me the most delight-ful experience of my life. One perfect night during the middle of May, all the world white with tree bloom, touched to radiance with brilliant moonlight, intoxicating with countless blending perfumes, I placed a female Cecropia on the screen of my sleeping-room door and retired. . . . Past midnight I was awak-ened by soft touches on the screen, faint pullings at the wire. I went to the door and found the porch, orchard and night-sky alive with Cecropias holding high carnival. I had not supposed there were so many in all this world. From every direction they came floating like birds down the moonbeams. I carefully removed the female from the door to a window close beside, and stepped on the porch. No doubt I was permeated with the odour of the moth. As I advanced to the top step, that lay even with the middle branches of the apple trees, the exquisite big creatures came swarming around me. I could feel them on my hair, my shoulders, and see them settling on my gown and outstretched hands. Far as I could penetrate the night-sky more were coming. They settled on the bloom-laden branches, on the porch pillars, on me indiscriminately. I stepped inside the door with one on each hand and five clinging to my gown. Then I went back to the veranda and revelled with the moths until dawn drove them to shelter.

Admit one or more of the males to the female's chamber, and she will soon be mated. Eggs will appear, the size of glass pinheads, on curtains or wherever she can crawl. Then you can launch a new generation according to the methods offered in Chapter 13. The big, beautiful moths have large and striking larvae as well. Cecropia's thick, apple-green caterpillar bears red and yellow and blue tubercles that give it a decorated look. You may be surprised by their appetites. The first batch of Cecropias I acquired as a boy came in the form of a couple of hundred eggs. I began by trying to feed each hatchling individually, but as they outgrew my patience I tossed them into a washtub with fresh foliage daily. Eventually I simply slung the lot onto my mother's lilacs—which they nearly defoliated by the time they spun their big-bag cocoons!

Searching for those cocoons in winter makes a fine treasure hunt. Each species has its own distinctive shape. Cecropia makes a drawn-out sack; Promethea's is narrower, wrapped in a leaf. Polyphemus, too, incorporates the leaf, but the cocoon is broad and bulky. The lovely green Luna spins up in a rounded silky ball. When the leaves fall in deciduous woodlands, thickets, and hedgerows, these and many moths' smaller cocoons stand out. Since most of the giant silkmoths feed on a variety of broad-leafed trees and shrubs, they occur in many rural and wildland habitats. And according to Gene Stratton Porter, "The Cecropia is a moth whose acquaintance nature-loving city people can cultivate." She noted several bushels of their cocoons in Indianapolis one winter. Well adapted to many ornamentals, nonethless they tend to spread out and seldom assume pest status.

But if Cecropia tolerates cities, an equally beautiful species positively prefers slums. Whereas Cecropia is colored in shades of russet and robin-red, the Cynthia Moth is honey-tan with lilac-pink bands. Imported from Asia as a potential silk source in the nineteenth century, the moth and its host plant (*Ailanthus*) became naturalized in the East. The sericulture project faded out, the cocoons being too difficult to unravel, but the adaptable *Ailanthus* continued to spread with its beautiful moth. Known as "the tree that grows in Brooklyn" *Ailanthus* has a penchant for slums, railroad yards, industrial sites, concrete jungles—anywhere it can get a roothold. So these are the kinds of places where

Polyphemus Moth full-grown caterpillar, prior to pupation. Giant silkmoth larvae are prodigious eaters of foliage, but seldom occur in damaging concentrations.

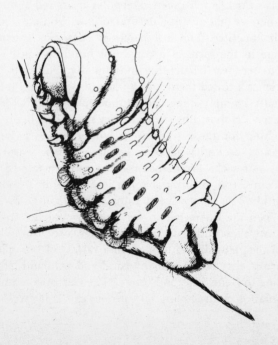

Polyphemus Moth cocoon. The pupa has been enshrouded in a silken bag, further secreted by a pair of oak leaves bound together for the purpose by the caterpillar.

Cynthia lives. The slender cocoons, wrapped in a leaf and lassoed to a twig by a silken tie, may be found in great numbers in these uninviting locales.

Silk-enclosed cocoons like these should be stored in a cool place and sprinkled lightly with water from time to time. There should be something for the emerging moths to climb on—twigs or rough wood or fabric. If you keep the cocoons in a warmer place indoors they may hatch early, like forced crocuses. Silkmoths lack mouthparts and live only briefly as adults, usually just a few days. Once having seen them in their pristine condition, every scale in place, you may prefer to release them. Be sure to do so in the proper habitat, and well away from strong lights, at dusk.

I shall never forget the pleasure of keeping Luna Moths in my lab at Yale. A friend sent me a batch of cocoons, which I kept over the winter. With spring they began to eclose: pale green shrouds with moist white mantles crawling out of silken bags sheared open with a tooth concealed in the ermine fur of their thoraxes. As they pumped fluid from their fat bodies into crumpled wings, their long tails unfurled and the green vanes took shape. I was deeply struck by these splendid moths, their sickle-shaped, crescent-tailed wings of the softest jade, rimmed along the leading edge with deep purple. At a frenetic and pressured time in my life the Lunas brought a very welcome note of tranquility and beauty, and a touch of nature for which I was grateful. They were the first I'd seen alive. It would be several years before I finally saw Luna in the wild in the Connecticut woods.

I have been speaking largely of the giant silk moths of the family Saturniidae, distant relatives of the domestic silkmoth. But there are many other groups of moths worth your attention. Their incredible diversity presents a real challenge in terms of identification. For many years Holland's *The Moth Book* was the only available reference that named and pictured even a smattering of American moths. Now there are detailed monographs of some families and selective field guides are beginning to appear. Still, it is no mean feat to identify correctly the moths you encounter. The family Noctuidae (commonly called millers) alone comprises some hundreds of roughly similar species. Our moths as a whole are rather poorly known. Where I live we haven't the scantiest picture of the moth fauna. Moths will continue to present new frontiers to lepidopterists long after the butterflies have been reasonably well documented. This seems appropriate for these mysterious night fliers. Somehow, with the dark as their curtain, I feel we may never know moths as well as we might like.

I hope you will not let the difficulty of identifying moths discourage you altogether. It is not difficult to get to know the commoner, more conspicuous species and the major families. For those who develop a deeper interest, names will come later as a product of the sort of involuntary research that is the handmaiden to enthusiasm.

Our moths may lack the charming common names with which the English species have been endowed—names like True Lover's Knot, Angleshades, Maiden's Blush, and Lesser Lutestring. Yet they possess no less charm. If "charm" seems a peculiar word to apply to a moth, I would ask your opinion again after you have seen a few of our elegant underwing moths or followed an Eight-spotted Forester making its rounds among the sweet rocket, in the company of Bumblebee Sphinxes or Nessus Hawkmoths.

As I write, a large geometrid moth with the not unattractive name of *Triphosa undulata* lies flat against my study wall. Its dark brown, scalloped, intricately striated wings resemble those of a butterfly basking in the late rays of the sun. A lightly hibernating species, it has come indoors for the winter and might remain with me till spring, flitting from room to room. No butterfly will do that. If you admire butterflies, you will be missing out on a great deal if you ignore these closest relatives, the moths—perhaps our most undervalued nature resource.

18

Great North American
Butterfly Spots

Henry David Thoreau was not the only naturalist known to take his pleasures chiefly in his backyard. The great eighteenth-century British naturalist Gilbert White observed plants and animals almost within the bounds of his rural parish in Hampshire. Yet from these two stay-at-homes' notebooks emerged the greatest nature classics of their time: *Walden* and *The Natural History of Selborne*. It is still true today that observant writers draw much of their material from their immediate precincts. Annie Dillard at Pilgrim Creek, Sue Hubbell on a Missouri bee farm, and Anne Zwinger in her Colorado aspen grove are but three examples.

For the entomologist in particular, any plot of ground offers enough diversity to occupy an hour or a lifetime. Witness Frank E. Lutz, the eminent entomologist of the American Museum of Natural History, who recorded several thousand species of insects within his small Brooklyn yard and garden. This he recorded in a backyard wildlife masterpiece entitled *A Lot of Insects*. Had I his energy, enterprise, and knowledge, I know that Swede Park, the old homestead on which I dwell, could occupy me for the rest of my life with its insects. Even studying them in a casual way gives me a lot of pleasure and new insights into the odd mixture of habitats we share.

Yet I find that I wish to travel, to seek fresh fields (greener pastures are unimaginable), and to see unfamiliar butterflies on their home ground. Even Thoreau roamed about to a degree, and this enabled him to compare his Concordian vision to other rivers, other landscapes. Our best-known modern nature writer, the late Edwin Way Teale, roamed the entire country with his wife, Nellie, to see nature at large, after portraying his close-to-home insect garden in *Near Horizons*. Wider horizons beckon most of us from time to time. We are fortunate to live on a continent where travel is as simple as anywhere in the world (wanting only a lot more trains), yet where the diversity of landscapes, habitats, plants, and animals is exceptionally high. Without straying far from major transportation corridors in North America north of Mexico, the butterfly enthusiast can find some 700 species and hundreds more subspecies of butterflies. If the advice of the previous chapter be heeded and moths tossed into the bargain, the possibilities become too great to grasp.

Even so, most of us lack the key to the highway—the ability to roam when and where we wish to watch butterflies or fish for trout or simply follow the white lines or forest paths. Because of work, economic constraints, and family responsibilities, most people have to fit their travel wishes into a more or less rigid framework of weekends and vacations. I often think of the vacation as one of the worst torments ever invented. With all the wonder that exists out there, all the mountains and beaches and parks and places, how is one to decide where to spend the measly two or three weeks grudgingly allotted most workers for refreshment? A specific enthusiasm can help in narrowing down the impossible range of options. A good butterfly spot—that is, one that offers high diversity and abundance, especially attractive species, or aggregations—can make a worthwhile destination. In these few pages I certainly could not describe all the good butterfly spots, even if I knew them. But I can suggest a few favorite places that, weather willing, will brighten any entomological itinerary.

First, a word of caution regarding the land, its ownership, and its proper use. Many naturalists prefer the Amerindian concept of the land belonging to no one and everyone—especially when they spot a special bird or mushroom on the other side of the barbed wire. But landowners and county sheriffs don't see it that way. I seldom find landowners hostile if asked in advance for permission to trespass. But when I have been lazy or impatient and have hopped a fence without asking, I have had to explain myself to a few (understandably) indignant farmers and ranchers. Keep this in mind, especially where land is posted.

Watchers have the advantage that they do not need to obtain collecting permits, which are required in certain parks and reserves for collectors. A use fee may be stipulated on some kinds of public land, for example, Wildlife Recreation Areas in Washington. The Nature Conservancy restricts access to some of its preserves to permit holders, for the protection of fragile sites. Make it a point to know the status of the land you intend to visit and to comply with use regulations. Wherever you go, respect the common sense rights of the land, its owners, and other users. These are well summed up in the English Country Code, which is just as applicable in this country:

THE COUNTRY CODE

Guard against all risk of fire
Fasten all gates
Keep dogs under proper control
Keep to the paths across farm land
Avoid damaging fences, hedges and walls
Leave no litter
Safeguard water supplies
Protect wildlife, wild plants and trees
Go carefully on country roads
Respect the life of the countryside

Your behavior in the countryside has a lot to do with how welcome naturalists will be in the future. In these days of overcrowded public facilities and growing protectiveness by private landholders, this becomes an important consideration.

For the duration of the chapter, I will roam vicariously around and across the continent, naming an arbitrary selection of excellent butterfly localities and regional characteristics. No very logical route will be adhered to; I would not recommend trying to follow this itinerary in a season. And I wish to make four disclaimers.

First, all butterfly watching is dependent on the season and the weather. If you arrive at Trail Ridge Road in the Colorado Rockies with twelve feet of snow on the ground, I guarantee no success. Second, habitats change so rapidly these days that a butterfly paradise one year may be an asphalt hell the next. I have tried to minimize such disappointments by referring chiefly to protected areas. Third, this is not a collecting guide, for the same reason. Many of the areas I name have rules against collecting or require permits. Finally, this bag of butterfly hot-spots is by no means all-inclusive or complete. Every state and province has dozens of rich sites that I am unaware of or lack room to mention.

I find much of my most memorable observation along the roadside, in unsung pullouts, or down irresistible side roads. Doubtless you will find the same, if you can avoid being glued to the highway between major destinations. Roam. Wander. Explore. Lepidopterists tend to be a conservative lot, revisiting the same tried-and-true localities from year to year and seldom trying new places for fear of getting skunked. They also tend to collect near major roads. If you are willing to walk, take back roads, and reject the comfortable lure of the known quantity in favor of the wide-eyed gamble from time to time, you will be rewarded with some fine spots that no one knew to tell you about.

If, like mine, your butterfly yearning begins to throb in January or so and you live in the North, a butterfly vacation to warmer climes may be in order. Let us then begin in the southernmost states, then move, as Teale did in his famous American Seasons books, "north with the spring."

Late winter and very early spring are the best times to seek butterflies in the southwestern deserts. The several federal reserves dotted across the Mojave and Sonoran deserts in southern California and Arizona can be very inviting at that time, particularly after a wet winter when the wildflowers bloom exuberantly. Joshua Tree, Organ Pipe, and Saguaro National Monuments are some of the best of these. At Patagonia, in the Huachuca Mountains of Arizona, a TNC (The Nature Conservancy) reserve has gained fame for its birdwatching in winter; it is just as good for butterflies. The deserts and canyons of the Southwest offer the chance to see butterflies with Mexican affinities and species that fail to penetrate much farther north. These include colorful specialties such as the Pima Orangetip, Red-eyed Brown, Red Satyr, and Arizona Pine White, as well as the Desert Swallowtail, Dogface Butterfly, and Great Purple Hairstreak. The brilliant metallic blue of the last-named long-tailed gem is matched by that of the Pipevine Swallowtail, represented in the region by a furry-bodied subspecies that flies at the Grand Canyon, among other places. If you are very lucky, you may see a giant skipper shoot past the ubiquitous yuccas it feeds on.

From here you can follow a band of good butterfly diversity all along the Rio Grande, through Big Bend National Park and Big Thicket National Reserve in Texas, down to the river's delta. Much altered by agriculture, the lower Rio Grande Valley nonetheless still is well known for its butterflies. The Santa Ana National Wildlife Refuge west of Brownsville continually produces butterflies never before recorded north of the border, as well as a good cross-section of regional skippers, blues, sulphurs, hairstreaks, nymphs, and others.

The crescent of the Gulf of Mexico rewards the naturalist with a kaleidoscope of wildlife, except where erased by oil, industry, or agriculture. The visitor to New Orleans will find some of the butterflies indigenous to Louisiana along the Mississippi levee path, which runs near the airport. Less common and adaptable species need to be sought along the wilder bayous such as the Atchafalaya. Much of the Southeast is butterfly mecca and it is difficult to pick favorites until we have rounded the Gulf and come to rest in the Everglades. Pausing in the hammocks, or on wooded islands in the flooded glades, you may spot purplewings, blue wings, daggerwings and longwings, or Pearly Eyes flitting through the dappled sunbeams. Or remain until dusk and watch the butter-and-black Zebra butterflies gather for their communal nocturnal roost. If one spot is to be recommended in Everglades National Park, it is Shark Valley, otherwise known as Alligator Alley, off the Tamiami Highway. This old canal into the glades offers excellent bird and 'gator watching as well as splendid butterflying. Queens and Gulf Fritillaries crowd the beggar's tick beside the water, as great, full-winged Palamedes and narrower Giant Swallowtails dip to nectar on the blue pickerell weed. White Peacocks, orange Anemones, and many another butterfly

The larvae of giant skippers burrow into the roots of yuccas. Butterfly watchers in the southern yuccalands should be alert for the large, speedy adults.

dwell here as well. Or seek giant sulphurs and Long-tailed Skippers at Royal Palm, along the Anhinga Trail.

Perhaps the rising heat will induce you to abandon the gaudy butterflies of the deep Southwest and head north. A Carolina lane may tempt you with Tawny Emperors, or Spicebush Swallowtails will draw you to a halt in a Georgia park. But carry on to Tennessee and catch the Blue Ridge Parkway. This long, scenic avenue, a green umbilicum connecting Great Smoky and Shenandoah National Parks, runs tantalizingly along the spine of the lush Appalachians. Practically anywhere you stop will be rewarding. In particular I recommend Big Meadow in Shenandoah, in Virginia. Swallowtails and Monarchs by the score glide over the mauve ironweed expanse, as Large Wood Nymphs negotiate the mountain grasses. Or drop down the ridge, across the Shenandoah River, and up again into Shenandoah National Forest. I have never seen so many Red-spotted Purples as here, basking in the road and showing off their metallic blue, brick-red-dotted wings, rising constantly in front of one's car. Wet meadows and marshes along the forest fringe sometimes secrete crimson patches of cardinal flower, where Great-spangled Fritillaries and Eastern Tiger Swallowtails take nectar.

Now it is summer, and all around Chesapeake Bay the butterflies abound. Before heading farther north, stop at the Dismal Swamp on the Virginia–North Carolina border, near the shore. Despite its name, the Dismal Swamp is anything but for the naturalist. Largely protected today, this great wetland can be plied by canoe or boardwalk. This is a good place to become acquainted with skippers: A large proportion of the eastern species haunt the Dismal Swamp, where pickerel weed is their preferred nectar source. If the array of tawny wedges seems too much to deal with, just enjoy their color, behavior, and variety. No shortage of bigger butterflies awaits the visitor to the Great Dismal, for almost all the eastern swallowtails abound in the swamps and on their edge along with many other species.

Just across Delaware Bay is Cape May, New Jersey, another famous birdwatching spot. Jumping ahead in the season for a moment, this is a spot to return to in autumn. Just as millions of birds mill about the Cape before heading off south again, migrating butterflies do the same. Nowhere else have I encountered emigrating Buckeyes and sulphurs in such numbers, along with the truly migratory Monarchs. I found it to be a unique and strange thrill to watch thousands of Sharp-shinned Hawks passing by on high, hordes of butterflies doing the same lower down following different schemes and planes of passage.

One way to go northward into New England is to follow the traprock Palisades from New Jersey well into Massachusetts, and a good place to stop along the way is New Haven, Connecticut. Yale University, famed for butterfly research and collections, lies very near one of these formations, West Rock. Yale Professor Charles Remington attributes the richest butterfly fauna in New England to this outcrop. This is because northern and southern elements meet and mingle here in a varied blend of habitats. If you visit West Rock State Park in the spring, you may be sure (on a sunny day) of seeing the delicate and lovely Falcate Orange-tip near historic Judges Cave. As the season progresses, Baltimore Checkerspots and many other species emerge.

In Vermont and New Hampshire, various recreational areas

in the White Mountain National Forest offer glimpses of northern forest butterflies such as Compton Tortoiseshell, various angle-wings, and the White Admiral. Mt. Washington is famed for the White Mountain Butterfly, a post-glacially stranded arctic, and for a purplish race of Titania's Fritillary on its arctic-alpine slopes. Up in Maine, a relative of the White Mountain Butterfly known as the Katahdin Arctic abides near the summit ridges of Mt. Katahdin in Baxter State Park. Trails through this wilderness lead to many intriguing habitats, whether or not you make it all the way up to see the dusky brown arctic.

A rule of biology has it that as latitude north from the equator increases, diversity decreases while abundance rises. Certainly the flies and mosquitoes of the north country prove the latter point, and the butterflies demonstrate the former. The Maritime Provinces of Canada proffer no great variety of butterflies. Some very special butterflies, however, are to be seen here in some very scenic settings. The vanishing habitat of the fisherfolk's cottage garden has been re-created along with others attractive to native butterflies in the Oxen Pond Botanic Garden at St. John's, Newfoundland (mentioned in Chapter 12). Here one can hope to see the mysterious nordic Jutta Arctic and the real specialty of the Maritimes—the colorful orange, yellow, and blue-spotted Short-tailed Swallowtail.

The related Old World Swallowtail flies across the Canadian North. One traditional locality for Far North butterflies involves a railroad journey. This is Churchill, Manitoba, on the western shore of Hudson Bay. In few other Canadian places can one get onto the arctic tundra with such relative ease. Here, on warm days, the tundra comes alive with brown-and-russet alpines, lesser fritillaries with the names of Norse deities, and certain sulphurs that live only in such places, from Siberia to Lapland, Labrador to Alaska.

Alaska itself might not seem at first thought like the most promising butterfly habitat. Only about seventy-five species live in the largest state. But as Dr. Kenelm Philip's Alaska Lepidoptera Survey has shown, this small fauna holds many interesting surprises, and certain spots are quite rich. The most visited spot for Alaska butterflies may be Eagle Summit, outside of Fairbanks toward the Brooks Range. When the Lepidopterists' Society met in Fair-

The Compton Tortoiseshell may be seen in the northeastern woods. The patterns of its underside blend beautifully with those of treebark, which it visits to rest or to drink from sap flows.

banks some years ago, a field trip to Eagle Summit took place. The members were said to have vanished into the vast tundra landscape in search of arctic varieties like raindrops on the desert. Dr. Paul Opler and others brought back some fine slides of rare arctic satyrs, sulphurs, and fritillaries. On any other day you might not see such a sight, though you might well see a net or two waving in the distance—a good field mark for prime butterfly sites. But like Denali (formerly Mount McKinley), the butterflies of the Alaskan arctic might not appear to view at all unless the sun shines on the permafrost. This can be a rare enough event, even in the short midsummer of the Midnight Sun. So watch for the clouds to clear when you travel in the North Country.

Our extended midsummer runs right down the Continental Divide, through the many national parks from Jasper to the Grand Tetons. Don't miss the Beartooth Plateau, northeast of Yellowstone in Montana, for its astonishing scenery and arctic-alpine butterflies, including American Coppers and Beartooth Fritillaries. Northern butterflies follow the cool ridges of the Rockies southward. Numberless fine butterfly habitats dot the range. Most celebrated among them, parts of Colorado, lie such that their butterflies reflect the fauna of all parts of the country. I recommend Trail Ridge Road in Rocky Mountain National Park, where motorists may gain the arctic-alpine zone with ease, trails lead for miles into the wilderness, and entirely different lowland habitats on both sides of the Continental Divide are close by. Rock Cut on Trail Ridge Road has a nature trail for tundra wildflowers where the gorgeous burnt orange Mead's Sulphur may be followed with the eye—less easily on foot at this altitude. Across the road, a rockslide noted for its ground squirrels, pikas, and marmots is the easiest place I know to see my favorite butterfly: the black velvet Magdalena Alpine. Along with the fiery orange Lustrous Copper and the Rockslide Checkerspot, Magdalena dwells only on the high country screes.

The Colorado Front Range south of there is some of the best butterfly country around. Dr. Ray Stanford's Gilpin County Fourth of July Butterfly Count routinely turns in the highest tally, very nearly one hundred species seen in a single day. Drop down any of the canyons for a taste of this diversity. Half a dozen western swallowtail species at damp gravel, hordes of silver-spotted fritillaries greedily sucking thistles, and amethyst Colorado Hairstreaks darting over the scrub oaks: These are the kinds of spectacles to be seen in canyons such as Deer Creek, Boulder, South Platte (no motors—good walking), and many others. Red Rocks Park near Denver is a particularly attractive and accessible site for most foothills butterflies. In fact, myriad mountain canyons throughout the ranges of Colorado, New Mexico, Utah, and Wyoming will be just as rewarding; not a one should be lacking the glorious black-and-white hang-glider known as Weidemeyer's Admiral or a great array of blues, hairstreaks, and pretty coppers like the Lilac-bordered, Ruddy, and Blue.

As difficult as it is to pick out special spots in the butterfly-rich Rockies, so is it a challenge to highlight the Midwest. Worthwhile butterfly areas are so numerous in the eastern hardwood zone that you can do no better than to check with the local butterfly clubs (see Appendix). The doyen of the Society of the Kentucky Lepidopterists, Dr. Charles Covell, may be able to direct you to a special hollow where the prized Diana Fritillary turns up faithfully. The sight of Diana's deep-blue female and Halloweencolored male is a magnificent spectacle I have yet to enjoy. Or the Ohio Lepidopterists may suggest a tamarack swamp where the rare Mitchell's Marsh Satyr flies in good numbers with Swamp Metalmarks and Pearl Crescents.

Possibilities have diminished over the vast Great Plains, where most of the natural grasslands have gone the way of the plowshare. The Schlitz Audubon Center in Milwaukee presents a good introduction to the Great Lakes fauna, which may be enhanced by a visit to Indiana Dunes National Lakeshore in Indiana, E. W. Teale's boyhood haunt. Other tips: Wolf Road Prairie south of Chicago; Nebraska's Sand Hills, Niobrara River, and Fontenelle Forest Preserve near Omaha; and a string of Nature Conservancy prairie preserves from Minnesota to Montana south to Kansas and Oklahoma. Perhaps the best remaining tract covers part of the Flint Hills near Wichita, proposed for a tallgrass prairie national park.

Should you find yourself in any of these prairie remnants (check with the Conservancy for directions and rules) you may be fortunate enough to see our greatest silverspot, the Regal Fritillary, nectaring among a guild of special prairie skippers on purple coneflower. These grassland specialists have all but disappeared with the native prairies. Eyed Browns and Prairie Ringlets have adapted better (except for a wet prairie race of the former, which is endangered), and you should find them with other skippers in a broader range of eastern grassy spots. At the risk of being terribly selective, I cannot resist mentioning one hot-spot in eastern Colorado where I have had some of my most pleasurable butterfly days. This is Bonny Lake Reservoir and State Park. A cottonwood-rimmed lake on the high plains, Bonny lies on the very edge of the tallgrass-shortgrass prairie interface. Truly eastern butterflies such as Queens and Pipevine Swallowtails and Little Wood Satyrs may be found there along with species of the Midwest and West, all in good numbers nectaring on extravagant stands of milkweed. Acadian Hairstreaks punctuate the flowerheads and interact with Great Gray Coppers on sultry summer afternoons.

A different kind of grassland ranges across the Great Basin, really a shrub steppe and sage desert. To find butterflies here, look for moisture, verdure, or elevation. Bear River National Wildlife Refuge in Utah, and the courses of the Colorado, Green, and Snake rivers and their tributaries, concentrate butterflies in the

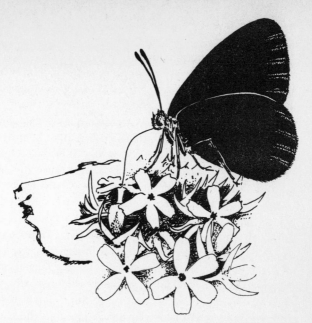

The all-black Magdalena Alpine dwells on the high-country rock-slides of the Rocky Mountains. Difficult to follow but highly rewarding to watch, Magdalena may be approached as it pauses for nectar at pink patches of moss campion.

cold desert, as this hot country is classified. And by the Snake we come to the Columbia Basin and the Pacific Northwest, where pale aridity runs into wet verdure along the Cascade Crest. As in the Rockies, the canyons cutting into the east side of the range offer the richest conditions for butterflies. The Okanogan Highlands, the Chelan country, and the Yakima area in Washington claim some 125 species of butterflies in their canyons and meadowlands, uphill from the agricultural valleylands. Short-tailed Black Swallowtails, Oregon Swallowtails, several species of buttery sulphurs, and many species of gossamer wings join checkerspots and fritillaries to make the Cascades of Washington and Oregon great butterfly country. Rise to their alpine meadows around any of the Cascade volcanoes (Mts. Baker, Rainier, Adams, Hood, and others) to see fritillaries, parnassians, alpines, and blues. Other favorites: Tiffany and Moses Meadows, Okanogan National Forest; Big Summit Prairie, Ochoco National Forest; Camp Sherman on the Metolius River; and the transcascadian pass routes.

Across Puget Sound, drive up Hurricane Ridge in Olympic National Park for a look at a rich, isolated alpine fauna. Special here, the puma-colored Valerata Arctic flies alongside cinnamon-spotted Vidler's Alpine, while pretty Sara's Orangetips drink at lush subalpine waterfalls with blues and crescents. The rain-shadowed, oak-and-grass-dominated San Juan Islands and Victoria, British Columbia, environs are totally different, though very near. Ferries go to these destinations, where butterflies are more numerous than in most of the Maritime Northwest.

The Coast Ranges to the south of the Olympic Mountains, where I live, may arguably be called the poorest butterfly region in North America. Pale Tiger Swallowtails and Clodius Parnassians, two large and attractive pale butterflies, are common here. In Oregon these subtle green hills, mostly logged off, rise a little higher and two particular eminences deserve the butterfly trekker's attention. Saddle Mountain State Park harbors isolated populations of the tawny Nevada Arctic and the stonecrop-loving Moss Elfin; and Mary's Peak, west of Corvallis, recalls to me the memorable image of Western Meadow Fritillaries nectaring prolifically on Columbia lilies with many other butterflies about. Elsewhere in Oregon, butterfliers return again and again to the Siskiyou Mountains near Ashland, the Wallawa and Blue Mountains near LaGrande, and isolated Steens Mountain—a long, high ridge on the alkali flats well east of the Cascades. Nowhere else are the desert and arctic-alpine species so closely juxtaposed, and special races of the Mormon and Hydaspe Fritillaries, Anicia and Leanira Checkerspots fly only here.

California I leave for last. The state is quintessential butterfly country, from Death Valley and Mt. Whitney to Yosemite and the Redwood Coast, wherever the state's overpopulation has not crowded out the natural habitats. All the national parks are worthwhile butterfly destinations. In Yosemite, look for the green Behr's Sulphur after snowmelt in Tuolumne Meadows. The Sierra Nevada boasts this and several other butterflies that fly nowhere else. Dozens of species flit among the giants of Sequoia National Park: As a ranger-naturalist there, I had difficulty seeing the trees for the butterflies. Mineral King Valley makes a butterfly-and-wildflower transect from chaparral to the spectacular arctic-alpine.

Parnassians are butterflies of the cool northland, restricted in the New World to the West. In the Pacific Northwest you may encounter the crimson-spotted Clodius Parnassian. This nectaring female shows the sphragis on the end of her abdomen, a device deposited by the male to keep her from mating more than once.

In California, all you have to do to find butterflies is watch for the nets. Many lepidopterists here visit the Mojave Desert in spring and the Sonoran Desert after the fall rains (e.g., Mitchell's Caverns or Anza Borrego State Park, respectively). They seek out the chaparral in June, and haunt the west slopes of the Sierra Nevada and the Trinity Alps through summer. Legendary habitats include the American and Merced rivers, Donner Pass, and the hills around the Napa Valley, where you can see Muir's Hairstreak on Sargent Cypress at Mt. St. Helena in May.

Near San Francisco, try San Bruno Mountain, Mt. Tamalpais, and any of the East Bay regional parks; around Los Angeles, the San Gabriel, San Bernardino, and Providence mountains. Or take the ferry to Santa Catalina Island. Perhaps our most narrowly restricted full species of butterfly, the Avalon Hairstreak, appears abundantly in the hills above Avalon. A unique orange-tip may be observed nearby. Seeing a few butterflies in their sole homelands can be as stimulating as watching scores of more widespread types altogether.

But the best known of all butterfly locales in California must be the Monarch groves. Celebrated in everything from granite statues and children's parades to Beach Boys' songs, the Monarchs of Monterey Bay are firmly lodged in California folklore. Citizens of Pacific Grove recently passed a bond issue to protect one of their main Monarch cluster sites, after losing others to ill-advised development. Thanks to the voters, Western Monarchs will still return to the place that calls itself "Butterfly Town, U.S.A.," to rest between their autumnal and vernal migrations. The sight of a thousand Monarchs clinging to a eucalyptus bough like their own scales to their wings will never be forgotten. Pacific Grove, Carmel, and Monterey may be the classical sites, but a larger colony can be found most winters in Santa Cruz. Here, in Natural Bridges State Park, visitors are invited to walk gently among the clusters and marvel at the tens of thousands of winter resters. West Coast Monarch groves occur from Mendocino south to Baja California. Monarch scientist John Lane and the Xerces Society's Monarch Project have surveyed these sites and worked to conserve them.

As winter-bunching Monarchs show, no part of the year is without its butterflies somewhere. One day in late January I was visiting my sister Susan and her husband, Ted Kafer, in San Jose. It looked as if I were doomed to spend that glorious sunny day watching the Super Bowl. Instead, I telephoned lepidopterist Robert Langston and asked where I could find the first new butterflies on the wing. Then I called butterfly gardener Barbara Deutsch: Could she arrange a trip? Kick-off time found us watching the incredibly brilliant Sonora Blue—a lifer for me. Minute bits of blue foil daubed with fire-engine orange flickered over the succulent Duddleyas of nearby Alum Rock Park. The Forty-niners romped, but I felt we'd had the better day.

We complete our imaginary tour just as the Monarchs begin to stir, mate, and launch their return migration. The same is happening deep in the mountains of Mexico, where the bulk of the North American population congregates in winter, in much larger numbers than the California sites hold. Before they leave, let us join them there. What better way to cross the border (and the chapter) than on the wings of a butterfly?

19

Butterfly Watching Abroad

Imagine yourself basking in the sun high on a Mexican mountainside. It is January and there is some snow in patches on the ground, yet you are warm. Still it is snowing—snowing butterflies. Monarch butterflies fill the sky and eclipse the sun; Monarchs falling, drifting, sailing, and gliding; Monarchs every shade of orange, as the sun backlights or falls full upon them: pumpkin, salmon, or flame. They alight on every surface, and every purple senecio supports a dozen drinkers, every bough a hundred baskers. Monarchs alight on your boots, your belly, your face, give you a physical and mental massage of softly beating wings. So many butterflies flutter that a soft, rushing whir fills the mountain air— yes, you can actually hear the Monarchs.

The rustle keeps up, unabated for a second, until the sun begins to fall below the firs. Only then do the millions of migrants start to settle back onto the oyamels for the night, clinging to every needle so thickly they form a pelage like reddest fox fur. Then it becomes a still world of orange butterflies—walls of Monarchs, curtains, solid tree trunks, boughs, and whole forest groves of Monarchs, with scarcely a green needle showing through. The sun goes down, and a chill rises. Having caught the last beams to warm them against it, the masses close their wings and become ashen scales against the dark foliage of the firs. It is time to descend to the valley below, to seek the warmth of a village hearth, order "una cerveza, por favor," and recount the day's adventure with friends as overwhelmed by it all as you. You will sleep well after the walk at high altitude, and dream of Monarchs—you can't help it—and for days afterward your mind will be graven with the flickers of a million moving, golden gliders. And for the rest of your life you will carry the image of the greatest butterfly show on earth among your most vivid memories.

Since 1975, when Professor Fred Urquhart of the University of Toronto and his associates found the overwintering grounds of North American Monarchs in Mexico, only a relatively small number of people have been able to see them. Out of concern for the butterflies and the possible harm that might come to them from fire or disturbance, the precise localities were at first undisclosed. In more recent years, research and conservation efforts led by Professor Lincoln P. Brower, University of Florida biologist, have brought about several Monarch reserves. The governments of Mexico, the state of Michoacan, and the local towns hope to protect this incomparable resource in perpetuity. The major threat comes from logging: either the roost trees themselves are cut or the forest is opened up, in which case it loses its ability to insulate the clusters from freezing at night. It has become evident that for the reserves plan to work, alternative forms of income must be generated to make up for the loss of timber revenue in the local economy. This means that tourism, carefully managed to avoid killing the golden geese, is inevitable. All of us involved in Monarch study and conservation believe that the spectacle should be available for the world's nature lovers to see for themselves.

A beginning has been made in this direction. Visitors may now make their way to the overwintering area, obtain a local guide (obligatory), and be taken to see a major colony that has been designated as the first tourism use and study site. All other sites will remain off limits, for purposes of protection and research, for the time being. To see the Monarchs, visit either El Rosario or Angangueo (west of Mexico City, east of Morelia, north of Zitacuaro) between November and March. Prepare for cold weather but hope for hot. The guides will find you as soon as you show up looking like gringo butterfly watchers. Spend freely. Whether on a tour or on your own, you will be part of this important experiment in ecotourism. Good luck! The roads, the weather, the vagaries of the butterflies—none is predictable.

The winter roosts of migratory Monarchs comprise the grandest of butterfly spectacles. A threatened phenomenon, the roosting occurs in coastal California and montane Mexico.

These butterflies represent the entire North American summer population, excepting those from the Far West that migrate to Californian sites. No one yet knows how they find their way. Yet, while they return to the same general area year after year, actual cluster sites may shift according to weather and perhaps other factors from year to year. A few years ago, El Rosario was thought to be all but abandoned by the butterflies; then in 1982–83, it supported the largest colony of all—some twenty acres of solid butterflies! There is no guarantee of seeing a spectacle quite like the one I describe, but you should at the very least see a great many overwintering Monarchs. They are the visible sign of one of nature's strongest, most amazing mass movements. For the first time, the miracle of Monarch migration is accessible to naturalists. Virtually our national butterfly, the Monarch—and its migratory phenomenon—can be saved only through international cooperation. It is appropriate that ordinary citizens have a chance to see the zenith of the cycle that begins anew each spring across the milkweed meadows of North America.

You would be forgiven for thinking that, after the Monarchs of Mexico, all else would be anticlimax. But butterflies, like loved ones, should never be compared outright. Each has its own unassailable charm and beauty. I have been thunderstruck each time I have visited the Monarchs of Michoacan; but I have been as moved by a single common ringlet in a golden September meadow or a blue on a clover head. So the Monarch spectacle need not spoil you for what follows. For example, subtropical swallowtails and pearly white morphos frequent the canyons below the town of Tuxpan, near the Monarchs. Much of Mexico offers superb butterfly watching, with many giant sulphurs and dozens of species of swallowtails. Any spot away from development or intensive agriculture will do nicely, at all but the driest times of year. The jungles of Chiapas are said to be the best of all, but they are going fast, as is much of the neotropical rain forest.

As you continue south, butterfly diversity soars. Costa Rica boasts over 2,500 species, including tens of brilliant blue hairstreaks and extravagant metalmarks. I was privileged to be led to a forest near San José by Dr. Paul Opler, where over a hundred species of butterflies were on the wing on a single day. In one ravine, perhaps twenty butterflies of four families were flying together, all evolved according to the same orange, yellow, and black mimicry theme. Their predators must have been as confused as I was. In the same spot, clear-winged ithomiines fluttered spectrally through the dappled jungle light, while immense eye-spotted owl butterflies perched upside down on tree trunks. Iridescently flashing preponas and green Malachites lit up the glades, as scarlet-patched longwings nectared on passion flowers or flitted along the edge. Similar assemblages may be found in several of Costa Rica's national parks, of which there is an excellent system. Monte Verde is considered by discriminating naturalists to be one of the best joint butterfly and birding places in Central America. Quetzals spread their emerald wings overhead as 88 Butterflies (named for

Certain ithomiines and satyrs of the New World tropics (this is one of the former) have lost most of their scales and become transparent. This makes them difficult to follow as they flutter among the green of the jungle, but very beautiful to observe at rest.

the pattern of 88 on their wings) and kite swallowtails crowd the puddles on the jungle floor.

My greatest butterfly thrill in Costa Rica, and one of the most memorable of my life, could just as well have occurred in the entomological paradises of Belize or Panama: my first look at a living morpho, one of the fabled metallic blue giants of the New World tropics. We were walking down a forest path in Santa Ana National Park, when a blue flash of incredible brilliance ignited straight ahead. It flashed again, then disappeared, over and over, as the sun caught the flapping wings of a big morpho. (Only at the right incidence to the light does the tinsel blue show; the wings go drab and colorless in the shade.) The powerful creature sailed right past our eyes and then out over the Caribbean, where the blues blended into a single field of sapphire sky, sea, and butterfly wing. I have seldom been so awestruck, and I was taken back to the first morpho specimen I received as a young collector. As I gazed at the lifeless but splendid specimen in its cigar box, I wondered whether I would ever see one in real life.

The legendary home of morphos is the Amazon. But in Brazil, as in much of South America, it is becoming increasingly difficult to find a patch of moist tropical forest large enough to support much of the native wildlife. Of course a trip up the Amazon, or to the middle of Rio for that matter, would prove exciting to a first-time visitor interested in insects. To experience the phenomenal richness of South American butterflies that so thrilled H. W. Bates, Darwin, and Beebe, however, you should visit a rich rain forest remnant such as Rondonia, in Brazil; then help to save it. Ecuador and Colombia have proven very popular with lepidopterist tours in recent years for the great variety and abundance they furnish in certain concentrated areas. Tinalandia, near Santo Domingo de los Colorados in western Ecuador's montane rain forest, is rapidly becoming known as a butterfly nirvana.

Of all countries, Peru may have claim to the richest assemblage of butterflies. At least 3,500 species are reckoned to live there, and that estimate is probably low. In fact, in a single two square kilometer area in the Tambopata Natural Reserve in the Department of Madre de Dios, Dr. Gerardo Lamas has recorded over 1,000 species of butterflies. Another area visited by butterfly tours for its prolific blue morphos and other brilliant butterflies is Tingo Maria Parque Nacional and vicinity. The traveler could do worse than to follow the tourists to Macchu Pichu, then descend to Iquitos in the headwaters of the Amazon to sample a share of Peru's butterfly diversity. These are the spots scheduled for delegates to an international butterfly biology conference to visit on their excursions, so they must be held in high regard by the Peruvian lepidopterists. Dr. Lamas welcomes all to come and enjoy Peru's butterflies while adding knowledge of the country's fauna. Roger Tory Peterson recommends Explorer's Lodge as a butterfly base.

Don't neglect the Latin satyrines. Soft-colored creatures in the north, in the neotropics they might be clear-winged with rose or lavender patches (*Cithaerias*), or, on the shoulders of the Andes, entirely metallic silver (*Argyrophorus argenteus*): suitable satyrs for an extravagant biology.

When visiting a challenging new country to seek butterflies, it can be a boon to go with a group or seek out lepidopterists who reside there. Usually they will be only too happy to provide tips for prime viewing localities or go out in the field with you. The membership list of the Lepidopterists' Society (see Appendix) gives names of such contacts. Butterfly-oriented tours are becoming more common, although still far fewer than those for bird-watchers. Few travelers would see South America's fabulous *Agrias* butterflies, which look like scraps of brightest red and blue foil pasted together, on their own. A leader knowledgeable about local conditions and baits could make it possible. One cautionary note: Most of the organized butterfly tours to date cater to collectors; so to avoid having the object of your devotion netted out from under your nose you may have to get away some distance from the other tour members. More and more, general nature tours are learning the value of tropical butterflies as a valuable resource. See Appendix III for tour companies.

More tours of this kind visit Africa than any other continent. A drier land with fewer forests, it hasn't the diversity of its former neighbor in Gondwanaland, South America. Nonetheless, butter-flying is good almost all over Africa except in bad droughts or where the land has been grazed clean by hoofed animals or locusts. The game parks, where most naturalists end up, abound in butter-flies, but they can be frustrating, because one is not permitted generally to walk about in them. Spotting elephants from a Land Rover is one thing, but swallowtails beg for closer inspection. So try to spend some time on the veldt outside the parks, but always watch out for larger game while on insect safari; it can be danger-ous. One particularly rewarding area is the Kenyan coast, where the Shimba Hills National Park runs down to meet Shimoni Marine National Park. There we have watched roan and sable antelope at close range in the morning, snorkled to spy on live cowries and corals in the afternoon, and made the acquaintance of dozens of new butterflies along the way.

The jungles of Zaire, Rwanda, and other central and west African nations beckon for their butterflies as well as gorillas and leopards. There, in the African rain forest, you can see some of the few truly red butterflies in the world, the flaming *Cymathoes*, and an array of the robust and colorful *Charaxes*. On Madagascar, you might be fortunate enough to see the Sunset Urania—the world's most brilliant moth—if you can find a patch of undisturbed habitat. Malagasy forests and their rich insect fauna are the subject of a Xerces Society survey and conservation project.

Another conservation project addresses the Blue Mountains of Jamaica, sole homeland of the huge Homer's Swallowtail (*Papilio homerus*). Each of the islands of the West Indies offers distinctive biology where the landscape is intact. Trinidad and Tobago, Puerto Rico, and Hispaniola, for example, are all rich in endemic butterflies.

Butterflying in Kenya and Bermuda may lead to a taste for things British as well as the desire to see the butterfly fauna upon which modern Lepidoptera studies were based. Probably the best known butterflies in the world, and consisting of only some seventy species, the British butterflies are well worth experiencing. Visit National Trust lands on the North and South Downs of Surrey, Sussex, and Kent in spring and summer to see the set of blues favoring chalk soils on these green hills. The Chalkhill Blue has a pallor as though its larvae actually took in some of the Downland chalk through their host plants, while the Adonis Blue may be the deepest, most shimmering of all the blues, like mini-morphos. They fairly swarm some years on Ranmore Common, a National Trust Site. On an English butterfly tour, eight of us reveled among rare Lady Glanville Fritillaries and Green Hairstreaks on the Isle of Wight. Here or in Bernwood Forest on the Oxfordshire-Buckinghamshire border, where two-thirds of British butterflies live, you may be richly rewarded by the sight of the Purple Emperor flying around sallows or high oaks. Monks Wood National Nature Reserve is a classic spot for watching the rare Black Hairstreak, the White Admiral, and many others. But with all the NNRs, you should gain the permission of the overseeing agency, English Nature, before entering. Not far away (both lie in western Cambridgeshire), Woodwalton Fen National Nature Reserve supports a reintroduced colony of the Large Copper. This brilliant big gossamer

*The Blue Mountains of Jamaica are home to Homer's Swallowtail, the
largest butterfly in the New World. The fortunate visitor might spot it
nectaring on garden hibiscus near the forest edge.*

wing became extinct in Britain when the extensive fens were
drained long ago; the present line comes from German stock.
Another tiny fenland remnant, Wicken Fen (north of Cambridge),
was Darwin's favorite beetle haunt. The British Swallowtail became
extinct there but may still be seen in parts of the Norfolk Broads,
an extensive system of lakelands and marshes northeast of Nor-
wich. A superb thatched visitors' center tells the story of the swallowtail. Finally, one must try to see a true English cottage garden
in high summer, where Peacock butterflies should be gathering
with Small Tortoiseshells, Red Admirals, and Commas on the Buddleia.

Continental Europe harbors many butterflies absent from Great
Britain. The Alpine ringlets, only hinted at by the Scotch Argus
of the Highlands and the Mountain Ringlet of the Lake District
in England, reach their center of diversity in the Alps. Gross
Glockner Pass in Austria, Simplon Pass in Switzerland, and the
Dolomites around Cortina in Italy will all satisfy the scenery-

seeker as well as the *Erebia* watcher. Different species occur in the Pyrenees between France and Spain, both countries rich in butterfly life. South of Madrid, on the road to Toledo, is a remnant of the original maquis vegetation known as "El Regejal." Here, in a newly cretaed reserve, you may find a very small swallowtail, *Zerynthia rumina minima,* the endemic local race of the Spanish Festoon.

The striking black, red, and cream festoons occur across the Balkans and into Asia Minor. If you were to follow a similar path, you would doubtless hear about and visit the famed Valley of the Butterflies on the Greek island of Rhodes. The so-called "butterflies" are a migratory kind of tiger moth, as brightly colored with red, yellow, brown, and white as many a nymphalid. They congregate in a certain grotto where tourists have marveled at their bright masses for a very long time.

Oases concentrate wildlife throughout the Middle East and North Africa. Ein Geddi on the Western Dead Sea Plain is one example of a biologically important oasis where many butterflies may be found. Throughout the arid Arabian Peninsula and nearby lands, moisture is the key for finding butterfly concentrations. Water multiplies to the east, all across the Indian subcontinent, and butterflies do the same. In spite of its vast human population, India teems with butterflies. Some of the rarer species, such as the superb Green Page Butterfly of the Himalaya have apparently become rarer, but many colorful common species abound. What might have been here prior to massive human alteration of the landscape? We will never know. But I am reminded of an anecdote belonging to Torben Larsen, an authority on butterflies of the Middle East. Writing of a butterfly excursion to India, he reported being so thickly surrounded by curious villagers wherever he went with his net that he found it almost impossible to use. At its most dense, the crowd exceeded one hundred. I have encountered a similar phenomenon (albeit smaller crowds) in heavily populated tropical locales. Here is where the observer has the advantage, for in such situations any visitor receives attention, but not nearly so much as a visitor with a butterfly net.

It is also worth noting that local customs, regulations, and feelings should be observed at all times. The traveler needs to be adaptable and considerate, even if this means abandoning the chase temporarily. In New Guinea I found that village boys and men often wanted to wield my net for me. The result was less than optimal, but it created a lot of good will. Edwin Way Teale believed that the best way to be a naturalist in a strange land is to be inconspicuous and unobtrusive, and this is no doubt true, although it may be difficult if your language and clothing mark you as a tourist.

Common sense and courtesy open many doors, but can't budge closed borders. With Russia, its neighbors, and China opening up, opportunities are broadening constantly. Great Graylings and Queen of Spain Fritillaries greeted me in a Turkmenian gorge, and an Asian Monarch graced the Caspian Sea tamarisk. Tibet remains mostly off-limits, but trekkers in Nepal see many butterflies among the icy summits.

In Japan, a pleasing array of large red and black swallowtails and other butterflies may be found, especially in the mountains. Quoting from W. J. Holland's 1931 *The Butterfly Book*, a digression entitled "Collecting in Japan" reads in part:

> In the morning, the drops glittering on every leaf, we started out to walk through the fields to Oiwake . . . intending to loiter all day amid the charms of nature. Seven species of lilies bloomed about us in the hedges and the fields; a hundred plants, graceful and beautiful in blossom, scented the air with their perfume, and everywhere were butterflies and bees. Above us hung in the sky a banner, the great cloud which by day and by night issues from the crater of Asama-yama; five species of Fritillaries flashed their silvery wings by copse and stream; great black Papilios soared across the meadows; blue Lycaenas, bright Chrysophani, and a dozen species of Wood-nymphs gamboled over the low herbage and among the grass.

Hong Kong is a butterfly watcher's paradise, largely because of watershed reserves that maintain native forest. Giant orangetips, Rice Paper Butterflies, and neon-winged swallowtails roam at large through the parks and gardens of this most urban and populous city. Taiwan, Korea, and the Philippines boast the many colorful species that make them centers of the butterfly curio industry. In spite of the millions of butterflies removed for these purposes, visitors claim that forested canyons in these lands remain densely populated with a rainbow of butterflies.

Just about anywhere in Southeast Asia and Indochina that has not been devastated by Agent Orange or shifting agriculture will give good butterfly results. As Alfred Russel Wallace found a century and a half ago, the whole of the Malay Archipelago exudes great allure for the entomologist. One area continually mentioned in the chronicles of traveling naturalists is the Cameron Highlands of Malaysia. Here too the butterfly trade makes itself very evident. One of its main objects is Rajah Brooke's Birdwing—a splendid emerald and black creature with a scarlet-slashed body and wings expanding more than six inches. My colleague Dr. Michael Morris of the British Institute of Terrestrial Ecology, who traveled to Malaysia and elsewhere to investigate butterfly farming, reported that Rajah Brooke's Birdwing may still be found in packs puddling beside mountain streams. What a sight to see! Another: shimmering Dead Leaf Butterflies visiting ripe papayas on the jungle floor.

I had the opportunity not long ago of working with the giant birdwing butterflies of Papua New Guinea. Here the butterfly trade takes a different shape, with farming accounting for much of the output, and habitat reserves actively set aside for birdwings and other wildlife. If the Monarchs of Mexico constitute the grandest butterfly spectacle *en masse,* the New Guinea birdwings are the greatest in size. Queen Alexandra's Birdwing, largest of all butterflies, measures up to a foot in wingspan. It inhabits the Papuan coastal plain, but its habitat is now reduced to a tiny area because of logging and oil palm planting. The males of all the birdwings display resplendent greens, golds, and/or blues, while the larger females are salt-and-pepper in color. Nowhere will you be guaranteed of seeing the rarer birdwings, but the Goliath Birdwing often makes an appearance over the cliffs of Varirata National Park, near the capital, Port Moresby; and nearby Brown River gives a good rain forest cross-section, including additional birdwing species. Over much of Papua New Guinea you will surely see the common Green and Black-and-gold Birdwings, as well as the big blue Ulysses Swallowtail—almost morpho-like, but black-velvet-bordered and -tailed. Arguably the world's loveliest butterfly, Weisk's Swallowtail dwells in the New Guinea Highlands. It is a neon-lavender and grass-green creation of incredible brilliance.

Among the most spectacular butterflies of all, the birdwings of Papua New Guinea offer an insect counterpart to the birds of paradise. Most species are rare, but the Common Green Birdwing may easily be seen over much of the island.

Mt. Kaindi, near the Wau Ecology Institute in Morobe Province, often has this butterfly hilltopping near its summit. Should you find yourself in that area, drop in on the Insect Farming and Trading Agency at Bulolo, where entomologists may be able to direct you to prime butterfly spots or an operating butterfly farm.

Elsewhere in the New Guinea Highlands, Mt. Wilhelm National Park offers fine trails and a rich array of the beautiful *Delias* butterflies—colorful relatives of our humble whites. Bayer River Bird of Paradise Sanctuary promises not only the celebrated birds but also many Highland butterflies such as forest nymphs and kites. As you descend from the Highlands, consider visiting the islands. Bougaineville has its own special birdwing, Queen Victoria's. A cruise to the Trobriands, New Britain, or Manus will enable you to see many tropical swallowtails, coke-bottle green relatives of the Monarch known as crows, huge amethyst hairstreaks, and the pearl-and-ruby swallowtail called *Cressida*. Papua New Guinea (and Irian Jaya, the Indonesian half of the island) is a kind of butterfliers' Valhalla—the place to go if ever all else should seem commonplace.

Perhaps you will be able to visit Australia, but not New Guinea. You can still see Green Birdwings and Ulysses Swallowtails in the rain forest of North Queensland, where the jungle is New Guinean. Perhaps no other place, for an American, combines such ease of travel with such a degree of novelty and natural diversity as Australia. So varied are the butterflies, so many the good spots to go, that I cannot begin to choose for you. Townsville offers the best snorkling reefs anywhere (for butterfly fish) alongside rich bird and butterfly forests. Beyond that I recommend simply wandering wide-eyed or consulting the government entomologists of Commonwealth Scientific and Industrial Research Organization (CSIRO) in Canberra or the entomological societies for hot tips.

Tasmania and New Zealand have subtler butterfly faunas, but number among them some fascinating satyrs in the mountain and southern beech forest parks. South Island's alps even has a butterfly so similar to the Alpine *Erebia* that it was first considered to be one. Later, when it was realized that this could not possibly be, it was renamed *Erebiola*. Seek it among the alpine tussocks.

A leap across the water brings us back to our own land in mid-Pacific. Hawaii, as the most isolated major islands in the world, never evolved a diverse butterfly fauna. You might expect this tropical paradise to be butterfly heaven; in fact, only two native butterflies live there. Happily, unlike many Hawaiian birds and snails, both are common and widespread. The Kamehameha Butterfly, named after a legendary Hawaiian king, is a large and deeply colorful version of a Painted Lady or Red Admiral. Both these relatives have been introduced, so you can see them all together, to the Kamehameha's distinct advantage. Blackburn's Bluet, a charming mite, shows bright green beneath and brilliant blue above. You can find both native butterflies together in Kipuka Puluau, an island of older forest vegetation surrounded by lava flows in Hawaii Volcanoes National Park on the island of Hawaii. There I have seen Blackburn's Bluets by the dozens flitting and ovipositing on a host, as some sixty Kamehamehas sucked sap from seeping *Hibiscadelphus* trees.

Although only two species of butterflies were involved, this was one of my most memorable butterfly watching experiences. Only two butterflies—yet of such color and vibrancy that the encounter rivaled a fifty-species day in Colorado, a birdwing morning in Papua New Guinea or a Monarch time in Mexico. But as I said before, one mustn't compare too closely. Each butterfly watching experience is individual, each is a whole unto itself, a unique vision that can never be duplicated or taken away. And here is the treasure and the joy of butterfly watching. No matter where you do it, no matter how common or tattered the subject, the moment is a pure and unique encounter—just you and the butterfly. Whether you use a net, a lens, your eyes, or some other sense to "catch" it—no matter that it may fly away afterward—the image, scent, or touch of the butterfly will be yours. And your life will be richer for it.

I hope you will have the opportunity to hear the whir of the Monarchs' wings in Mexico one day. But even if it is only the click of a Mourning Cloak taking flight in your own backyard, hearken to Tennyson:

> *Hast thou heard the butterflies*
> *What they say betwixt their wings?*

Listen. And watch.

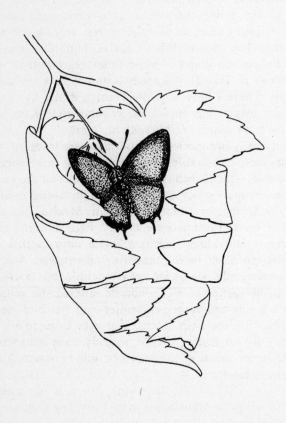

Epilogue

Recently I visited a forest above a deep lake in Olympic National Park, Washington. A small, purplish-brown butterfly known as Nelson's Hairstreak flew more abundantly than I have seen it before, along the forest road. I watched it at length. Visiting vine maple, the hairstreaks clambered over the palmate leaves sucking up shiny droplets of sap exuded from the leaves. They visited the red-and-white panicles of the maple flowers themselves as well, digging in to drink deeply. As I watched them tip over to bask toward the southwest sun, interact, nectar, and otherwise carry on, I learned new things about this common butterfly. I also re-learned something about myself, something always partly forgotten over the long winter.

There is serenity to be found in butterflies. Watching Nelson's Hairstreak that afternoon I achieved a degree of tranquility that I hadn't enjoyed for a long time. Perhaps it amounts to a kind of meditation, with butterfly as mantra. Or is it Thoreau's transcendental tonic? The peace of Pan? Whatever, it lent a profound personal serenity whose palliative effect I felt long afterward.

My own approach to peace calls for personal responsibility to be peaceable. I believe that no one filled with the love of nature can become very interested in violence. Many retired soldiers have become lepidopterists, but I have never known of a butterfly-lover who started a war. Butterflies offer serenity to anyone willing to seek it. And in that way, they offer a broader promise of peace in a world more reverential of nature than ours.

Appendix:
Help for Butterfly Watchers

I. BUTTERFLY CLUBS

By joining these groups you will be able to meet other butterfly enthusiasts in your area, learn of meetings or outings, and keep up on current information and new findings through their journals and newsletters. Check with your nearest natural history museum or university to find out about community entomology groups in the area, and to learn of insect displays and events.

The Lepidopterists' Society. This is the primary international learned society connected with butterflies and moths. Publishes *News* and *Journal of the Lepidopterists' Society.* Membership information: Fay H. Karpuleon, 1521 Blanchard, Mishiwaka, IN 46544.

Lepidoptera Research Foundation. Promotes better understanding of the Lepidoptera through dissemination of information. Publishes *Journal of Research on the Lepidoptera.* Membership information: Santa Barbara Museum of Natural History, 2559 Puesta del Sol Rd., Santa Barbara, CA 93105.

The Xerces Society. Dedicated to the conservation of rare invertebrates and their habitats, emphasizing butterflies. Publishes the newsletter *Wings* and the journal *Atala.* Membership information: Xerces Society, 10 S.W. Ash Street, Portland, OR 97204.

Southern Lepidopterists' Society. Promotes scientific interest and knowledge related to understanding the Lepidoptera fauna of the southern region of the United States. Publishes *Southern Lepidopterists' News*. Membership information: Secretary-Treasurer, Tom Neal, 3820 NW 16th Place, Gainesville, FL 32605.

Society of Kentucky Lepidopterists. Organizes field trips and gatherings, publishes *Kentucky Lepidopterist*. Membership information: Dr. C. V. Covell, Jr., Dept. of Biology, University of Louisville, Louisville, KY 40292.

The Ohio Lepidopterists. Involved in field trips, development of collections and inventory, conservation and communication. Publishes *The Ohio Lepidopterist* and research reports. Membership information: Eric Metzler, 1241 Kildale Sq. N., Columbus, OH 43229.

Utah Lepidopterists' Society. Holds monthly meetings, encourages study and discussion, and actively pursues mapping of Utah butterflies. Publishes *Utahensis,* a bulletin. Membership information: Joel M. Johnson, 59 East 400 North, Payson, UT 84651.

High Country Lepidopterists. Devoted to the study and conservation of the Lepidoptera of the High Plains and Rocky Mountain states. Membership information: Dr. Paul A. Opler, 5100 Greenview Court, Fort Collins, CO 80503.

Idalia Society of Mid-American Lepidopterists. Open to all with an interest in butterflies and moths of the central states. Publishes a newsletter, *Idalia.* Membership information: Suzette Slokomb, 219 W. 68th St., Kansas City, MO 64113.

Nebraska Lepidopterists' Newsletter. C/o Steve Spomer, 1235 N. 50th St., Lincoln, NB 68504.

New York City Butterfly Club. C/o Guy Tudor, 111-14 76th Ave., # 107, Forest Hills, NY 11375.

Northwest Lepidopterists' Association. A loose confederation of Pacific Northwesterners interested in the order. Publishes occasional bulletin. Contact Wayne P. Wehling, SE 535 Jackson St., Pullman, WA 99163.

Association for Tropical Lepidopterists. Publishes the color journal *Tropical Lepidoptera* and promotes study of this subject. Contact John Heppner, 4300 NW 23rd Ave., Suite 100, Gainesville, FL 32606.

Butterfly Conservation (formerly British Butterfly Conservation Society). Dedicated to perpetuation of British butterflies and their habitats. Contact Director Andrew Phillips, P.O. Box 222, Dedham, Colchester, Essex CO7 6EY, England.

In addition, two general entomology groups offer a great deal of encouragement and information to students of the Lepidoptera:

Sonoran Arthropod Studies, Inc., P.O. Box 5624, Tucson, AZ 85703.

Young Entomologists' Society. 19 Peggy Place, Lansing, MI 48910.

Many cities and states lacking a Lepidoptera club nonetheless have entomological societies. Commonly, many of the members will be interested in butterflies and moths. Seek these groups out, or consider starting your own butterfly interest group. Don't be put off by the "professional" sound of the societies; all of them welcome fully amateur and beginnning members as well as experts. The membership lists of the Lepidopterists' Society and the Xerces Society will give you the means of contacting other butterfly lovers in your town or state, whether or not they have formed a club. There is no substitute for companionship in building enthusiasm, knowledge, and enjoyment.

II. FURTHER READING

A book of this length addressing a broad topic can only begin to introduce the many subjects it discusses. Many readers will wish to pursue these subjects in greater detail. While a complete bibliography is beyond the scope of this appendix, here you will find several sources for greater understanding of each chapter heading. In your reading, always check the bibliographies for additional titles you might not know but will wish to seek out. The journals and newsletters of the societies mentioned above are full of articles further expanding on various butterfly topics, and deserve close attention. While only a few titles can be given here, your own research will quickly reveal many pertinent writings. Some areas, little explored or written about to date, await the pen of observant future butterfly watchers.

CHAPTER 1: *Why Watch Butterflies?*

Hewes, Laurence Ilsley. 1936. Butterflies: try and get them. *National Geographic* 109:667–78.

Matthews, Patrick. 1957. *The Pursuit of Moths and Butterflies:* an anthology. Chatto and Windus, London.

Measures, David. 1976. *Bright Wings of Summer.* Prentice-Hall, NJ.

Nabokov, Vladimir. 1966. *Speak Memory:* An autobiography revisited. See chapter, "Butterflies." Putnam, New York.

CHAPTER 2: *About Butterflies*

Brewer, Jo. 1976. *Butterflies.* Abrams, New York.

Brewer, Jo. 1967. *Wings in the Meadow.* Houghton Mifflin, Boston.

Brewer, Jo, and Dave Winter. 1986. *Butterflies and Moths: A Companion to Your Field Guide.* Prentice Hall, New York.

Dickens, Michael, and Eric Storey. 1972. *The World of Butterflies.* Macmillan, New York.

Douglas, Matthew M. 1986. *The Lives of Butterflies.* U. of Michigan Press, Ann Arbor.

Ehrlich, Paul R., and Peter H. Raven. 1967. Butterflies and plants. *Scientific American* 216:104–113.

Ehrlich, Paul R., et al. 1975. Checkerspot butterflies: a historical perspective. *Science* 188:221–28.

Emmel, Thomas C. 1975. *Butterflies:* Their world, their life cycle, their behavior. Knopf, New York.

Ford, E. B. 1975. *Butterflies.* Revised edition. Collins, Glasgow.

Gilbert, Lawrence E., and Michael C. Singer. 1975. Butterfly ecology. *Annual Review of Ecology and Systematics* 6:365–97.

Nijhout, H. Frederick. 1991. *The Development and Evolution of Butterfly Wing Patterns.* Villard, New York.

Owen, D. F. 1971. *Tropical Butterflies.* Clarendon, Oxford.

Sbordoni, Valerio, and Saverio Forestiero. 1988. *The Butterflies of the World.* Crescent, New York.

Smart, Paul. 1991. *The Illustrated Encyclopedia of the Butterfly World.* Crescent, New York.

Urquhart, Fred A. 1987. *The Monarch Butterfly: International Traveler.* Nelson Hall, Chicago.

Vane-Wright, R. I., and P. R. Ackery, eds. 1983. *The Biology of Butterflies.* Royal Entomological Society Symposium 11, London.

Watson, Allan, and Paul E. S. Whalley. 1975. *The Dictionary of Butterflies and Moths in Color.* McGraw-Hill, New York.

Williams, C. B. 1930. *The Migration of Butterflies.* Oliver and Boyd, Edinburgh and London.

CHAPTER 3: **Watching versus Catching**

Morris, Michael G. 1976. Conservation and the collector. In *The Moths and Butterflies of Great Britain and Ireland,* ed. J. Heath, Vol. 1. Curwen/Blackwell, London.

Pyle, R., M. Bentzien, and P. Opler. 1981. Insect conservation. *Annual Review of Entomology* 26:233–58.

Rindge, Frederick H. 1965. The importance of collecting—now. *Journal of the Lepidopterists' Society* 19:193–95.

Xerces Society Policy on Insect Collecting. 1975. *Atala* 3:24.

CHAPTER 4: **How to Find Butterflies**

The annual Season's Summary published in the *News of the Lepidopterists' Society,* the Fourth of July Butterfly Count reports published by the Xerces Society, and contact with other lepidopterists through the clubs listed above will prove helpful here. Regional, state, and local butterfly books often name productive localities, as do the newsletters of the butterfly clubs. Bird-finding guides such as those listed in Stephen Kress's *Audubon Society Handbook for Birders* (Scribners 1981) will guide the butterfly watcher as well as the bird-watcher to useful sites. Also note the places selected for field trips by native plant societies and other natural history clubs.

CHAPTER 5: **Watching Butterflies**

Newman, L. Hugh. 1977. *Looking at Butterflies.* Collins, London.

Pyle, Robert Michael. 1974. *Watching Washington Butterflies.* Seattle Audubon Society.

Whalley, Paul. 1980. *Butterfly Watching.* Severn House, London.

CHAPTER 6: **Butterfly Watching Equipment**

Gray, Alice. Direction Leaflets published by the American Museum of Natural History, Department of Insects and Spiders. These pertain largely to collecting techniques, but apply to observation equipment as well.

Heath, J. 1970. *Insect Light Traps*. Amateur Entomologists' Society Leaflet No. 33. Available, along with other helpful leaflets and handbooks, from the AES Publications Agent, 137 Gleneldon Road, Streatham, London SW 16, England.

Platt, Austin P. 1969. A lightweight collapsible bait trap for Lepidoptera. *Journal of the Lepidopterists' Society* 23:97–101.

Townes, H. 1972. A lightweight Malaise trap. *Entomologists' News* (U.K.) 83:239–47.

The Brown Company, Yawgoo Pond Road, West Kingston, Rhode Island 02892, offers butterfly hibernation boxes, nectaring stations, and field guides. Also helpful are the catalogues of such supply firms as Bioquip Products (P.O. Box 61, Santa Monica, CA 90406) and Carolina Biological Supply Company (Burlington, NC 27215).

Chapter 7: *Names and Identification*

Bailowitz, Richard A., and James P. Brock. 1991. *Butterflies of Southeastern Arizona*. Sonoran Arthropod Studies, Tucson.

Christensen, James R. 1981. *A Field Guide to Butterflies of the Pacific Northwest*. U. of Idaho Press, Moscow.

Dornfeld, Ernst J. 1980. *The Butterflies of Oregon*. Timber Press, Portland.

Ebner, James A. 1970. *The Butterflies of Wisconsin*. Milwaukee Public Museum.

Ehrlich, Paul R., and Anne H. Ehrlich. 1961. *How to Know the Butterflies*. Wm. C. Brown, Dubuque.

Emmel, Thomas C., and John F. Emmel. 1973. *The Butterflies of Southern California*. Natural History Museum of Los Angeles County.

Ferris, Clifford D., and F. Martin Brown, eds. 1980. *Butterflies of the Rocky Mountain States*. U. of Oklahoma Press, Norman.

Garth, John S., and J. W. Tilden, 1986. *The Butterflies of California*. U. of California Press, Berkeley.

Harris, Lucien, Jr. 1972. *Butterflies of Georgia*. U. of Oklahoma Press, Norman.

Heitzman, John Richard, and Joan E. 1987. *Butterflies and Moths of Missouri*. Missouri Dept. of Conservation, Jefferson City.

Hooper, Ronald. 1973. *Butterflies of Saskatchewan*. Saskatchewan Museum of Natural History, Regina.

Howe, William H., ed. 1975. *The Butterflies of North America*. Doubleday, New York.

Kimball, Charles P. 1965. *Lepidoptera of Florida*. Florida Dept. of Agriculture, Gainesville.

Klots, Alexander B. 1951. *A Field Guide to the Butterflies of North America, East of the Great Plains*. Houghton Mifflin, Boston.

Macy, Ralph W., and Harold H. Shepard. 1941. *Butterflies:* A handbook of the butterflies of the United States, complete for the region north of the Potomac and Ohio rivers and east of the Dakotas. U. of Minnesota Press, Minneapolis.

Miller, Jacqueline, ed. 1992. *The Common Names of North American Butterflies*. Xerces Society/Smithsonian Institution Press, Washington.

Miller, Lee D., and F. Martin Brown. 1981. *A Catalogue/Checklist of the Butterflies of America North of Mexico*. The Lepidopterists' Society, Memoir No. 2.

Mitchell, Robert T., and Herbert S. Zim. 1964. *Butterflies and Moths:* a guide to the more common American species. A Golden Nature Guide, Golden Press, New York.

Morris, Ray F. 1980. *Butterflies and Moths of Newfoundland and Labrador*. Agriculture Canada, Hull.

Opler, Paul A. 1992. *A Field Guide to Eastern Butterflies*. Houghton Mifflin, Boston.

Opler, Paul A., and G. O. Krizek. 1984. *Butterflies East of the Plains:* An Illustrated Natural History. Johns Hopkins University Press, Baltimore.

Peterson, Roger Tory, Robert Michael Pyle, and Sarah Anne Hughes. 1983. *A Field Guide to the Butterflies Coloring Book*. Houghton Mifflin, Boston.

Pyle, Robert Michael. 1981. *The Audubon Society Field Guide to the Butterflies of North America*. Knopf, New York.

Pyle, Robert Michael. 1974. *Watching Washington Butterflies*. Seattle Audubon Society.

Royer, Ronald A. 1988. *The Butterflies of North Dakota*. Minot State University, Minot.

Scott, James A. 1986. *The Butterflies of North America.* Stanford University Press, Palo Alto.

Shapiro, Arthur M. 1974. *Butterflies and Skippers of New York State.* Cornell University, Ithaca.

Shull, Ernest M. 1987. *Butterflies of Indiana.* Indiana Academy of Science, Bloomington/Indianapolis.

Tilden, J. W., and Arthur C. Smith. 1986. *A Field Guide to Western Butterflies.* Houghton Mifflin, Boston.

There are many additional titles dealing with the butterflies of states, provinces, and regions, and new ones appearing annually. Check your library and bookseller to keep up with these.

CHAPTER 8: *Records and Field Notes*

Crawford, R. L. 1982. A scientific system for recording specimen collection localities. *Proceedings of the Washington State Entomological Society* 44:630–32. (Also see *Systematic Zoology,* December 1983.)

Heath, John. 1971. *Instructions for Recorders.* Nature Conservancy, Biological Records Centre (Monks Wood Exper. Stat., Huntingdon, Cambs., England). Also see other publications of the BRC.

Herman, Steven G. 1980. *The Naturalist's Field Journal: A Manual of Instruction Based on a System Established by Joseph Grinnell.* Buteo Books, Vermillion, S.D.

Pyle, Robert Michael. 1982. Collections and Field Notes. In *Interpreting the Environment,* ed. Grant W. Sharpe. Wiley, New York.

CHAPTER 9: *Listing and Mapping*

Heath, John, and J. A. Thomas. 1984. *The Atlas of Butterflies of Britain and Ireland.* Penguin, London.

Heath, John, and Paul T. Harding. 1981. The Biological Records Centre and insect recording. *Atala* 7:47–48.

Lutz, Frank E. 1941. *A Lot of Insects.* Putnam, New York.

Pyle, Robert Michael. 1982. Butterfly ecogeography and biological conservation in Washington. *Atala* 8:1–26.

Stanford, Ray E. County dot atlases of western North American butterflies. Self-published, updated periodically. Contact R. E. Stanford, 720 Fairfax, Denver, CO 80220.

Chapter 10: *Counting Butterflies*

Ehrlich, Paul R., and Susanne Davidson. 1960. Techniques for capture-recapture studies of Lepidoptera populations. *Journal of the Lepidopterists' Society* 14:227–29.

Nielsen, Vanessa, and Julian Monge-Najera. 1991. A comparison of four methods to evaluate butterfly abundance, using a tropical community. *Journal of the Lepidopterists' Society* 45:241–43.

Owen, D. F. 1975. Estimating the abundance and diversity of butterflies. *Biological Conservation* 8:173–83.

Pollard, E. 1981. Monitoring changes in butterfly numbers. *Atala* 7:68–69.

Sheppard, P. M., and J. A. Bishop. 1973. The study of populations of Lepidoptera by capture-recapture methods. *Journal of Research on the Lepidoptera* 12:135–44.

Swengel, Ann B. 1990. "Monitoring Butterfly Populations Using the Fourth of July Butterfly Count." *American Midland Naturalist* 124:395–406.

Xerces Society, Fourth of July Butterfly Count Instructions and Reports. Information from the Xerces Society, address above.

Chapter 11: *Butterfly Behavior*

Chinery, Michael. 1989. *Butterflies and Day-flying Moths of Britain and Europe*. U. of Texas Press, Austin.

Davies, N. B. 1978. Territorial defense in the speckled wood butterfly (*Pararge argia*): The resident always wins. *Animal Behavior* 26:138–47.

Dowdeswell, W. H. 1981. *The Life of the Meadow Brown*. Heinemann, London.

Evans, Howard Ensign. 1968. *Life on a Little-Known Planet*. Dutton, New York.

Gilbert, L. E. 1972. Pollen feeding and reproductive biology of *Heliconius* butterflies. *Proceedings of the National Academy of Science* 69:1403–07.

Rothschild, Miriam. 1967. Mimicry. *Natural History*, February.

Scott, J. A. 1974. Mate locating behavior in butterflies. *American Midland Naturalist* 91:103–17.

Shields, Oakley. 1967. Hilltopping. *Journal of Research on the Lepidoptera* 6:69–178.

Tinbergen, Niko. 1969. *Curious Naturalists*. Doubleday, New York.

CHAPTER 12: *Butterfly Gardening*

Brewer, Jo. 1979. Bringing butterflies to the garden. *Horticulture,* May.

Brewer, Jo. 1982. *Butterfly Gardening*. Xerces Society Self-Help Sheet No. 7.

Collman, Sharon J. 1983. The butterfly's world. Notes of a butterfly gardener. *University of Washington Arboretum Bulletin* 46 (2):16–26.

Cribb, Peter, ed. 1982. How to encourage butterflies to live in your garden. *Insect Conservation News* (Amateur Entomologists' Society, UK) 6:4–10.

Donahue, Julian P. 1976. Take a butterfly to lunch. A guide to butterfly gardening in Los Angeles. (Includes poster.) *Terra* (Natural History Museum of Los Angeles County) 14(3):3–12 plus poster.

Heal, Henry George. 1973. An experiment in conservation education: the Drum Manor Butterfly Garden. *International Journal of Environmental Studies* 4:223–29.

Jackson, Bernard S. 1981. The Oxen Pond Botanic Park as a reserve for common native butterflies. *Atala* 7:15–22.

Kulman, H. M. 1977. Butterfly production management. *U. Minnesota Agricultural Experiment Station Technical Bulletin* 310:39–47.

National Wildlife Federation. 1974. *Gardening with Wildlife*. NWF, Washington, D.C.

Owen, Denis F. 1976. Conservation of butterflies in garden habitats. *Environmental Conservation* 3(4):285–90.

Reinhard, Harriet V. 1970. Gardening for butterflies. *Pacific Horticulture* 48 (4).

Rothschild, Miriam, and Clive Farrell. 1983. *The Butterfly Gardener*. Michael Joseph / Rainbird, London.

Schneck, Marcus. 1990. *Butterflies: How to Identify and Attract Them to Your Garden*. Rodale Press, Emmaus, Pennsylvania.

Sedenko, Jerry. 1991. *The Butterfly Garden*. Villard, New York.

Teale, Edwin Way. 1942. *Near Horizons*. The story of an insect garden. Dodd, Mead, New York.

Tekulsky, Mathew. 1985. *The Butterfly Garden*. Harvard Common Press, Boston.

Tufts, Craig. 1988. *The Backyard Naturalist*. National Wildlife Federation, Washington.

Tylka, Dave. 1987. *Butterfly Gardening and Conservation*. Missouri Dept. of Conservation, Jefferson City.

Xerces Society and Smithsonian Institution (various authors). 1990. *Butterfly Gardening: Creating Summer Magic in Your Garden*. Sierra Club Books, San Francisco, and National Wildlife Federation, Washington.

CHAPTER 13: *Rearing Butterflies*

(References for moth-rearing are given here too, since the techniques are similar.)

Crotch, W. J. B. 1956. *A Silkmoth Rearer's Handbook*. The Amateur Entomologist 12:1–165.

Dickson, Richard. 1976. *A Lepidopterists' Handbook*. Amateur Entomologists' Society (U.K.).

Dirig, Robert. 1975. *Growing Moths*. 4H Members' Guide M-6-6. New York State College of Agriculture and Life Sciences, Cornell University, Ithaca, New York.

Oliver, Charles G. 1983. Culturing satyrids. *News of the Lepidopterists' Society*, May/June. (Also see this newsletter for the periodical feature "Culture Corner," of which this article is an example.)

Stone, John L. S., and H. J. Midwinter. 1975. *Butterfly Culture*. A guide to breeding butterflies, moths, and other insects. Blandford Press, Poole, Dorset, U.K.

Villiard, Paul. 1969. *Moths and How to Rear Them*. Funk and Wagnall, New York.

Monarch butterfly livestock can be obtained from Merle's Monarchs, 1030 Neil Creek Road, Ashland, OR 97520.

CHAPTER 14: *Butterfly Photography*

Allen, James. 1985. How to photograph butterflies. *Terra* 23(5):25–30.

Blackford, William M. 1986. Techniques in butterfly photography. *PSA Journal*, March, 20–23.

Dalton, Stephen. 1975. *Borne on the Wind.* The extraordinary world of insects in flight. Reader's Digest Press, New York.

Findlay, J. A. 1980–81. Butterfly photography in the field—theory and practice. (Parts 1–3). *News* of the British Butterfly Conservation Society, October, April, October. (This is a very detailed and worthwhile set of articles. The *News* often contains other articles pertaining to butterfly photography, rearing and watching as well as conservation. Address: BBCS, Tudor House, Quorn, Loughborough, Leicestershire, England LE12 8AD.)

Hall, John. 1978. Caught in action. *New Scientist,* 21 September (concerns the photography of Stephen Dalton).

Meyer, Gladys L. 1989. Moth and butterfly photography. *PSA Journal,* May, 15–17.

Shaw, John. 1984. Splendor in the grass: Tips from a professional on how to photograph insects. *Blaire & Ketchum's Country Journal,* June.

Shin, Chin Fah. 1987. Using a butterfly shooter: How you can get good shots of butterflies and other flighty subjects. *PSA Journal,* July, 24–27.

Sunset Magazine. 1977. The fascinating insect world in your garden. May.

Zuckerman, Jim. 1989. Butterflies: They're spectacular and they're free! *Peterson's Photographic Magazine,* June, 54–58.

CHAPTER 15: *Butterfly Conservation*

Brewer, Jo. 1972. How to kill a butterfly. *Audubon* 74(2):77–88.

Collins, N. M., and J. A. Thomas, eds. 1991. *The Conservation of Insects and Their Habitats.* Academic Press, Troy, Missouri.

Ehrlich, Paul R., and Anne H. Ehrlich. 1981. *Extinction: The Causes and Consequences of the Disappearance of Species.* Random House, New York, NY.

Fry, Reg, and David Lonsdale, eds. 1991. *Habitat Conservation for Insects—A Neglected Green Issue.* Amateur Entomologists' Society, Colchester, England.

Orsak, Larry. 1981. Why save an insect? *Xerces Society Educational Leaflet* No. 7. Also see other leaflets by the same author.

Pyle, Robert Michael. 1975. Create a community butterfly reserve.

Xerces Society Self-Help Sheet No. 4. Also see other X.S. Self-Help Sheets.

Pyle, Robert Michael. 1976. Conservation of Lepidoptera in the United States. *Biological Conservation* 9:55–75.

Pyle, Robert Michael. 1981. Butterflies: Now you see them . . . *International Wildlife,* January/February.

Pyle, R. M., M. Bentzien, and P. Opler. 1981. Insect conservation. *Annual Review of Entomology* 26:233–58.

Soulé, Michael E., and Bruce A. Wilcox, eds. 1980. *Conservation Biology:* an evolutionary-ecological perspective. Sinauer, Sunderland, MA.

Vietmeyer, Noel D., ed. 1983. *Butterfly Farming in Papua New Guinea.* National Academy Press, Washington, D.C.

Wells, Susan M., Robert M. Pyle, and N. Mark Collins. 1983. *The IUCN Invertebrate Red Data Book.* IUCN, Gland, Switzerland.

CHAPTER 16: *Teaching and Learning with Butterflies*

Ayars, James S., and Milton W. Sanderson. 1964. *Butterflies, skippers and moths.* Whitman, Racine, WI.

Best, Richard L. 1978. *Living Arthropods in the Classroom.* Carolina Biological Supply Co., Burlington, N.C. / Gladstone, Oregon.

Braus, Judy, ed. 1986. Incredible insects. *Ranger Rick's Naturescope* 1(1):1–65.

Brewer, Jo. 1967. *Wings in the Meadow.* Houghton Mifflin, Boston.

Farb, Peter. 1959. *The Story of Butterflies and Other Insects.* Harvey House, New York.

Klots, Alexander B. 1951. *A Field Guide to the Butterflies of North America, East of the Great Plains.* Houghton Mifflin, Boston.

Lemmon, Robert S. 1956. *All About Moths and Butterflies.* Random House, New York.

National Wildlife Federation. 1978. Official birds, mammals, trees, flowers, insects, and fish of the U.S., Territories and Possessions. Leaflet available from NWF, 1412 Sixteenth Street, Washington, D.C. 20036.

Simon, Hilda. 1969. *Milkweed Butterflies: Monarchs, Models and Mimics.* Vanguard, New York.

Stokes, Donald, and Lillian and Ernest Williams. 1991. *The Butterfly Book.* Little, Brown, Boston.

Teale, Edwin Way. 1953. *The Junior Book of Insects*. Dutton, New York.

Xerces Society. Educational leaflets, self-help sheets. See address above under "Butterfly Clubs."

Chapter 17: *Moths—Learning to Love Them*

Covell, Charles V., Jr. 1984. *A Field Guide to the Moths of Eastern North America*. Houghton Mifflin, Boston.

Dickens, Michael, and Eric Storey. 1975. *The World of Moths*. Macmillan, New York.

Dominick, R. B., D. C. Ferguson, R. W. Hodges, et al. 1971. *The Moths of America North of Mexico*. Wedge Entomological Research Foundation, Washington. A series in 41 fascicles, in progress. Major fascicles completed to date include silkmoths and sphinx moths. Information from E. W. Classey Ltd., P.O. Box 93, Faringdon, Oxon. SN7 7DR, England.

Holland, W. J. 1968 edition (orig. publ. 1903). *The Moth Book*. A guide to the moths of North America. Dover, New York.

Mitchell, Robert T., and Herbert S. Zim. 1964. *Butterflies and Moths: A Guide to the More Common American Species*. Golden Press, New York.

Novak, Ivo. 1980. *A Field Guide in Colour to Butterflies and Moths*. Octopus, London.

Porter, Gene Stratton. 1912. *Moths of the Limberlost*. Doubleday, Page, New York.

Sargent, Theodore D. 1976. *Legion of Night: The Underwing Moths*. U. of Massachusetts Press, Amherst.

Chapter 18: *Great North American Butterfly Spots*

(Also see titles and suggestions given for Chapters 4 and 7.)

Benedict, Audrey DeLella. 1991. *A Sierra Club Naturalist's Guide to the Southern Rockies*. Sierra Club Books, San Francisco. (Also see other titles in this series, such as Stephen Whitney's for the Sierra Nevada.)

Frome, Michael. Annual editions. *Rand McNally National Park Guide*. Rand McNally, Chicago, New York, San Francisco.

Glassberg, Jeffrey. 1992. *A Guide to the Butterflies of the Washington—*

New York–Boston Corridor: How to Find and Identify Them in the Field. Cornell University Press, Ithaca (tentative title and date).

Hilts, Len. 1976. *Rand McNally National Forest Guide.* Rand McNally, Chicago, New York, San Francisco.

Perry, John, and Jane Greverus Perry. 1983. *The Sierra Club Guide to the Natural Areas of Oregon and Washington.* Sierra Club Books, San Francisco. (The Perrys have also written natural areas guides for California and the Eastern States.)

Peterson, Roger Tory, and James Fisher. 1955. *Wild America.* Houghton Mifflin, Boston.

Riley, Laura, and William Riley. 1979. *Guide to the National Wildlife Refuges.* Anchor Press/Doubleday, New York.

Stephenson, Marylee. 1983. *Canada's National Parks: A Visitor's Guide.* Prentice-Hall Canada, Scarborough, Ontario. (Gives special attention to insects.)

Sutton, Ann, and Myron Sutton. 1974. *Wilderness Areas of North America.* Funk and Wagnall, New York.

Also see the annual Season's Summaries in the *News* of the Lepidopterists' Society, and the Fourth of July Butterfly Counts of the Xerces Society.

CHAPTER 19: *Butterfly Watching Abroad*

Brown, F. Martin, and Bernard Heineman. 1972. *Jamaica and Its Butterflies.* E. W. Classey, Faringdon, England.

Corbet, A. S., and E. M. Pendelbury. Revised by J. N. Eliot, 1978. *The Butterflies of the Malay Peninsula.* Oliver and Boyd, London.

D'Abrera, Bernard. 1984. *Butterflies of South America.* Hill House, Victoria, Australia.

D'Abrera, Bernard. *Butterflies of the World.* A series in progress. Volumes now or soon available for the Australian, Afrotropical, and Neotropical regions. Inquire of E. W. Classey Ltd., P.O. Box 93, Faringdon, Oxon. SN7 7DR, England.

Daccordi, Mauro, Paulo Triberti, and Adriano Zanetti. 1987. *Simon and Schuster Guide to Butterflies and Moths.* Simon and Schuster, New York.

DeVries, Philip J. 1987. *The Butterflies of Costa Rica and Their Natural History: Papilionidae, Pieridae, Nymphalidae.* Princeton University Press, New Jersey.

Higgins, L. G., and N. D. Riley. 1980. *A Field Guide to the Butterflies of Britain and Europe*. Collins, London. (A simpler, updated version by Lionel Higgins and Brian Hargreaves is also available; Collins, 1983.)

Lewis, H. L. 1973. *Butterflies of the World*. Follett, Chicago.

Matthews, Patrick. 1957. *The Pursuit of Moths and Butterflies:* an anthology. Chatto and Windus, London.

Parenti, Umberto. 1978. *The World of Butterflies and Moths*. Putnam, New York.

Riley, N. D. 1975. *A Field Guide to the Butterflies of the West Indies*. Collins, London.

Sbordoni, Valerio, and Saverio Forestiero. 1988. *The Butterflies of the World*. Crescent, New York.

Smart, Paul. 1977. *The Illustrated Encyclopedia of the Butterfly World*. Chartwell Books, New York.

Smith, Colin. 1989. *Butterflies of Nepal*. Techpress Service L.P., Bangkok.

Thomas, J. A. 1986. *RSNC Guide to the Butterflies of the British Isles*. Hamlyn, Twickenham, U.K.

Thomas, Jeremy. 1991. *The Butterflies of Britain and Ireland*. Dorling Kindersley/National Trust, London.

Williams, John G. 1971. *A Field Guide to the Butterflies of Africa*. Houghton Mifflin, Boston.

Wynter-Blyth, M. A. 1957. *Butterflies of the Indian Region*. Bombay Natural History Society.

Also see current guides to national parks of the world, a number of which are available.

III. BUTTERFLY HOUSES AND TOURS

As described in Chapter 12, butterfly houses have arisen all over the world. These hothouse conservatories exhibit living butterflies from the tropics, flying, nectaring, reproducing, and metamorphosing before the visitor's eyes. A butterfly house allows you to encounter a glorious array of butterflies in person, up close, in a compact area. A visit to such a place cannot possibly replace a butterfly walk in a real jungle, a wild habitat. But when you cannot jet to Belize or cruise to Papua New Guinea, a butterfly house might be the next best way to experience exotic insects. Generally, butterfly houses also offer interpretation, butterfly gardening and conservation displays and advice, programs, bookshops, and other amenities for education and enjoyment.

Following are the addresses and telephone numbers of the butterfly houses that are open in North America as of this writing.

The Cecil B. Day Butterfly Center at Callaway Gardens, Pine Mountain, GA 31822 (404-663-2281).

Butterfly World, Tradewinds Park, 3600 W. Sample Road, Coconut Creek, FL 33073 (305-977-4400).

Butterfly World, Highway 97C, Okanogan Valley, British Columbia, Canada (604-769-4408).

Butterfly World, Coombs, near Parksville, Vancouver Island, British Columbia, Canada (604-248-7026).

Butterfly World, Marine World Africa USA, Marine World Parkway, Vallejo, CA 94589 (707-644-4000).

Papillon Park, 120 Tyngsboro Rd., Westford, MA 01886 (508-392-0955).

New facilities are planned for Cincinnati, Austin, San Diego, and Denver. Watch for these and others opening in the future, and for the many butterfly houses abroad, especially in Great Britain. The best known of these, the London Butterfly House, is located at Sion Park, near Kew Gardens and close enough to Heathrow International Airport for a visit in transit.

Butterfly tours are conducted by the following firms.

Holbrook Travel, Inc., 3540 N.W. 13th St., Gainesville, FL 32609 (1-800-451-7111). Offers numerous butterfly tours to tropic locales.

Joseph van Os Nature Tours, P.O. Box 655, Vashon Island, WA 98070 (1-206-463-5362). Annual tours to the Mexican Monarchs.

Green and Pleasant Tours, 369 Loop Road, Gray's River, WA 98621.

Index

Monks Wood National Nature
    Reserve, 113
morphos, 22, 239–40
Morris, Dr. Michael, 246
Moss Elfin, 232
Moth Book, The (Holland), 212, 218
mothing sugar, 47
moth observation, 207–15
    sugaring and, 211–12
    use of female for, 214–15
    use of lights for, 208–10
moths, 4, 204–19
    anatomy, 204
    butterflies distinguished from, 12–
        13
    charm of, 214–15
    compared with butterflies, 205
    Cynthia, 216–17
    discriminating from butterflies, 57
    dislike of, 205–6
    diurnal, 206–7
    identification of, 218–19
    Lunas, 218
    pests, 205
    See also moth observation
Moths of the Limberlost (Porter),
    214–15
moth walks, 214
Mourning Cloaks, 4, 6, 17, 24, 68,
    149–50, 188–89
mud-puddle clubs, 128
mud-puddling, 37, 128, 201, 239
Muellerian mimicry, 132

Nabokov, Vladimir, 1, 3, 190
National Geographic, 143, 167
National Grid, 88
national recreation areas (NRA), 25
    regulations on butterfly collection,
        25
National Wildlife Federation, 192
    Backyard Wildlife Program, 144
    Conservation Summits, 198
Natural History of Selborne, The
    (White), 220
natural history societies, 96
Nature Conservancy, The, 28, 96, 192,
    222, 230
nature study
    and butterfly and moth walks, 198–
        202
    decline in schools, 194–95

designation of state insects, 197–98
for disabled people, 5, 202
education and, 194–203
increased interest in, 195
Klots' instructions for, 196–97
teaching assistants and, 202–3
teaching materials related to
    butterflies, 196
use of butterflies in, 194–203
Near Horizons (Teale), 221
nectar, 37
    butterflying and, 145–46
    butterfly bush as source of, 40
    plant sources, 40–41
    sources of, 121
    specific preferences, 41–42
nectaring behavior, 123–26
    of moths, 208
Nelson's Hairstreak, 251
nettle-feeding butterfly, 150–51
New Guinea, 246–48
    butterfly cultivation in, 31
    conservation in, 190
    giant birdwings of, 10
Newman, L. Hugh, 144
Neyhart, John and Vikki, 182, 183
nocturnal butterflying, 4–5
North America
    butterfly catalog for, 98
    butterfly families, 82–84
nymphalidae, 13, 23, 24, 84
nymphs, 37

Ochre Ringlet, 45
Old World Swallowtail, 227
Olympia Marblewings, 188
Opler, Dr. Paul, 228, 238
Orange-tip, 9
Oregon Swallowtail, 167, 197
ovaries, 23
overwintering, 24
Owen, Dennis, 154

Painted Ladies, 6, 41, 45, 57, 81, 189
    See also Cosmopolitan Butterfly
Papilionidae, 13, 83
parasite cycles, 44
parnassians, 83
"patrolling," 138
Peacock butterflies, 40
Pearl Crescents, 136, 230
"perching," 138

sex, 23, 159
  listing and, 102
  ratio, 92
sex-determining chromosome, 5, 12
sex scales. *See* Androconia
shape, identification and, 78
Shapiro, Adrienne and Arthur, 99
Shields, Dr. Oakley, 138
Short-tailed Black Swallowtail, 153
Sierra Club, 192
silkmoths, 204, 217–18
Silvery Blues, 140
size, identification, and, 78
skippers, 82
Small Tortoiseshells, 40
Small Whites. *See* European Cabbage
  Butterfly
Solitary Blue, 80
Sonora Blue, 234
Sooty Hairstreak, 80
Speckled Wood butterfly, 137–38
spermatophore, 23, 159
Sphinx moths, 208
spider webs, escape from, 22
Springtime in Britain (Teale), 29
Spring Whites, 138
Stanford, Dr. Ray, 229
state insect, 197–98
stumps and hollows, 39
sugaring, for moths, 211–12
sulphurs, 83, 139
sunlight, 38–39, 133–34
Sunset Urania, 242
survival behavior, 130–32
swallowtails, 37, 42, 83
Swamp Metalmarks, 230

Tailed Blues, 60
Tawny Emperor, 127
Teale, Edwin Way, 29, 221, 230
Teale, Nellie, 221
territoriality, 136–39, 142
Thomas, Dr. Jeremy, 129
thorax, 20
Thoreau, Henry David, 65, 76, 220,
  221
Threatened Oregon Silverspot, 38
Tiger Swallowtails, 136
Tinbergen, Niko, 137
Titania's Fritillary, 227
topo sheets, 46

tortoiseshells, 127, 130
tours, 241
tree sap, 127
true butterflies, 13
tweezers, 68–69

U.K. National Grid, 105
U.S. Fish and Wildlife Service, 189–
  190
U.S. Geologic Survey topographic
  maps. *See* topo sheets
Ulysses Swallowtails, 51, 246
Uncompaghre Fritillary, 45
Universal Transmercator Grid, 88,
  105
urine, as butterfly attractant, 48, 128
Urquhart, Fred, 236

Valerata Arctic, 232
Valley of the Butterflies, 244
Variegated Fritillary, 60
Veined Whites, 120–21, 123, 142
vertical baskers, 133
Viceroy, 6
  avoidance by birds, 131–32
  caterpillar of, 161, 163
Vidler's Alpine, 232

Walden (Thoreau), 220
walkabout caterpillars, 162
Wallace, Alfred Russel, 96, 246
Washington Lepidoptera Survey, 106
Washington State butterflies, 102–8
Watching Washington Butterflies
  (Pyle), 25, 172
weather
  butterfly survival and, 132–34
  butterflying and, 4
  effects on butterfly population,
    120–21
  field notes on, 91
  variations in, 44
weeds, butterflying and, 150–51
Weidemeyer's Admirals, 127, 152, 188
Weisk's Swallowtail, 246–48
Weist's Sphinx Moth, 191
West Coast Lady, 48–49, 133
Western Meadow Fritillaries, 232
Western Monarchs, 234

White, Gilbert, 76, 220
White Mountain Butterfly, 227
Wilderness Society, 192
wineries, as butterfly sites, 40, 127
wings, 20–23
winter
  butterflying in, 4, 38, 49–50
  keeping larvae through, 168
Wolf, Hazel, 5
Woodland Skippers, 59
Wood Nymphs, 188
World Wildlife Fund, 190

Xerces Blue, 184, 189, 193
Xerces Society, 31, 75, 118, 144, 187,
  189, 192, 253
  conservation and, 190–91
  teaching and, 196
  See also Fourth of July Butterfly
  Count

Yellow Brimstone, 49–50

Zebra butterfly, 4, 82
Zwinger, Anne, 220